GERRY FRANK'S

FRIDAY SURPRISE

A COLLECTION OF HIS COLUMNS
FROM
The Oregonian

Gerry Frank's Friday Surprise
A collection of his columns from the Oregonian

©1995 Gerry's Frankly Speaking

Printed in the United States of America

ISBN 1-879333-99-6
Library of Congress 95-94441

First Edition 1995

For additional copies (quantity prices available), please write or call:
Gerry's Frankly Speaking
P.O. Box 2225 • Salem, Oregon 97308
Ph: (503) 585-8411 • Fax: (503) 585-1076
1-800-692-2665

Contents

It's Friday Surprise in new guise from a true local 1

Namesake pales in light of the 'real' Claire Luce 3

Following Dad's footsteps, but staying much drier 5

Telegram stirs memories of encounters with Nixon. 7

Legendary secretaries served the public well 9

What's 'in', what's 'out'; and what life's all about 11

Portland of yesteryears had few good eating spots 13

The Reagans characterized by inauguration day style. 15

Paris mission attempts to break POW deadlock 17

Hatfield assistants plant Vietnamese 'seeds' early 19

Chocoholic judge at work 21

The heart of the matter was downtown Portland 23

Mideast challenges wise men 25

Latest bombing recalls department store blast 27

Woman power driving government, civic affairs 29

Oregon hospitals reach out, send vital aid to Afghanistan 31

Portland personalities add luster to hometown 33

All aboard! Trains are back on track with speed and style 35

Oil spill mileage? 4 smiles per gallon of industry greed 37

Regal presidency takes toll on decent men's lives 39

When the 'stars' shine, these guys do polishing 41

Mid-century Lincoln High broke walls of prejudice 43

Take tip from Nepal and tackle sales tax issue now 45

First Interstate leaders serve Oregonians well. 47

Leadership of U.S. Bank constructive force in state 49

Americans learn lesson, tighten up purse strings 51

Business tycoons often trip over their own egos 53

Vision and service give Toys 'R' Us retail lead 55

Icy life at South Pole station supports Antarctic science 57

Imprisoned in own country, Czechs throw off shackles 59

Approval ratings shadow White House retirees. 61

Sweetland transformed Oregon political history 63

Mayo Medical Center is masterpiece of logistics 65

Play your kings, queens, Trump card is biggest deal. 67

Prominent couples abound as Portland enters the 1990s 69

Visit to Ethiopian Emperor proves eye-opener 71

The ghost of Aunt Rosie still smiles on the Benson 73

Luminaries pay tribute to son of immigrants 75

Chief-of-Staff guards desk where buck stops in capital. 77

One man's foresight leads to vibrant east side activity 79

Efforts of former governor revealed during trip to coast 81

Library dedication speaks volumes about presidency. 83

Downtown buyers fill up shopping bags and Saks 85

Tiny town pours its heart into an artistry in bronze. 87

For Kam Sang Kwan, it's always year of work horse. 89

Glenn Jackson led effort to add commuter airline 91

Historian rubs shoulders with colorful governors 93

1991's the year to display Bernard Baruch-type sense 95

We've lots of bright stars to lead Oregon's future 97

Conflict in Gulf produces impact throughout world 99

Fear stalks neighborhoods as America shrinks inward 101

Thatcher's 'iron fist' proves right technique for the time 103

Good as we know we are, we know we can be better 105

Senate holds strengths, weaknesses of humanity 107

Memories of Liz Taylor: always the star of the show. 109

Echoes from the past still ring at 'Little Grey Home' 111

Great White Way lassoes American folk hero. 113

When playing world stage, character rules everything 115

Surprise! It's Friday already, and time for page in history. 117

Photographs 119

Map of Oregon 124

The Best of Oregon: destination attractions, places to visit, eat, and more. 126

Photographs 129

Putting best face forward, growth industry of the '90s 133

John Hancocks document history and personalities 135

Chocolate cake contest tests judge's stamina. 137

Called piddling, this pond has some very big fish 139

Miss Arbuckle great story; her desk another column. 141

Got your bellhop caps on? It's a quiz on historic hotels 143

Whom do folks admire most? Those who make life better 145

It's time to chew the fat over life as a food critic 147

Studies of bias in schools lead to look at leaders. 149

Speaking of farms, phones, more phones, and stress. 151

In shadows of headlines lurk real legislative issues 153

There's really no show biz like store biz, even on Broadway 155

'Detectives' sift through treasure trove in archives 157

Dull knives never carve out that well-honed retail niche 159

In the presence of a king? Awe, shucks, it was great 161

Lose people's trust, lose the whole ballgame. 163

Eat, drink in old Portland? Speak easy, it's nostalgia. 165

Heed fresh tip for success, then milk it for all it's worth 167

Oregon's reputation sparks NY callers, internal challenge 169

Yes, Virginia, there is an Oregon with gifts galore 171

Bob Straub tallest tree; have to go a fir piece to beat him 173

Frankly speaking, he made Portland 'my kind of town' 175

Musings on what lies ahead for the new year 177

No matter who we are, U.S. still best place to be 179

Mickey's boss does well, but public smells a rat. 181

And now for the real story behind political squabbles 183

Andy Rooney keeps dinner lively with non-stop talk 185

G.I. relives World War II from KP to Lucky Strike. 187

Times may be a-changin'; but names often retained 189

Holocaust memorial brings back more memories of World War II. 191

Politics, parades, paving; the news doesn't change 193

Fallout from Clinton's haircut may have him pulling it out 195

Three pioneers in their fields carved their own Oregon Trail. 197

Taking a stand guides Hatfield's long service. 199

Portland's past peopled with fabulous characters 201

The jolly yule elf got a ho ho for wearing a 'mirthday suit' 203

Now, more than ever, Oregon needs ingenuity 205

Strategies for taking U.S. to the top of the mountain 207

What a difference a day makes – a century ago 209

Olympic Star Dan Jansen sets pace for all to follow 211

Around-the-world jaunt begins in exotic Bangkok 213

From amazing India to the ancient kingdom of Sheba 215

Mouth-watering memories of old Portland eateries. 217

Oregonian adds his voice to London conversation 219

Green fields of N. Ireland seen through bulletproof windows. 221

Citizens in the limelight held to different standard 223

Serving Oregon a way of life for Otto Frohnmayer, family 225

Oregon's visionary leaders mark places in history book. 227

Much today goes awry due to lack of discipline. 229

Whale of a time a shoo-in in Warner Bros. proposal 231

Good or bad, foreign policy rests with the president. 233

Modern marketing means you always get to choose. 235

Special group of 10 VIPs are major community asset 237

Veteran institution at bank closes account on career 239

Where there's an old will, there's interesting reading 241

The President, "The King" and a man from Oregon 243

Ceremony stirs memories of outstanding careers. 245

1905 Portland Automobile Club frolics at Sandy River clubhouse 247

Preface

*I*t is always a thrill for me to reflect on the fact that I am part of a seven-generation Oregon family whose roots are deeply seeded in native soil. I love this state and I know, from the sum and substance in my daily mailbag, that my feeling is shared by my readers.

Those who are new to Oregon may wonder where the title for my column originated. I am happy to tell you, as it speaks to my family's strong ties here. On Friday, April 29, 1887, a weekly sales event called Friday Surprise was inaugurated at the family store, Meier & Frank, and soon became a long-standing social tradition which many people remember with genuine fondness for "the good old days." This weekly occurrence ended with the sale of the firm, although recently it has been periodically revived, and finding the concept had many applications, I called my column "Friday Surprise."

Over the years, the "Friday Surprise" column has featured stories of historical interest and others with a more current twist, often relating the past to the present and showing the strong sense of purpose and commitment which began with our pioneer ancestors and continues to this day. I have also tried to keep my readers informed on national and international events which, whether Oregonians feel their impact directly or not, affect us one way or another as we all grow closer through advanced technology.

A career in merchandising, a memorable stint in the field artillery during World War II, studies at Cambridge University, England, civic and business involvement throughout Oregon and twenty-six years of association with Senator Mark O. Hatfield in Oregon and Washington, D.C., gave me the opportunity to visit every continent and some 130 countries and to meet, first-hand, presidents and kings and even modern-day saints. In this volume, I share some of these experiences, in and out of Oregon, with you. It is exciting and fun and sometimes humbling to recall the proud heritage of our state and its people, and to describe the life and times of other people whose lives touch our own.

My thanks and appreciation go to Catherine Glass, Tim Prock, Linda Wooters, Cheryl Johnson, Louise Martin and Karen Kaplan for their assistance in making this compilation possible. I am also indebted to my editors at the *Oregonian:* Jud Randall, Bob Caldwell and Dick Johnston, for their interest and advice over the years.

FRIDAY SURPRISE

It's Friday Surprise in new guise from a true local

*I*t didn't occur to me back in my Ainsworth Grammar School days that several decades later I'd be asked to write a regular column for the *Oregonian.*

Kate Protzman, a legend for all who attended Ainsworth in those days, was the able and tough eighth-grade English teacher. It was an accepted fact that her students would pass college entrance English tests with flying colors.

I suppose it was partly because of Miss Protzman and partly because I always enjoyed writing that I was inspired to become editor, publisher and distributor of the *Weekly Chatter,* a sort of in-house chronicle of unimportant information about our household, my school, local football scores and various other bits of trivial news.

In those days, the mimeograph was the way to get things duplicated, and I would take my manuscripts to my father's office at Meier & Frank, where his secretary, Rosalia Happe, would find time in her busy day to keep the boss' son happy.

From there it was to the mimeograph department on the 13th floor of the old "Friday Surprise" store where Lillian Heltzel would find time to help the budding publisher. She would, that is, on condition that I brought some of those great chocolate caramels that mother made. It was a fair trade. That's how the *Weekly Chatter* got going. Being

full of merchant genes, I would sell "lifetime subscriptions" knowing full well that the life of that newspaper would probably be rather short.

That enterprise lasted long enough to let me try out whatever budding ability there was to write. And on to Lincoln High School where Mabel Southworth, a mother image for countless students, directed the fortunes of the *Cardinal,* the school paper, and was a source of encouragement to all novice writers.

My contributions to the *Cardinal* were menial at best, but I did have the opportunity to work with Sylvia Schnitzer, now Mrs. C. Girard-Davidson, who was then, as she is now, a brilliant and productive individual. So the interest in journalism is really nothing new.

When the editor of the *Oregonian* first broached the possibility of a weekly column, I wondered if there would be enough time.

After all, I have a full-time job as chief of staff to Senator Mark Hatfield, besides a rather full platter of business and civic activities, plus trying to run a Konditorei in Salem and write and publish a book on New York. Sort of an eclectic life.

The folks at the *Oregonian* said the sky was the limit on subject matter, that I could comment on a multitude of my interests and activities in Oregon, in Washington, D.C., in New York and

1

overseas, including, but not limited to, views and comments on personalities, business, government and travel.

One subject, however, that is off limits, is the senator. This column in no way is to be a forum for his positions and his views.

Those being the guideposts, herewith is the first effort, a "Friday Surprise" if there ever was one. Old-time Oregonians will remember the Friday Surprise name, I am sure.

This famous merchandising event at Meier & Frank was originally conceived to be a vehicle to get rid of old lots of merchandise, put out at a special price just one day a week. The fame of the event spread rapidly.

Buyers soon learned to buy specifically for this event. It was easy because most merchants around the country couldn't use relatively small lots of sale goods, and manufacturers weren't too worried about giving special deals to a store way out in Oregon.

Friday became the big shopping day of the week all over Portland, and many Oregonians remember the crowded sidewalks outside the Friday Surprise store at 9:30 A.M.

What they didn't see on the inside was Ludwig Hirsch, a mere wisp of a gentleman, long-time treasurer of the firm, standing on his tiptoes to ring the bell on the first floor to let the bargain-hungry folks in. This was an event that Mr. Hirsch wouldn't miss for anything, a weekly ritual that both he and store employees looked forward to. Of course, the name Hirsch still is a familiar one in the area. Ludwig Hirsch, related to the Meier and Frank families, also shared a relationship with Harold Hirsch, head honcho at Hirsch-Weis and still an important player in art and philanthropic activities in the Rose City.

Well, so much for the beginnings of my journalism career.

Wouldn't my grandparents have a good chuckle if they could see this column perched near a Meier & Frank ad, 130 years later?

Namesake pales in light of the 'real' Claire Luce

*T*he recent passing of Claire Luce, a legendary figure in the artistic and political life of our country for decades, brought back memories of a most unusual set of circumstances that involved this talented and charming lady.

While I was attending Stanford University in the mid-1940s, one of the most popular and attractive coeds on campus was my classmate, Ann Claire Brokaw ("Ace" for short), a young lady who did not let her famous mother overshadow her own life.

Tragedy (a fatal automobile accident) struck this young lady while she was a college student, and left a lasting mark not only on her parents, but on all those who had known her, including myself.

Several years later, while a student at Cambridge University in England, I noticed in the London papers that Claire Luce was appearing on stage in London. Having never been able to personally tell her how saddened I was about the death of her daughter some years back, I thought I would seek to see this famous actress on stage, to take the opportunity to renew my acquaintance and recall some of the happy days I had spent with her daughter.

I sat through what I thought was a rather boring and unimpressive performance by the lady whose fame as an actress had spread all over the world. I thought that perhaps I just didn't appreciate the finer things in life.

Afterward, with every hair in place, shoes carefully polished, and somewhat sweaty palms, I made my way to the stage door entrance and asked the "bloke" guarding the door if it was possible to see Claire Luce in person.

After severe scrutiny, and what seemed like an eternal wait, I was finally ushered back to the lead dressing room where I found myself in a small and cluttered room, ablaze with mirrors, lights, discarded clothing, flowers and a dog.

I reintroduced myself to the actress, recalling our previous meetings and my affection for her daughter, only to be greeted by blank stares.

In looking at Mrs. Luce, I thought to myself how much she had aged since I had seen her years before, and how she didn't look like the very classy lady I had known. Perhaps it was the make-up, or perhaps she was very tired after her performance.

Our conversation went from not very stimulating on my side to absolutely zero on her side.

This, indeed, was not the Claire Luce I had known. Yes, it was a lady by the same name. Yes, she was an actress. But there was absolutely no relationship between the two women.

How in the world did I get myself into such a situation, and, most important at the moment, how in the dickens did I get myself out?

By this time the perspiration was coming down in buckets, not only from the bright lights in the cozy and intimate dressing room, but also because of my extreme embarrassment at the confusion.

I made some lame excuse about how someone was outside waiting for me and exited from the encounter.

During the ensuing years, I followed with some interest the career of the "real" Claire Luce, hoping that someday I would have the chance to see her again.

Out of the blue one day in Washington, D.C., came a call from Dan Boorstin, who was then the librarian of Congress, a good friend and author, who said that he and his wife, Ruth, were planning a black-tie dinner for the opening of a special exhibit at the library and would I like to escort Claire Luce to the event?

Would I? You bet.

For days, I battered back and forth in my mind whether to tell her of the London event.

When I arrived to pick up Mrs. Luce, I learned that she and a member of her family had been engaged in an unpleasant family discussion. It seemed that the family member had wanted to take her to see a recent portrait of herself at a gallery in Washington, only to learn that the portrait in question was of her English namesake.

Mrs. Luce thought she was being purposely embarrassed by the family member.

Well, my story then fit perfectly into place, and the great lady was fascinated and touched by the whole episode.

I couldn't believe how two such distant experiences had melded together.

The "real" Mrs. Luce, of course, turned out to be a most attractive and vivacious lady in her later years, full of wit and entertaining stories of an event-filled life. Her feelings about her English namesake were colorful, to say the least.

I didn't have to go to the gallery to see that painting.

FRIDAY SURPRISE

Following Dad's footsteps, but staying much drier

I was brought up in the family of a "fire chaser." Many are the times I can remember at the family dinner table that the phone would ring and my dad would jump up to be told by the American District Telegraph operator where a major fire had been reported.

He had some kind of a deal with these people; they were instructed to find him wherever he might be.

No, he wasn't a fireman, but Aaron Frank, like so many who loved their community and appreciated those who helped make it a safe and comfortable place to live, was a great supporter of the fire service.

This fascination led to all sorts of consequences, some amusing and some with far-reaching implications.

One time, Dad was told of a major blaze taking place in the heart of downtown, a multi-alarm job with all available equipment on hand. In those days there weren't handy connections, so lengthy hoses were strung all along the area of the blaze. Firemen and police lined the perimeters, admitting only those on official business.

Because of his long-time interest and support for their cause, the firemen had made Dad an Honorary Fire Chief. He showed this badge with great pride as he went through the fire line, much against the advice of the local authorities.

He had been called from a summer party and was dressed up in his best white "ice cream suit."

Sure as the dickens, as he approached the center of action, one of the fire hoses burst right in front of him. He was covered with water, debris and the humiliation of being completely drenched in full view of all those in back of the fire lines. He learned his lesson.

The sight of firefighters working on cold winter nights led him to donate a hot coffee wagon to the fire services. Jay Stevens, a close friend of my dad's, was the fire marshal in Portland at that time, in the 1930s. Dad went to him, told Jay of his desire to provide a multi-use piece of equipment for his troops and asked his help in designing it.

Some time later, the Jay W. Stevens Disaster Wagon came into existence. It was the first of its kind in the nation.

It was later to be copied by fire departments around the world. It resembled a large bus, with the latest emergency equipment housed in its interior. Of course, it had facilities to provide hot coffee and food.

The Portland Fire Bureau planned a major, formal ceremony at the Portland Auditorium to receive the wagon. It was to be presented to the city, with fire and civic officials participating and the public invited.

My dad said the only way he would consent to attend was if he could just sit like anyone else in the audience, not be introduced, and have absolutely no mention or fuss made of him. This was promised, with fingers crossed behind.

The night of the presentation, we all watched with pride as the ceremonies proceeded.

Dad was delighted. But all of a sudden a voice over the wagon's loud speaker commanded that the donor be brought to the stage for "official thanks." Dad was furious and tried to leave the auditorium. But two burly firemen appeared, literally picked him up and carried him kicking and fighting all the way up the aisle to the stage. He (at 130 pounds soaking wet) was no match for his captors.

I have kept up the family interest. Each year, the Marion County Firefighters present the Gerry Frank Meritorious Service Award to someone in the area who has performed an outstanding humanitarian deed.

Several weeks ago, I had the pleasure of giving the 1987 award to Orville Rice of Turner, relief operator of the Wheatland Ferry that plies the Willamette River. In February 1987, Orville responded to the screams of a frantic father whose son had fallen into the cold river trying to rescue his dog, Scout.

Cold and scared to death, the boy was caught in the water. Quick-witted Orville docked the ferry, launched an auxiliary boat, sped to the side of Matt Nys, thirteen, of Brooks and, along with another man recruited to help, rescued the boy.

A few more minutes and the results would have been tragic. As it was, the boy was rescued unharmed.

There probably are numerous such acts going on every day all over the country. It is certainly rewarding to know that in our own communities we still have firefighters and other support personnel who put service and concern for their fellow human beings at the top of their priority list.

FRIDAY SURPRISE

Telegram stirs memories of encounters with Nixon

*W*hen the 1988-89 edition of my book, *Where To Find It, Buy It, Eat It in New York,* was launched with a special party and promotion by Bloomingdale's in New York, I felt it was pretty heady stuff. But the most impressive part of the whole episode was the personal telegram of congratulations that I received from former President Nixon, who is attracting attention to himself these days while he promotes his book, *1999.*

In retrospect, this thoughtful remembrance was vintage Nixon, a shrewd and skilled politician who never forgets anything or anybody. Whether or not one agrees with his political philosophy, few would disagree that he will be remembered as one of the most talented political operators of our time.

My first meeting with Nixon was over Santiam beans and Oregon strawberries at a luncheon in Salem in 1959 when he was in Oregon to help celebrate our centennial. He was vice-president at that time.

I found him to be sharp and probing, and not much interested in matters other than politics and sports.

He was fascinating to watch: no comment went unnoticed, and when the political discussion became heated, he was in his element like no one I had ever met.

Some months later, as he was developing his team for the 1960 presidential race, he somehow remembered the rag merchant from Salem with whom he had broken bread, and asked me to join a national group headed by Chuck Percy, then chairman of Bell and Howell, to come up with a platform for his upcoming race.

At that time, I was pretty well committed to other tasks, so I felt I could not accept the offer.

My career path changed when Meier & Frank was sold to the May Company. And new fields opened in Washington, D.C.

Nixon had become president, and I was overwhelmed to receive an invitation from him and Pat Nixon to a state dinner at the White House.

When my time came to greet my host and hostess in the receiving line, before I could utter a stumbling word, the President said to Pat: "Gerry comes from a very well known department store family in Oregon." His memory was absolutely amazing.

There were more occasions during his presidency where we met under one circumstance or another.

Each time there was the same recognition and the same recounting of some personal identification.

The next major association was at the 1968 Republican convention in Miami. Nixon was going to be the nominee, but still in question was his choice of a vice-president. Senator Mark O.

Hatfield, with whom I was associated, was a top contender for the position.

There was one major stumbling block: they didn't see eye-to-eye on our Vietnam involvement. I was asked to be the intermediary with the selection committee headed by John Mitchell, Nixon's trusted associate and campaign chief.

To say the least, I learned what the real rough and tumble of high-level politics is like.

It was a different Nixon at our meeting in San Clemente, California. Watergate was history, and the scars were visible. He was obviously in pain, distracted and uncomfortable in his relationships with his guests.

One could not help but have compassion for a proud man, now rejected and discarded.

The most memorable association was a private dinner in Georgetown, at the home of a mutual friend. There were eight in attendance at a stag dinner. The company included then Senator Howard Baker, former Senator William Fulbright and Nixon. Nixon captivated the audience by holding forth for the best part of four hours with fascinating stories of his associations and evaluations of world leaders.

Most recently I enjoyed a pleasant luncheon at the home of Vice-President George Bush and Barbara Bush, where Nixon was also one of the guests. The occasion was a reception to honor the marriage of former Portlander Esther Jantzen and Richard Moore, who was a member of the Nixon White House. Many of the former Nixon crew, including Rosemary Woods and John Mitchell, were present. It was Nixon who held the center of attention.

When history is written, it will be kinder to Nixon than we can presently imagine. No one in contemporary America is more skilled and knowledgeable on foreign affairs. No leadership post will come his way again, of course. But this very complex, very able person must take some sort of satisfaction when he walks unannounced into a New York restaurant and the entire assemblage rises and cheers. I was cheered, too, to think that this man of history would take time to remember a fledgling author.

Legendary secretaries served the public well

*L*ast week was Secretaries' Week, and it brought to mind that many of those persons who previously were called "secretaries" are called "administrative assistants" in today's world. No matter what the title, the old-time executive secretaries were very valuable persons, just as their counterparts (with different titles) are today.

Leolyn Barnett knew everyone in Oregon, or at least everyone who was prominent in community affairs. She served as the No. 1 secretary, schedule-maker and doorkeeper for five governors, starting with Earl Snell in 1943.

She had a natural political sensitivity and knew how to take care of those folks who "just had to talk to the governor directly." Barnett was unfailingly courteous; even when she had to say "no," she did it with such finesse and class that no one could have been offended.

The demands for personal appearances for the state's chief executive were not as intense in the early days that Barnett kept the schedule book. She would put the invitations in the back of the book, and then periodically show them to her boss. As time went on and the invitations multiplied, just doing the scheduling became almost a full-time job.

Her memory of people, places and incidents made her an asset to one governor after another, each one benefiting from her world of experience. Barnett capped her career with service in the Senate, where she also was revered as "one of a kind."

In Southern Oregon, and particularly in the Medford area, Glenn Jackson was the area's best known and most influential citizen. Although he spent a great deal of time in Portland at the Pacific Power and Light Company, his Medford office was most important to him.

When he was present there, and more important when he wasn't, Marina Gardiner was the expediter. She knew Glenn like the back of her hand and could answer nearly any question that would be posed to him.

Gardiner was very much a community person. Because Jackson was involved in such a diversity of activities, from ranching to power to transportation to politics, the contacts that she made on the staff level in all of these areas were of particular value. She knew where the right buttons could be pressed.

Glenn Jackson was a constant pipe smoker and coffee drinker. He had to have his hands free to take care of these needs. Thus the speaker-type telephone was in constant use in his office, and visitors were intrigued to be listening in on conversations with individuals ranging from Wayne Morse to the baggage handler for Air Oregon. Gardiner listened also and thus knew just about everything that was going on. She then could take care of the details without any participation from Glenn himself.

In the forties and fifties, not much went on in Portland that Eddie Sammons, Paul McKee, Dave Simpson, E.B. MacNaughton, Phil Jackson and Aaron Frank were not involved in. The women who ran the offices of these busy men had a network all to themselves.

One of the most able members of this group was Florence Millsaps, who worked at the *Oregon Journal* and soon became the eyes and ears of Phil Jackson, the publisher.

Millsaps was also the alter ego of this civic leader, taking care of his office, writing his letters, serving as the sounding board for his ideas, keeping him in touch with his newspaper organization.

But there was another side to this highly intelligent, inquisitive and productive secretary. She took it upon herself to be the contact person for the hundreds of *Journal* employees who were in the service during World War II by publishing the *Armed Forces Extra,* a house organ that kept them up-to-date on what was going on at home. In addition, she was the regular correspondent to dozens of sons and daughters who were overseas. Through that activity, she became one of the best-loved persons in Portland.

Those who knew Lee Luders Ebersole, secretary to Harold Wendel, manager of Lipman's in Portland, remember her as one of the most attractive and stately women in the city. She served as the right hand of this merchant and also was a fashion model in his store.

Ebersole was the counselor and teacher of dozens of young people starting up the ladder in the retail business. One of her pupils was Phil Hawley, who later became the chief executive of one of the largest retail store chains in the nation. Ebersole capped her career as a secretary to Tony Yturri of Ontario, minority leader of the Oregon Senate for fifteen years. When the Senate was not in session, she served in various positions in the governor's office.

No fancy titles or fancy offices for these talented women. However, their impact on the State of Oregon, although not officially recognized in the history books, was of immeasurable significance and value.

FRIDAY SURPRISE

What's "in" what's "out"; and what life's all about

What's in and what's not? Depending on what you read and whom you listen to, you can get all kinds of different answers to that question. I have been fascinated to observe the trends and changes as I travel around our country and around the world.

One of the areas that certainly is the trendiest these days, outside of clothing, is what we eat and where we eat it.

Light foods are very much "in." Where it used to be that a big juicy slab of roast beef was considered the ultimate, today's choice would be much on the lighter side. Steaks are out; seafood, especially the fresh variety we are so fortunate to have in Oregon in abundance, is very much "in."

Salads and fresh vegetables are high on the hit parade, with vegetable soup right at the top of the list. Rich, creamy, heavy soups are definitely "out," as are any high-cholesterol foods.

A trend that is strong in the East, and spreading all over the country, is the purchase of already prepared dishes in the gourmet departments of grocery and specialty food operations. With Mom and Dad both working, and food preparation time limited, the "in" way to eat these days is to buy the dinner meal on the way home.

Wine, light beer and diet drinks are the popular choices. Hard liquor is on the decline. "Smoothies" made with a mixture of fresh fruits, healthy and satisfying, are "in." The setting for our pleasures in eating also has changed. The backyard barbecue has again become popular; the TV dinner is "out." Inexpensive ethnic restaurants are much the rage.

In jobs, the "in" place to find employment is Florida, with the Santa Ana-Anaheim and the San Jose regions of California running second. On the other side of the coin, the "out" regions are Decatur, Illinois; Dubuque, Iowa; and Great Falls, Montana. In types of jobs, the fastest-growing "in" occupations are paralegals, medical assistants and physical therapists in percentages of increase, but retail sales, waiters and waitresses in total numbers.

Jobs considered the "best" these days include being an actuary, a computer programmer or a computer systems analyst. On the opposite end of the scale are migrant workers and fishermen; their jobs are considered the toughest because of low salary, stress, tough work environment and little job security.

Long hair, short skirts, big hats and baggy clothes are all on the "outs." Taking their place are refined, comfortable clothes that can be used season after season. Suspenders, "walking" shoes, clothes without designer names or initials are "in." Undershirts for men are "out"; pocket watches on a chain are high on the "in" side.

Answering machines are on the "out" list, especially those with the pre-recorded message from some well-known personality. Personal pocket computers and data books are "in." Very "in" is a new pocket computer that does more than its big brothers and fits into a coat pocket besides.

Portable telephones and personal pagers that make a loud noise in public places are at the top of the "out" list. Small, thin, portable compact disc players are "in," not only for the young people but for all who enjoy good music. Large, ostentatious stereo installations are "out."

Politicians who are not afraid to admit a mistake, and who do not begin every sentence with an "I," are "in." Those with pat answers to everything, and those who promise the moon and stars to every group they talk to, are sinking on the rating scale. Drugs and crime are the "in" issues; single-issue partisan groups are "out."

In the home, large and well-equipped bathrooms are becoming the most important room in the house. Formal sitting or living rooms are "out." Easy to clean and easy to use kitchens with lots of storage space and work areas are "in." Bedspreads are "out;" sexy, comfortable comforters are "in."

And just to finish the list, good manners and taking a gift along when invited out to dinner have been and continue to be very much "in." Smoking in confined space, hand-carried music machines, complaining about those in positions of responsibility, and lack of interest in elderly friends and relatives are at the top of the "out" list.

So much for the trendy talk. But if we're enjoying life and helping others, isn't that all that really counts?

FRIDAY SURPRISE

Portland of yesteryears had few good eating spots

*P*ortland did not always provide the wide variety of good places to go for a meal that it does today. As a matter of fact, before liquor by the glass was legal, it was not easy to find many really fine eating spots in our Rose City.

There was just one great place to get hamburgers, and that was Yaw's Top Notch in the Hollywood district. Win Yaw himself was much in evidence, greeting the loyal clientele by name and by interest.

In the days when it was mainly a counter operation, folks thought nothing about standing behind someone's seat, sort of urging them along to eat a bit faster so they could sit down. The hamburgers were large, juicy and well anointed, and the accompanying milk shakes were the real thing.

Alas, management changed, and the old-style operation gave way to tables. The charm and the outstanding food faded away, and now that landmark is no more.

When counter service was desired downtown, the place to go was Jolly Joan on Broadway. This was the meeting place for couples after a movie at the old United Artists, Rivoli, Orpheum or Paramount theaters.

At the noon hour in downtown Portland, the place to go was the Tea Room on the 10th floor of "Murphy and Finnegan." Folks would begin to line up at the entrance well ahead of the opening hours, as they knew that the food quality was superb, the price was reasonable, and the service sure to be special.

The chef, Don Daniel, was a Portland fixture. Early members of the Meier & Frank family (especially "Grandma Meier") would frequent the kitchen to make sure that only the finest ingredients were being used. The ladies who did the serving had been with the store forever, and knew most customers by name or sight.

Adjoining was the Men's Grill, where a community table for men dining alone was the gathering spot for the movers and shakers of the city. Frank Callahan, who operated one of the city's major meat provision houses, would amuse the clan with his Irish wit. Jesse Rich would bring the latest edition of the *Oregonian, Oregon Journal,* or *News-Telegram* from his newsstand. Many a major community project was conceived, planned, financed and executed at this table.

If it was seafood that one was after, two of the most famous and popular spots are still in business. Jake's Famous Crawfish Restaurant, today one of Portland's most popular gathering spots, was a great attraction not only for the locals, but also for folks coming from out of town, wanting to try the delicious crawfish and seafood dishes.

The old-time waiters were a tradition in themselves. Some (such as Julius Eneidi) served Portlanders for more than a half-century.

For more than seventy years, the Oregon Oyster Company (on S.W. Ankeny Street), still a great place to eat, has attracted folks who find a trip to the coast a long excursion for fine seafood. Three generations of the Wachsmuth family have not wavered from their hands-on operation.

On Sunday morning, when a platter of pancakes and bacon, or delicious crispy waffles was desired, the Original Pancake House (at 8600 S.W. Barbur Boulevard) was the place to go. Founder Lester Highet was there smiling as hordes of hungry Portlanders would sometimes wait for an hour to be seated.

If German pancakes were desired, no one could fix them quite like Henry Thiele. Thiele himself was one of Portland's best known personalities. He would move his considerable frame around his restaurant at West Burnside and 23rd Avenue to insure that all his patrons knew he was present.

Huber's has been in the same location in the Oregon Pioneer Building (320 S.W. Stark) for 78 years. Before that, it was known as the Bureau Saloon, founded in 1879 by W.L. Lightner. Frank Huber (later the sole proprietor) was hired as bartender in 1884, and he hired Jim Louie as chef seven years later. The Louie family has been in charge since 1891.

For the special evening occasion, there was just one place to go in your finest dress-up clothes: the old Portland Hotel dining room, located on the block that now is known as Pioneer Square. Just above what is now Powell's Travel Bookstore was the magnificent and stately main dining room of the hotel, looking out on Morrison and Sixth.

Skilled, white-jacketed waiters served great food with grace and dignity, on tables covered with well-starched white linen cloths, sparkling crystal, and specially made china. The waiters doubled as stewards on Union Pacific's "City of Portland," serving the route from Portland to Chicago in the days when dining on a train was a memorable experience.

When restaurants in Oregon were allowed to serve liquor, the whole scene changed. Perhaps the number of choices is better today, but the personal service and family traditions of the old-time favorites never will be forgotten.

The Reagans characterized by inauguration day style

*W*hat would you think about if you found yourself all alone on the first floor of the White House on the evening of the inauguration of the President of the United States?

Frankly, I had never given any thought to such a possibility. But it happened, and it was an experience long to be remembered. Not just because of the surroundings, but also because it gave an unusual insight into the people who were to inhabit that awesome establishment for the next eight years.

The date was Tuesday, January 21, 1981. That morning I had been involved in the inaugural activities at the Capitol; my assignment for the event was the new Cabinet. I had to assemble them, brief them, get them in order for the line of march, and answer a hundred questions much like the questions any large group would ask before a ceremony begins. The only difference was that these folks, I thought, should have known the answers.

In any case, the two hours that were spent in getting things organized gave me a rather quick, but nevertheless incisive, look at the folks who would be running the government for the next few years. Alexander Haig, surrounded by a retinue of aides and security people, was running back and forth to the telephone with the latest information on the release of the hostages. The years to come would not be especially good to him.

The ceremony itself was most impressive, particularly because Oregonians put it on. Senator Mark O. Hatfield, for whom I was working, was producer and director of the inauguration that year.

But the evening was the momentous time for me. I was invited by Nancy Reynolds, a friend of the Reagans who had served as Nancy Reagan's press secretary in California governor days, to be her escort for the evening's festivities.

We first went to Blair House, directly across the street from the White House, for dinner. This series of historic buildings is used by the government to house official visitors to our nation's capital.

Well, just being inside this home was exciting enough, but the company was even more so. The President's family was all there, although he was not. This was part of the excitement, just sizing up the first family.

After dinner, we walked across the street to the White House, and without too much pass-showing and inspection, Reynolds and I were ushered in to the first floor area of the great house. The others stayed behind at Blair House to get dressed for the evening's galas.

Reynolds indicated that Nancy Reagan wanted her to come to the family quarters to help her get dressed, so that left yours truly by himself in this historic home at this historic time. The Reagan troops were not yet organized and in place, and the Carter people had left.

Soon I looked around, and there I was, all by myself, without another soul in sight. I pinched myself. What an opportunity! What could I do? Well, I thought, I am going to go room by room and just look.

While inspecting the family dining room, I did run into the Chief Usher of the White House, who regaled me with stories (he had served through several administrations) about Lyndon Johnson.

In about an hour, the president and Nancy Reagan came downstairs. He was the epitome of graciousness, almost as if he was wondering what in the world he was doing there at that time. Nancy Reagan seemed much more occupied with showing off her inaugural gown.

Family pictures were taken (by this time assorted children and relatives had arrived). Obviously, this was not a close family group, sharing love and concern. The egos were apparent.

Then off with the junior members of the family to several of the galas, and much mixing with people who were important, and more who thought that they were.

My feelings during the past seven and a half years about the personalities involved have certainly been colored by my personal observations from that day's and evening's activities.

Ronald Reagan is a pleasant human being, above all. No matter what political views we may have, it would be difficult not to like him personally. Whether he was the right person in the right place at the right time remains to be seen. But what does one think about at that time, by oneself, in the location of so much history? That only in America could this happen.

FRIDAY SURPRISE

Paris mission attempts to break POW deadlock

Go undercover to talk to the Vietnamese at the Paris peace talks concerning the release of non-military prisoners?

Are you kidding? The closest this former operative in Meier & Frank ever came to any undercover activity was counting the number of customers in the housewares department at Lipman's during a sales event.

But it certainly sounded exciting, and here starts a story that isn't over yet, seventeen years later.

This experience was brought to mind by the recent story in the Sunday *Oregonian* about the FBI files on Wayne Morse, the late Oregon senator, and Wes Michaelson, a former staff member for Senator Mark O. Hatfield.

The mission was to persuade the Vietnamese negotiators at the Paris talks that a starting point for a peaceful solution to our tragic involvement would be to release some prisoners who were not involved directly in the military aspects of the war.

Hatfield had been an outspoken opponent of our involvement in this struggle from the beginning, and was very much concerned about ending it before more lives were lost. Through contacts he and members of his staff had with American Friends Service Committee personnel, it was learned that it would be possible for representatives of the senator to be received in Paris to discuss the situation.

The time was early December 1971, and the complex and secret arrangements for the meeting had come to the point where a decision had to be made. Who would go? What were the chances of any success from such a private mission?

It was obvious that the senator himself could not go, so next best was to send some senior members of his staff. He decided that the two who should go would be Wes Michaelson, chief legislative assistant at that time, who had been involved in all aspects of the Vietnamese struggle, and myself, then a fledgling in the intricacies of the whole affair.

The utmost secrecy surrounded who was going, where we were going, when we were going, and why we were going. Reservations were made for the flight to Paris under assumed names. Wes, now with the World Council of Churches in Geneva, was to be the "detail" man of the team; my mission, as the senator's top assistant, was to provide credence to the message we were bringing. Fortunately, office associates and friends asked few questions about what was going on.

On a dreary Friday afternoon the two of us left our downtown Paris hotel by taxi for Choissy-le-Roi, a suburb outside of Paris, and arrived at Avenue General LeClere a few minutes early, as we didn't want to take any chances of missing our appointment. At every turn of the way, on the plane, at the airport, at the hotel, on the streets of Paris, I was horrified at the thought that I would run into someone I knew. How would I field questions about what in the world I was doing there at that particular time and under those conditions?

The compound that we entered had a fortress appearance, or, more properly perhaps, a monastic look. Once inside we saw immediately the North Vietnamese red flag with a yellow star flying above the main building where we were headed. Frankly, it made my heart sink.

A gentleman by the name of Xuan Oanh greeted us (we had been told he was the primary contact) and guided us to the conference room where we would meet with a man whom we knew only as Mr. Vy, the head of the delegation. A Mr. Bo soon joined us, and as we sat under a glaring picture of Ho Chi Minh, we discussed the background and hopes of our mission, the political climate in our country, and the tremendous power of public opinion.

We were struck at once with how very knowledgeable these folks were about our country and the political situation here. They knew their American history.

We talked about the great public concern that had been aroused in the United States about the prisoners, and the fact that the president (Richard Nixon) had been able to successfully use this in support of his policy of Vietnamization.

To do this, of course, would require some gesture or symbol that would increase the trust between the North Vietnamese and the Americans who wanted to see the war end.

A possible step was suggested: Wes said that it was our understanding that in addition to the military prisoners of war, there were a certain number of civilian POWs. They included missionaries, nurses, volunteer workers, construction workers, journalists, and others. It was our proposal that with this group of people, some gesture might be possible to break the deadlock.

(To be continued–see next column.)

FRIDAY SURPRISE

Hatfield assistants plant Vietnamese 'seeds' early

*O*ur conversations at the Vietnamese mission in Paris continued for several hours. Mr. Vy, the chief negotiator, talked at length with us about the matter of trust and suspicion. He indicated that he and his fellow negotiators had not previously allowed discussions about releasing non-military prisoners, thereby implying that our meeting was really a historic one. This made the adrenaline run a little bit faster, thinking about the importance of these talks, and how they could affect the lives of so many people.

Vy emphasized repeatedly that the prisoner issue posed absolutely no problem, but that it must be considered in the context of settling the war. He referred to the nine prisoners who had been released in 1968-1969, pointing out that this was done as a symbol of hope for negotiations to continue. Vy felt that what was really needed was some kind of gesture from President Nixon, a gesture such as setting a date for complete withdrawal from the area.

We felt the three-hour exchange had been helpful, and we were impressed that we had met with the top negotiator, Vy, and his chief deputy, Xuan Thuy. At no time did they indicate that they had to check with any higher authorities on what they could say. We felt they were serious about peace.

In the report that was prepared as we flew home across the Atlantic, we noted that an idea had been offered, but, far more important, a relationship had been established. We wrote that the talks "had created a foundation on which some future meaningful contact, on the prisoner issue or on completely different matters, could easily result." Little did we think it would take sixteen years for those words to be proven correct.

Hatfield felt it was important to pass along the results of this mission to President Nixon and the secretary of state, which he did.

Nothing appeared in print about this trip. We felt good about our "cover," but unhappy that we couldn't share the story of this momentous occasion.

Many months later in Eugene, during a luncheon speech, the senator casually dropped word of this mission in an answer to a question about the progress of the peace talks. Although there were several members of the press in attendance at this meeting, none of them caught the significance of what he said, and his words went unreported.

In mid-1986, the senator felt it was an appropriate time to investigate the possibility of a visit to Hanoi to talk with the Vietnamese about the MIAs and about the eventual normalization of relationships between the two countries.

He sent Jim Towey, his chief legislative assistant, on an advance mission to Vietnam to see whether it would be possible to arrange a meeting with top officials of that country.

As fate would have it, some of those whom Towey initially contacted were the same people we had talked with in Paris sixteen years earlier. They remembered the occasion, and appreciated the basis of our mission at that time.

After several extremely difficult days of negotiations with this belligerent and suppressive government, Towey was satisfied that a visit to Hanoi could indeed be profitable.

As is the custom there, however, no promises were made. When Hatfield and Senator James McClure, R-Idaho, and some staff members arrived in Hanoi in January 1987, it was touch and go whether this long trip would prove to be successful.

When we saw the size of the composition of the greeting party at the airport, we knew the answer: it was positive.

Our delegation was received at the highest level. We had two days of significant talks with Prime Minister Pham Van Dong, Senior Adviser Le Duc Tho and Nguyen Co Thach, the foreign minister and the Politburo's rising star.

We also had an opportunity, informally, to see first-hand how downtrodden and tragically poor the country really was.

After reporting the observations to President Reagan and Secretary of State George Shultz, we were delighted to learn not too long afterward that the long-stalled talks about the return of the remains of the MIAs and the release of Re-education Camp prisoners had started again.

Coincidentally, the orderly departure program was reinstated, after a year of no interviews.

Perhaps that seemingly remote visit of two naive amateurs nearly two decades before had planted the seeds of acceptance and confidence so necessary in any kind of meaningful negotiations in this topsy-turvy world.

FRIDAY SURPRISE

Chocoholic judge at work

*W*hat do you end up doing if you are a chocoholic? Like me, you judge the chocolate cakes at the Oregon State Fair. Also like me, you open the Konditorei, a candy store where you can play with chocolate to your heart's content.

My passion for chocolate was inherited. I think I was probably weaned on chocolate milk. In any case, if there was ever a choice, I opted for chocolate.

My initiation was being around after mother and her friends made great creamy caramels for sale to raise money for various charitable causes. I scooped up the goodies left in the pans.

My merchandising days included some chocolate episodes, of course. We sold chocolate fudge every day at Meier & Frank. I got the idea of bringing in a small heating element and actually cooking up some fudge right before the customers' eyes. Who could pass by without stopping to get just "a little" bite? We sold over 1,000 pounds of the delicious stuff on one weekend.

A visit to Hershey, Pennsylvania, was another chocolate experience not to be forgotten. That is, of course, Chocolate City. A tour through the Hershey plant was a thrill, just looking at those huge vats of that beautiful creamy chocolate goo. I felt like jumping into the huge container myself. What a great place that must be to work.

The biggest chocolate phase of my life has been at the Oregon State Fair. For twenty-eight years, I have been the sole judge of the chocolate cake division. It has mushroomed into a major event in the Home Economics Department. Department heads including Maxine Mallicoat, Connie Hampton, Pat Wells, Cheryl Carlson, Sandy Brady, Jan Amling, and Janet Lee have put a great deal of effort behind the event, and as many as 130 cakes have been entered in the contest.

The recipe for one of the best chocolate cakes ever entered is included here.

The big event this year takes place at 2 P.M. Sunday in the Jackman-Long building on the Salem fairgrounds.

I take two bites out of each cake (frosting and inside) and assign points to the entries, which are known only by numbers.

I guess most of those in the audience wonder how much chocolate one person can eat at one time. The day's event provides chocolate saturation for weeks, believe me.

FRIDAY SURPRISE CAKE

1 1/2 cups granulated sugar
3/4 cup soft butter
3 eggs
2 1/2 cups sifted cake flour
1 tablespoon baking powder
1/2 teaspoon salt
2/3 cup unsweetened cocoa
1 cup cold water

1/2 teaspoon vanilla

Gradually cream the sugar and butter until light. Beat in eggs, one at a time. Sift together the sifted cake flour, baking powder, salt and cocoa. At low speed, beat together the dry ingredients and the water in small quantities. Blend in vanilla. Divide batter evenly in two 8-inch floured cake pans, and bake at 325 degrees for 35 to 40 minutes until just done when toothpick comes out clean.

FILLING
1/2 cup butter
1 8-ounce package cream cheese
1 pound powdered sugar
3/4 cup unsweetened cocoa
3 teaspoons strong coffee (or more if needed)
1 teaspoon vanilla
Dash of salt

Cream butter and cream cheese. Add sugar and cocoa and beat until fluffy. Add coffee and vanilla as needed for consistency and a dash of salt for taste. Spread between layers of cake.

FROSTING
3/4 cup unsifted powdered sugar
1/3 cup unsweetened cocoa
2 1/2 tablespoons all-purpose flour
3/4 cup soft butter
3 egg whites
3/4 cup powdered sugar

Mix the powdered sugar with cocoa and flour. Sift together then blend smooth with the soft butter and set aside. Beat the 3 egg whites to soft peaks. Gradually add unsifted powdered sugar and beat stiff. Add to the cocoa mixture and blend smooth. Spread on cooled cake.

The heart of the matter was downtown Portland

*B*efore the advent of the shopping centers, Portlanders made the downtown area their destination for personal and household needs. In those days, a journey to the heart of the city was considered entertainment, and many folks made it a weekly expedition. Those who lived in outlying areas of the state would save up their needs and come to Portland every month or two by car, bus or train with the kids to enjoy the excitement of the metropolis.

Many of the store names were household words that are now forgotten. Some doors were closed when the individual owners retired or passed on, and families were not interested in carrying on the business. Others were sold to out-of-state companies who changed the name or combined the store with another business.

On the block now occupied by the Galleria stood the once-proud store of Olds, Wortman and King, a favorite shopping spot for Oregonians. Founded under another name in 1852, Olds and King reached its strongest position under the leadership of the Schlesinger family (of San Francisco "City of Paris" fame) in the first third of the twentieth century.

The manager of the store during a portion of this period was a popular and dashing young man, Lee Schlesinger, whose interest in polo and other facets of the good life made him a well-known figure in the social life of the city.

When Schlesinger's car was found empty in the cold waters of the Columbia River in December of 1932, a massive search took place for his body. No trace was found; he was last seen visiting friends at Vancouver Barracks and was presumed to be on his way home when the accident occurred.

The mystery surrounding the disappearance of this highly visible businessman set tongues wagging in many a Portland living room. Because a considerable amount of insurance was involved, the insurance companies were not about to let the case be closed without a thorough investigation. Some years later they indeed did turn up Schlesinger, who was living in South America under the assumed name of Donald Moore.

Ernie Swigert, the ex-Hyster chief, long had been a close friend of Schlesinger, and in 1980, when Swigert's health was failing, Schlesinger returned to Portland to see him and others he had known decades earlier. As a next-door neighbor to the Schlesinger family, I had an interest in his life and that of his family. It was a special treat to spend a few hours with Schlesinger on this, his last and only return to his early haunts. Not once during the conversation did he make reference to the scandal that rocked the Portland establishment.

If you were looking for Hart, Schafner and Marx clothes in the early days, the men's store featuring this brand was Samuel Rosenblatt and Company, long gone from our retail scene. Rosenblatt himself was much in evidence on the floor of his store, helping the businessmen of the area with the important purchase of a new suit. Neither his son (who was the distinguished Dr. Millard Rosenblatt) nor his daughter took an interest in the family business. However, the merchandising genes did run in his grandson, Bob Freidenrich, who became a store manager for several of the Sears Roebuck stores in the Pacific Northwest.

It has been only a few years since the "Me too" store closed its doors for good. Known as Charles F. Berg, this fine ladies' specialty store got its nickname from the signs Berg placed in his window at Sixth Avenue and Morrison Street when neighbor Meier & Frank would advertise a big hosiery sale. An active participant in the civic life of his city, Berg passed along this concern to his son, Forrest, who expanded the store during his tenure as head man.

For years, the well-dressed ladies would let no one but Evelyn Gibson dress them in the city's finest. If fur wraps were included, Nicholas Ungar would charm the lady and raise havoc with her hubbie's wallet. If clothes were to be made at home, of course, the first stop would be the piece goods department of Roberts Brothers, where there were bargains galore.

Some of these great names are fond memories nowadays. Although there were indeed blood battles across the sales counters, that blood was closer in the operations of the two merchandising giants located across Alder Street on Fifth Avenue. In the days before

Lipman, Wolfe was bought by Roberts Brothers, it was owned by National Department Stores, headquartered in New York. The daughter of the president of National, Laura Schwartz, married Roger Meier (of the M&F Meiers), who later worked at Lipman's. Meier's boss and the longtime manager of Lipman's, Harold Wendel, was a first cousin of Ruth Frank, wife of Aaron, the president of M&F. To add to the connection, Jessie Lipman, wife of I.N. Lipman, former president of Lipman's and a member of that store's founding family, was a sister of Ruth Frank.

Quite an incestuous relationship in some of the pioneer merchandising families of the city.

FRIDAY SURPRISE

Mideast challenges wise men

*O*ne of the most important and complex dramas of our time is unfolding in the Middle East. No solution is going to be easy or satisfying to all parties concerned, for there are political, social, economic and religious factors intertwined in a part of the world that is deeply steeped in history, and at the same time is a major player on today's world stage.

In the Middle East countries, there are unique and different conditions and personalities. Years of work by top diplomats of our country, including such professionals as Henry Kissinger, Zbigniew Brzezinski and George Shultz, have been spent trying to unravel the problems of the past and suggesting possible solutions for the future.

I have had the opportunity to make nearly two dozen visits to countries throughout the Middle East and have visited with heads of state and their staffs. In these exciting and informative experiences, I have gathered a feel for the individual perspectives of the different nations. This background is vital if one is going to try to understand what is going on now in the long-anticipated talks between Yasser Arafat and the representative of the United States, Robert H. Pelletreau Jr., our ambassador in Tunis.

Of all the Middle East countries, Lebanon, and particularly Beirut, was probably the most charming. The Lebanese are a cultured, competent and highly motivated people. The social and political problems, however, are of enormous complexity, inasmuch as the country is divided almost equally between Christians and Moslems.

Nearby Jordan is a completely different world. A tiny and relatively poor country in natural resources, Jordan has been literally kept together by the intelligence, spunk and political acumen of one man, King Hussein. If there was any one individual on Earth who must thank his lucky stars to be alive each night when he goes to bed, it is this brave man who faces incredible presures in the divided country that he rules.

I have visited refugee camps in both Lebanon and Jordan several times. The ones in Jordan were particularly sad, with several generations of Palestinians living a most spartan existence under conditions that were ripe to be exploited by the troublemakers of the region. The fact that Hussein has been able to keep his country from breaking out into civil war is one of the great political achievements of our time.

Syria has strong and determined leadership, a necessity as they sit in a strategic position in relation to their Arab friends and the Jewish state of Israel. A trip to the Golan Heights is enough to convince one of the extremely volatile conditions that exist in this area. One of my most vivid recollections is a visit to the PLO headquarters in an old part of Damascus some years ago on a mission to try to bring about some meaningful dialogue with American officials. It was like stepping back several hundred years in time.

Saudia Arabia, on the other hand, is a rich and fascinating country, with two very distinct classes of citizens. The royal family and their many relatives live in medieval splendor in showcase castles in the middle of sand dunes, while hundreds of thousands of others live in poor and crowded conditions.

President Hosni Mubarak of Egypt, one of the wise men of the region, also occupies an important role in the drama. He has brought his poor nation into modern times through extended economic activity and an on-again off-again dialogue with his neighbors. In several personal visits with Mubarak, I have found him to be a highly motivated and sincere friend of our country, a practical man we can count on when things get tough.

Sitting in the midst of this fascinating web of different cultures and varying economic problems is the tiny country of Israel.

The hopes and struggles of their people are well-known, but today a new and important factor has surfaced. For the first time since the establishment of the current state, her citizens are divided about the methods necessary to bring about peace. The economy of the country cannot stand the continued pressures of turmoil.

Caught as pawns in all of this are the Palestinian refugees, literally a people without a country. Their need and right for a plot of ground to call "home" is the most unsettling fact of life in the area.

What a jigsaw puzzle to put back together! What a challenge for the wise men of our time who must try to find a workable formula. An extra special holiday prayer is in order.

Latest bombing recalls department store blast

*T*he bombing of the Pan American airliner over Scotland last week brings to mind an earlier incident in Portland, another example of this terrifying method of political revenge and extortion.

It started one mid-afternoon during a busy Friday Surprise sale at the Meier & Frank downtown department store in April, 1955.

A numbing blast rocked the fifteen-story building, sending customers into the street and salespeople scurrying around to see what in the world had happened on the south side of the building.

Restrooms are located in the center of several floors on the Morrison Street side.

It was immediately apparent that a bomb had gone off in the men's restroom on the third floor, the quietest in the building because no men's departments were located on that floor.

Soon, sirens and emergency vehicles were heard and seen throughout the entire area, and police and fire officials descended on the building.

At the same time as the blast, Aaron Frank, then president of the store, was returning to his office on the 12th floor after having lunch in the store's dining room.

His secretary handed him a typed note that had been left with her by a man who said it should be opened at once. As Frank ripped open the envelope, the drama nine floors below him was unfolding.

The note told him what had happened, and what was threatened in the future.

"Bud" Frank was a feisty and tough merchant, besides being my father. He was not about to give in to a threat, but at the same time he would not endanger the safety of any customer of the store.

At this period of my career, I was a merchant-in-training, having served in various departments of the store from the receiving room to the main floor bargain squares.

All of this excitement that Friday afternoon sent my adrenalin rushing, and I ran to the area of the explosion.

Just as I got there, one of the salespeople yelled to me that I was wanted on the telephone.

When I got to the phone, it was my dad. His voice and demeanor were even more stern than usual.

"Go get me two white carnations," he barked. I thought for a minute that he had lost his marbles!

"But, dad," I said, "we've got a bit of a problem here on the third floor and there are police and firemen all over the place."

"I know. You heard me." Bang went the phone.

I darted down the stairway, headed to Tommy Luke Florists, in the middle of the block between Sixth Avenue and Broadway on Morrison.

As I got halfway across the street, I felt someone grab me with the instructions, "Come with me."

"Sorry, I can't. I'm on assignment for my dad."

FBI badges flashed.

I thought maybe I had better take a different approach.

I told the agents what I was up to, and they suggested that I immediately return to my dad's office and they would complete my assignment.

His office was filled with law enforcement people, store officials and others. I learned that the note told of the bombing, and the writer demanded money or another bomb would go off the next day.

There were instructions on how the money was to be delivered, and the bit about the flowers. The delivering party was to have a carnation in his buttonhole.

The rest is history. There was no other bomb. No money was delivered.

It turned out that a partially blinded chemist, Clarence Peddicord, unhappy with the world, was the bomber. He was caught by expert crime detection work that matched typewriter samples from the extortion note and from a mail fraud case.

He had no beef with M&F, just chose it because it happened to be a visible target. He was convicted, served a lengthy jail sentence, and that part of the story has now been forgotten.

What hasn't been forgotten is what has happened since. Bombings and bomb threats have multiplied. The more publicity there was, the more incidents occurred.

We are all now painfully aware of the problem, of the enormous expense that many have suffered because of these hideous threats and acts.

But there is a slightly amusing twist to the event of that Friday afternoon.

A gentleman who was using the facilities on the second floor, directly underneath the spot where the blast occurred, was last seen that day running out of the building at high speed with his trousers at half mast. He probably was one of those most appreciative of the life he once had taken for granted.

FRIDAY SURPRISE

Woman power driving government, civic affairs

*D*on't be surprised if the "Golden Man" on top of the state Capitol in Salem is replaced one of these days by the "Golden Woman." Women are making their marks in this community, and a lot of folks are saying that it is about time.

The big news this week was when the three top community awards, Salem's First Citizen and the two Distinguished Service Awards, all went to women.

It was the first time in Salem history that this had happened and one of the few times that such a happy situation has taken place statewide.

Keeta Lauderdale, a transplant from Depoe Bay who has been a resident of the community for more than twenty years, was selected as the town's leading personage. Lauderdale, who married her childhood sweetheart, Ray, and has raised three children since, has been the sparkplug for so many good causes that one wonders how she has managed so much activity. Whether it was the Hospital, Boy's Club, Symphony or work on Tom Neilsen's mayoral contest or on Vic Gilliam's legislative race, Lauderdale was there with unbounded enthusiasm. In addition to her well-deserved new title, she is the chairwoman of the Salem City Planning Commission.

It must be the valley air, for this enormous energy and zest for life seems to be contagious in Salem.

One of the Distinguished Award winners is so "up" all the time that someone asked her if they could bottle all that energy.

Lorraine VanAusdell's answer was the best: "I just love everybody." And it shows. For years VanAusdell was the main public presence for the United States National Bank in Salem, taking care of all those "outside" duties the day-to-day bankers don't have time for.

The Chamber of Commerce and the March of Dimes and the United Way always looked to VanAusdell for inspiration and example. Now that she is retired, this very popular dynamo seems to be going at double speed.

The second Distinguished Award went to a member of one of the pioneer families of Salem, Edith Findley Brydon. Brydon always cared deeply about the maturing folks in the area. Salem's extremely busy and successful Senior Center is directly the result of her efforts. Brydon has been "distinguished" to the Grey Panther set for a long time.

Those three are not all.

Sue Harris Miller just turned over the reins as mayor after two busy terms, marked by the beginning of activity on how Salem's riverfront will be used for business and recreational purposes. Miller was no "part-time" executive. She devoted the majority of her time working for her fellow citizens.

The business community also has several able women with top responsibilities. The Salem Area Chamber of Commerce elected Lynda Stephens as president for the current year, the second period in three years that a woman has held this highly visible post.

Like predecessor Kay Rogers, Stephens is right at home presiding over a multitude of committees and projects, including the monthly Forum luncheons that attract some of the nation's best-known business and political leaders as speakers. Portland General Electric is having to share Stephen's time this year, as both hats top a very busy head.

Then the local voice of the city, Gannett's *Statesman-Journal,* has a new woman publisher, with roots in the Portland area. Sara Bentley, raised in the Rose City, worked in the journalism field in the Midwest and has recently returned to her native state. Although schooled on the fiscal side of the publishing business, Bentley is quickly establishing herself as a concerned local leader.

Down the street at the Capitol building, Vera Katz is back as Speaker of the House for the third time. Although not from Salem, Katz spends a great deal of time in the capital and is a well-respected person throughout the area.

Secretary of State Barbara Roberts has found time to get involved in a number of local activities. She follows in the very large footsteps of another talented Salemite, Norma Paulus, who now serves on the Northwest Power Planning Council.

At last count there were about forty-five cities in the state that have women serving as mayor. They run the gamut from well-seasoned old-timers like Jean Young in King City and Edith Henningsgaard in Astoria to relatively young leaders like Laree Linder in Eagle Point.

All have one thing in common: they are tenacious boosters for their communities.

FRIDAY SURPRISE

Oregon hospitals reach out, send vital aid to Afghanistan

*T*his week the airwaves and newspapers have been full of the details of the Soviet pullout in Afghanistan after years of bloody conflict. The tragic toll in human life and suffering is staggering. It is estimated that more than one million Afghans have been killed, that there are more than five million refugees and that the Soviets have lost 15,000 men, with twice that many wounded.

I was particularly interested in the story after reading what was happening in the Afghan city of Jalalabad, an area practically cut off by the guerrillas. It was said there might be a major attack on government forces in that city, with the push coming from the Pakistanis. Reliable sources feel that the fall of Jalalabad is a foregone conclusion; only the timing is in question.

Jalalabad is a city of about 60,000 people. It is important because it controls the road to Pakistan, which is Afghanistan's route to the sea. Being a landlocked country, this is particularly vital both militarily and economically.

I visited Jalalabad in the early 1970s, on a mission from the U.S. Senate. Looking back upon that experience, little did I think that this quiet town would one day be at the focal point of the world scene. But then Afghanistan is a strange country, as it sits at the crossroads of Central Asia. It has had a turbulent history, has suffered numer-

ous invasions and has a population as tough and as combative as any in the world.

During my time there, I had sessions with the prime minister and other Cabinet officials. I remember them being friendly enough to America but not particularly sympathetic to our view of what was going on in the Middle East.

The most important and most memorable part of my visit was the day spent with Peace Corps personnel. Our trip through the Kabul Pass was one of the most beautiful and rugged automobile trips I have ever taken. I remember that the Peace Corps vehicle was not the most modern. At times I wondered if we would ever reach our destination.

In Jalalabad, I visited the Nangarhar University Hospital, which was being aided by a medical team from Loma Linda College and Indiana University, with a good deal of extra help from the devoted men and women of our Peace Corps unit in that country.

The members of the medical team were existing on meager salaries and living in the most rudimentary accommodations. They were giving their all to this medical project, at the time the largest non-government funded project in the entire country.

About a dozen Peace Corps volunteer physicians, a number of nurses and lab technicians assisted the medical faculty. In addition there were seven American physicians and several Catholic Sisters on the same team.

The primitive conditions and lack of equipment were mind boggling. Having served on the board of St. Vincent Hospital and Medical Center in Portland, I was used to medical institutions of some sophistication. This hospital couldn't have been further from what we take for granted in our community.

There were 125 patients at the time I was there, with one electric suction machine for the entire hospital. There was one glass syringe. One emergency room light was used between the two operating rooms for surgery. My notes reminded me that they had one thermometer for every 30 patients.

They had enough linen for only one bed change every eight days. No adjustable beds for positioning seriously injured patients were available.

The surgeon told me that they frequently had to postpone operations for lack of gloves or sterile linen. No disinfectants were available for the communicable disease area.

To complete the sad picture, only one pressure cooker was in central supply, and no lab equipment for rudimentary blood tests was available. Often there was not enough anesthetic to complete an operation.

Because there were so few nurses, families of the patients lived in the rooms with their loved ones, cooking food for them right by the bed.

I was so moved by what was being done in this remote village that when I came home, I called upon several of our local hospitals to get together excess supplies for shipment to Afghanistan. In the true Oregon spirit, hospitals in Portland and Salem organized tons of equipment and medicine, and after a series of bureaucratic hassles, we did get them on their way.

Months later when the shipment arrived, we heard from the medical team in Jalalabad. Their joy was contagious; the generous folks in Oregon had made a difference. One wonders if there is joy today of any kind in this poor, sad and desolate country?

FRIDAY SURPRISE

Portland personalities add luster to hometown

With Portland and Seattle, cities of comparable size within the same geographic region, it is inevitable they should be constantly compared.

Which is healthier economically? Which is the better place to live? A recent issue of *Pacific Northwest* magazine went into great detail comparing the two cities and came to the same conclusion many people have before: the "best" depends on what you are looking for.

I'll put my chips on Portland, naturally. As a native-born, fourth-generation Oregonian, I have strong emotional ties to my city of birth and state of residence.

Most Oregonians share this love, for a variety of reasons. Some like our attractive downtown, others the easy commuting distance to recreational areas, others the cultural scene, still others have family and business bonds.

One of the great things that has made Portland a great place to live (and I suppose the same thing is true in many other cities) is the contributions during the years of a number of individuals who made the Rose City their home. Some have been household names during the years, others are remembered only by reputation, still others are unknown to many but were major players in the building and blossoming of our community.

If there was one factor in the past that differentiated the two communities, it was the stability of Portland and the rather transient profile of our sister city to the north. With the exception of World War II shipyard days, when Henry J. Kaiser brought tens of thousands of "outsiders" to work in his shipyards, the blue collar scene in Portland grew slowly.

The younger generation will not remember her, but old-time Portlanders will never forget one of the most colorful mayors we have ever had: Dorothy McCullough Lee. "Do Good Dottie," as she was fondly referred to by friends and enemies alike, was the local version of British Prime Minister Margaret Thatcher. Her nickname came from cleaning up some tawdry activities in Portland. She was unafraid to tackle the toughest hoodlums and chiselers in town.

In a totally different arena, the name James J. Richardson will be revered for the contributions he made to the world of sports in the Rose City. For many years, Richardson was the popular manager of the Multnomah Athletic Club. To him goes the credit for building this club into what it is today, the nation's premier private athletic facility. Richardson pioneered numerous events in what was then called Multnomah Stadium (then a part of the MAC), encouraged the club's Olympic championship "Cody Kids" swimming team (named after coach Jack Cody) and was prominent in a legion of worthwhile civic activities.

Every city needs a cheerleader, and Portland had a prize: Frank Callahan. It's not too often that a butcher fulfills such a title, but Callahan was no ordinary meat-market proprietor. In his own charming Irish manner, this lovable extrovert knew no bounds in promoting his native city.

Portlanders with a bit of gray around their temples probably will not remember the exact name of the gentleman who played Santa Claus for decades on the most popular Christmas radio program in the twenties and thirties. Of all things, he was an insurance salesman by profession. His name: Frank Sardam. Sardam gathered an unlikely crew of ham actors around him each December, wrote scripts himself for Mother Goose and all of the other characters, and read hundreds of letters sent in by young Portlanders who wouldn't go to bed until after this daily radio show. I should know about Sardam's talent; he recruited me to play Tinker on the show for many years. I got fired when my voice changed.

Then there was the colorful sometime innkeeper and man-about-town, Harvey Dick. The scion of a well-known Portland family, Dick was very much his own man and had little time for the trappings of life of his contemporaries. With considerable expense, and an uncanny way of sensing what the community wanted to do to have fun, Dick made the Hoyt Hotel THE place to see and be seen. Some of the most memorable parties of the century were held by Dick, whose later marriage to Hildamae Jensen, widow of movie house pioneer Claude Jensen, united two of the more charming folks in town.

Every city needs an ambassador-at-large. Portland's contribution was Frank Branch Riley, orator extraordinaire. On yearly, cross-country speaking excursions, Riley would recite, in the most colorful prose imaginable, the sights and sounds of his beloved city.

Of course, there were hundreds more who contributed their share. We are all a bit richer because of these folks and others like them, who have now passed on to be prominent chapters in Tom Vaughan's Oregon Historical Society annals.

All Aboard! Trains are back on track with speed and style

*W*hat little kid is not thrilled by trains...the real ones and the model variety? I was no different, and the fascination has never diminished. First it was the great model train set-up that a friend of mine had, the kind with all the stations and tunnels and special switching apparatus. We would play for hours imagining that we were the engineers, never dreaming that one day I would really be a train engineer, so to speak.

For my first honest-to-goodness train ride, it was the great yellow Union Pacific "City of Roses" that took part of three days and two nights to go from Portland to Chicago. This was the way to travel in those days, before the convenience of air travel.

The best part of the journey was eating; the dining car on this streamliner was special. Wonderfully courteous waiters, beautifully set tables with white linen and sparkling crystal, and delicious food made every meal an exciting experience.

Upon reaching Chicago, if you were going on to New York, you had to change stations for the rest of your journey. The final night was spent on the Twentieth Century Limited, in those days the last word in train travel. A red carpet was laid out for you at the station, and the evening and early morning passed much too rapidly.

These days, some train travel can be rather humdrum, but not all. One has to give credit to Amtrak, for what it is doing to bring comfortable and affordable train travel back to millions of Americans who for one reason or another prefer this mode of transportation. The Amtrak Metroliners that make the run between New York and Washington in little more than two and a half hours are great trains.

When you arrive in Washington, D.C., by train, a real treat is in store for you. The magnificent Beaux Arts Union Station, built in 1907, has finally been restored (for $160 million) to its original grandeur. The building features one of the finest complexes of stores anywhere in the nation, including one devoted just to trains and train memorabilia.

A number of eating places are scattered throughout, including a grand restaurant in the area that used to be the "holding room" for presidents who were going to travel by train. Downstairs is a food fair and a multi-screen movie setup. The building looks absolutely first class, and it has become a favorite destination for visitors and nearby workers.

Three of my train experiences stand out especially. Number one was in the Soviet Union, of all places. We went from Moscow to Kiev to attend the Dartmouth Conference, a meeting of top-level U.S. and Soviet officials. It was an overnight journey aboard a regular Russian train, equipped with one historic car that had seen its better days, but still had all the trappings that allowed one to imagine what train travel was like in that country in the days of the czars.

The next of the never-to-be-forgotten rides was on the famous "Orient Express" from London, England to Venice, Italy. This train is made up of famous old railcars that have been completely refurbished to bring them back to their original condition...and what beauties they are.

In France, one boards the magnificent sleeping cars, where you are assigned to your own special accommodation, complete with every kind of convenience that can be put into such a small space. The promotion material mentions getting "dressed up" for the dinner hour, and many of the passengers do just that. Some of the great looks of the twenties appear at the candlelight and wine dinner, and romantic music and great stories combine to make the overnight trip a true journey into the past.

The third of the memorable trips was on the private train of the chief executive officer of Union Pacific. The occasion was a cross-country inspection trip of the railroad's Western facilities, and what a journey it was. Imagine having your own train!

The CEO had his own car, complete with bedroom and shower, dining facilities and all the trappings of home. We were treated to super meals, prepared by senior stewards who had been with the company forever. But the real excitement of the whole experience was the chance to play engineer (with professional supervision, of course). Yes, I did get the chance to sit in the engineer's seat in the locomotive, and yes, I did get the chance to pull that cord and blow that whistle to my heart's content. I guess we never grow up. In the case of trains, I hope I never do.

Oil spill mileage? 4 smiles per gallon of industry greed

*M*aybe it is about time for the occupants of the corner offices of corporate America to give the keys to the executive washroom to their secretaries and spend a little bit more time on the firing line. If some of the happenings in the business world in recent months haven't shaken them up a bit, heaven knows what will.

We are numbed by the oil spill disaster in Alaska. It will surely go down in the history books as an enormous environmental tragedy. I am told by those who know him that Lawrence Rawl, the chief executive officer of Exxon, is one of the most enlightened of today's top executives. A lot of folks are wondering if that is an accurate evaluation.

It would seem that time was wasted in the initial stages of the spill in getting adequate equipment working to try and contain the damage. Fingers were pointed at both the company and government officials in Alaska and Washington, D.C. But there surely was little time wasted in raising the price of gasoline for the American consumer. Sure, there are lots of reasons given, like worry over future supplies and increased summer demand. But the finger points very suspiciously to just plain bad judgment at best and plain, ordinary greed at worst.

I wonder if the officials of Exxon would have taken such steps if they had sensed the depth of feeling the average citizen has concerning this tragedy. And would they have allowed one of their associates to announce that the American motorist would have to pay the enormous costs of the cleanup?

Where is the corporate social responsibility? Is this the kind of response that our future executives are being taught in the business classrooms at Harvard and Columbia and Stanford? I hope not. Are the screaming headlines of one Eastern newspaper to "Boycott Exxon" a forerunner of what is going to happen?

Then we are being treated almost daily to the spectacle of the dealings at Drexel Burnham Lambert. I have no idea if Mike Milken is guilty of the securities charges leveled against him. But I do have a feel for the public reaction to the fact that one employee earned more last year in commissions than the entire company posted as profit. Maybe he deserved it, but that will be a hard one to sell. The business pages last week hinted at the dangers lurking in the junk bond market. Are we going to witness a repeat of that October 1987 disaster that is still fresh in so many people's minds and portfolios?

What is the reaction of the man in the street when he sees a full-page ad printed in some of the nation's leading newspapers praising Milken and his dealings? The words of support were signed by some of the major executives of corporate America. What kind of message will that send to our young people if Milken is not found guilty? You can get away with anything, as long as you don't get caught. Are the folks at Drexel Burnham conscious of what is being said on the streets of mid-America?

For insensitivity at its extreme, one need look no farther than the Eastern Airlines mess. There is no question that Frank Lorenzo had an almost impossible job of trying to bring the troubled carrier back to health. But surely the recovery room ordeal would have been much easier if he had the cooperation of all the practitioners on the operating team. The depth of unhappiness among the thousands of Eastern employees, and the translation of that into inconvenience for millions of American travelers, must be taken into consideration by any socially conscious executive. Lorenzo obviously didn't think so. Even with the seemingly helpful efforts of the team put together by Peter Ueberroth, there was no give. Is one man's pride ("I want to go out vindicated") worth the price?

Perhaps if Lorenzo had traveled on a few of his planes and spoken personally with some of his people, he would have had some sympathy for their concerns. He might even have found that they were willing to meet him more than halfway. Wasn't it Voltaire who said, "I disapprove of what you say, but I will defend to the death your right to say it"?

There are many, many other examples that we are exposed to almost daily.

One person who does listen out on the firing line can make a difference. We need look no farther than The Dalles, where Brett Wilcox, a modern, bright, young entrepreneur, listened to his employees and then put together a viable, employee-ownership plan for Northwest Aluminum, when others couldn't make a go of the company. Today it is very healthy and very profitable. At the same time, Wilcox is showing outstanding corporate social responsibility in the good works for his community. His hearing aid is turned up; are the batteries dead for some of the others?

Regal presidency takes toll on decent men's lives

*W*hat would you do if the president of the United States (directly or through a top lieutenant) asked you to undertake a mission that seemed, on the surface at least, to be one of extreme importance? I would guess that most of us would not ask too many questions, believing that the president should know what is proper and what is legal.

Every time I think about the circumstances surrounding the Oliver L. North trial, I reflect on another not-so-dissimilar case that had ties much closer to home.

Egil Krogh, Sr., was looked upon in the merchandising world as one of the outstanding men in his field. Ethically and educationally, he was top drawer, the kind of person in whom you would have complete trust and confidence. After a career with Marshall Field in Chicago, he was recruited by my father to become general merchandise manager of Meier & Frank, a position he held with great distinction.

He moved to the Portland area with his family, including a son, Egil, Jr., "Bud," who, like his father, was an achiever in every aspect of his life. He was in the top section of his class at school, was an outstanding athlete and later became a respected member of the bar. It was a little later that he caught the eye of John Ehrlichman, a Seattle lawyer, who was to play an important role in the Nixon White House.

Although I did not know Egil, Jr., well, I did know of the deep religious roots that made his family such a close-knit and respected clan. I was excited to learn that he had been tapped to work in Washington, D.C., at the source of power and influence: the White House.

I recall well meeting him for lunch in the early 1970s in the White House "mess" that is reserved for those who occupy senior administration positions. One has a hard time paying attention to the food in this spot; all eyes are on the other tables where big deals and big decisions seem to be the major menu items.

I was impressed with how Krogh had grown and matured. He seemed to be happy, in full control of his destiny, making important and influential decisions that would affect the lives of many of his countrymen. I remember thinking how fortunate we were to have a fellow of his caliber in that position.

The next time I saw him, about a year later, he was brought to the visitor's room at Allenwood Prison in Pennsylvania, where he had been sentenced for two to six years for depriving citizens of their rights.

By this time, perhaps, his name will ring a familiar bell. He was co-head of the Nixon White House "plumbers," the group that in 1971 broke into the office of Daniel Ellsberg's psychiatrist.

Jail time (reduced to several months) was not easy for this proud, talented individual. Nor was it easy for his family. In the strain and turmoil that followed, Krogh lost two of the most important things in his life: his license to practice law and his wife. Quite a price to pay, obviously, for undertaking what I am confident was an order from the commander-in-chief that Krogh never thought to question.

Fortunately, the story of his life since those dark days has become one of true grit and renewed achievement. He was reinstated to the bar after some agonizing times, has remarried and is again a highly respected practitioner in the legal field. He now does work for some Northwest utility companies.

The circumstances that surround the Oliver North Iran-Contra affair are vastly different, of course. But there is a similar thread to the two stories.

It would be difficult to imagine that North was basically anything else but a hard-driving, overly ambitious, loyal and thrill-seeking Marine. It is probably also fair to say that the end product was much more important in his life than the means used in getting there.

The verdict of the jurors in that protracted and uncomfortable trial indicated that they felt North was neither a villain nor a hero.

The cases of Krogh and North point up a basic fact of life during the twentieth century in the United States. We have established an almost regal presidency, with many of the trappings of a monarchy but without that name. It is fair to say that no chief of state in the world today enjoys the kind of support personnel, equipment and influence that our president does. It is also fair to note that George Bush is trying to downplay a bit of that ostentatious lifestyle that sometimes got slightly out of hand in the Reagan White House.

But given working in these surroundings, and given the intense, competitive atmosphere that exists to be recognized and to please the boss in that pressure chamber, is it any wonder that we have seen so many cases of decent men's lives being destroyed because of their complete faith in one man and his causes?

FRIDAY SURPRISE

When the 'stars' shine, these guys do polishing

A popular and talented sports figure finds himself at the eye of a storm about his involvement in a charity golf tournament. A top business executive takes on yet another civic assignment to add to a lengthy list of community and in-house responsibilities. A Cabinet secretary spends a goodly portion of her time testifying in front of congressional committees while her department continues to operate in a smooth and orderly fashion. A once-disgraced president of the United States gets a standing ovation at a gathering of newspaper executives who not long ago could hardly find a nice word to say about him.

What do these people and these seemingly unrelated situations have in common? Just like a successful Broadway opening or an award-winning television show where the plaudits go to the star, there are people behind the scenes who make these headliners look good.

And so it is in real life, where individuals who are faced with some tough situations have some loyal and talented people who allow them to fulfill their complex assignments and look good doing it.

Peter Jacobsen, one of the most successful and engaging athletes that Oregon has ever produced, was besieged by questions about his part in the management fee structure of the Fred Meyer Challenge. At first he did not respond to press questions. Later he used some edgy words to describe the whole situation.

It was obvious that some professional advice was necessary to put the right spin on the story.

It was no surprise that the person to whom he and his advisers turned was Ron Schmidt, a longtime practitioner in damage control and perhaps the ultimate behind-the-scenes operator in the state today.

I first knew Schmidt some thirty years ago when he was the front man for the Oregon Shakespearean Festival in Ashland. It was obvious even then that this savvy young man had a brilliant future. When the new Lloyd Center needed a public relations person in the early sixties, I suggested to Dick Horn, the manager of the center, that he couldn't do better than bringing Schmidt aboard. The fit was perfect.. Schmidt was launched on a career that would lead him to become the person most responsible for making Tom McCall one of the state's most unforgettable political personalities.

Schmidt has never sought the limelight himself, but he has personally made sure that any number of prominent individuals have been put in the most favorable light possible.

McCall was the newsman's dream: outspoken, colorful, unpredictable.

Many was the time that Schmidt was able to put the best twist on a McCall statement, or was responsible for an event that allowed this charismatic state executive to best show off his talents.

After eight turbulent and eventful years in Salem, Schmidt became part of a major advertising and public relations firm in Portland.

In the corporate world, one wonders how the president of a large bank or major utility can run the outfit, serve as chairman of numerous civic committees, give dozens of speeches and be successful at all of these assignments. The answer again is some top staff help.

Two of the best are Floyd Bennett of First Interstate Bank and Hillman Lueddemann, Jr., of Portland General Electric.

Probably no one in the state has such sensitive eyes and ears to what is going on in the community as Bennett. He has served as the back-up man for six bank presidents and for more civic events than he is able to count.

Lueddemann is retiring at the end of this month from a career as the expediter for his company. Not one to put himself at the front, this unselfish son of a former First Citizen has never been properly recognized for the enormous efforts he has put forth with the Rose Festival, William Temple House, United Way, OMSI and dozens of other important activities. When a big name receives the plaudits for a Portland project well done, you can just about guess that Lueddemann was one of the guys in the back who did most of the nitty-gritty work.

And so it is on the national scene, too. When former President Richard Nixon is rehabilitated to the point that the press is actually writing favorable pieces about him, you can bet that John Taylor, his assistant, has worked hard to plant the seed for those words.

When Elizabeth Dole, labor secretary, receives applause for the management of her sprawling department, you can bet that she would say that Jenna Dorn, the deputy secretary who is an Oregon native, deserves a great deal of that credit.

The headlines and plaudits make a nice platform for the top folks to stand on, but the perceptive public figure knows that many times the foundation is laid by others whose talents make that position possible.

FRIDAY SURPRISE

Mid-century Lincoln High broke walls of prejudice

*I*t is hard to believe, but as recently as the middle of this century, Portland was not known as a city where ethnic and religious minorities mixed easily with the greater population.

In fact, most major social and athletic clubs either prohibited membership for blacks, Asians and Jews or had unspoken "quotas" established and administered by anonymous committees.

Although polite folks did not talk about it openly, discrimination was obvious in the marketplace, in schools, in property transactions and in many other aspects of the society.

When confronted by obvious injustices, community leaders would shrug their shoulders and almost act as if they didn't know what was going on. Nonsense.

One of the institutions at the center of the ethnic mix that has given this city its strong undergirding of talent over the years was Lincoln High School, formerly located in the South Park Blocks, in a building which is now part of Portland State University.

Lincoln was the only four-year public high school on the west side of the river in those days. Students were drawn from very diverse neighborhoods: South Portland, Portland Heights, Dunthorpe and Northwest Portland.

The backgrounds these young people came from were as different as the areas they called home. South Portland was known as a predominately Jewish area, with many of the students coming from close-knit family and neighborhood relationships. Most were not too affluent in the material sense.

On the other end of the scale economically were the sons and daughters of community leaders who lived on Portland Heights or in Dunthorpe. They represented well-known, old-time families. Ethnically and culturally, they had little in common with their South Portland classmates before they entered high school.

In addition, there were a number of Asian students, many of whom had been reared in Portland's Chinatown.

Some very savvy teachers and administrators knew full well the challenge and opportunity they had. In particular, Principal Henry Gunn, who came to Lincoln from Ainsworth Grammar School, the most affluent and "socially acceptable" school in town in those days, realized he could make a difference in how minorities would be treated in the latter half of the century in Portland. He sensed that he was molding the characters of many future leaders and influence builders of the community. Gunn was assisted by an outstanding array of teachers, counselors and coaches in the Portland School District.

On the athletic side, Wade "Whizzer" Williams molded the character of his diverse football crew, while "Wee Dave" Wright took his talented, combined South Portland and Portland Heights basketball team to many a victory.

In the classroom, unforgettable teachers, such as Mabel Southworth, journalism; Ruth Halvorsen, art; Ruth Arbuckle, English; Helen Critchlow, history; Emma Griebel, science; Calvin Foulk, biology; and others molded their heterogenous classrooms into strong units that would have made the United Nations proud. The results were spectacular.

Several weeks ago, those who were fortunate enough to have been trained in this forward-looking and unusual school setting gathered in their "almost 50" reunion to exchange stories and laughs. But the major message that came across from those who attended the evening event was much more profound.

Because of their high school experiences, these individuals were able to join a society that badly needed reforming. They had the background to do just that, and they did.

Harry Glickman went on to become one of the most successful professional basketball executives in the nation. Two former student body presidents, Bob Roth and Ames Hendrickson, became major executives in various areas of merchandising. James Wong, who in high school days was the first Chinese teenager to be elected a student body president in the United States, had an outstanding career in government service. Harold Schnitzer has achieved prominence in the business world. Sylvia Davidson used her talents in many decades of leadership service in the arts and humanities.

Several of the old-time teachers were on hand at the reunion, staged by Peryl Gottesman and her crew, to receive well-deserved accolades for the influence they had on so many lives.

Henry Gunn, who later became superintendent of the Palo Alto, California, school system, one of the nation's best, would have been especially proud if he had lived long enough to take in the evening program. But he and his associates can take credit for being instrumental in breaking down a long-established, unfair and intolerable prejudice that for years crippled the growth and flowering of our city.

FRIDAY SURPRISE

Take tip from Nepal and tackle sales tax issue now

The setting was almost beyond description. It was a base camp, called Namche Bazaar, at the foot of Mount Everest in Nepal. The village was inhabited by Tibetan refugees whose main occupation was hand-crafting some of the most unusual rugs one could imagine.

Although participants were on an inspection tour of projects partially financed by American aid and an oversight look at some Peace Corps activities, they found the temptation to bring home one of those beautiful pieces of craftsmanship overwhelming.

Our means of transportation was a small helicopter, so storage room was at a premium. Nevertheless, the pilot said "OK" if we promised to buy only the small ones.

There was much excitement among the camp settlers as the chopper sat in the middle of their picturesque area. The village chief soon made himself known, spoke only enough English to allow himself to be understood and offered to take us on a tour of his entrepreneurial activity. We jumped at the opportunity.

Soon we had made our choices and the eager workers bound the rugs tightly and even helped store them in our copter. How much did we owe them?

The price quoted was ridiculously low, given what pieces such as these would bring in the markets of our country. A sales slip was produced, but below the amount settled upon was another figure. What was this? "Sales tax," came the answer, with not even a hint of a grin.

A sales tax in the middle of one of the most remote areas in the world? It boggled our imaginations, but I guess it should not have. What is that old saying about death and taxes?

Our concern about taxes is raised to prominence several times during the year, either when we have to figure our own liability or when some tax measure is being discussed in Salem or Washington, or when we have to vote on a tax issue. Otherwise, most of us just take for granted that taxes are a part of our lives that we really cannot do much about except pay.

But things are happening in our society today that make it imperative that we address the tax issue with more concern than in the past. No longer can we take the posture that it is beyond our control, and that all we can do is complain. Those who set tax policy are taxpayers just like you and me, and they are very responsive to what we think, especially when they are up for election.

We would probably get little argument about the importance of quality education. When we examine the education being offered the young folks in Japan and Korea, and see its results, we know the kind of race for excellence that we're in. The other day there was a picture on the front page of a national metropolitan daily showing a group of twenty students who were winners of special scholarship awards. Nineteen came from Asian backgrounds.

Our school administrators tell us that we cannot continue the uneasy and unsafe "safety net" system under which too many of our Oregon schools are operating. Something drastic must be done to ensure a sound and predictable source of funds.

Those who are in the business of recruiting new payrolls for our state will tell you when their sales pitch faces rough going: when the personal tax liabilities are detailed. It takes a lot of good locations and fine workers and great fishing to overcome those pocketbook questions.

When the problems peculiar to our state are combined with the frustrations faced by taxpayers who were supposed to get relief from a so-called simplified federal tax plan, the average taxpayer flees to the accountant's office for some aspirin.

Most of the accountants are so busy trying to figure out the tax code themselves that they hardly look up from their own bottles of Maalox.

So where do we go from here? The problem is simply put. The answer is not quite so simple.

One thing is for sure. The voters in Oregon will never accept a sales tax unless they are convinced that such a major departure will eliminate our present dependence on property and income taxes. Nor will they unless convinced that the tax rate will not be inched upward year after year without their personal vote. Some mighty important "unlesses."

Control of spending is, of course, a primary necessity. And a sales tax is certainly not a perfect answer. But what is?

The leadership of this state must come to grips with the question. Could it be that Oregonians are faced with a necessity that even those mountain folks in Nepal could not escape?

First Interstate leaders serve Oregonians well

*W*hen two major statewide banks control about 57 percent of the deposits in the state, it is only natural that the individuals who head these institutions should play prominent roles in the affairs of the community. This has certainly been true for the chief executive officers of U.S. National Bank of Oregon, an affiliate of U.S. Bancorp, and the First Interstate Bank of Oregon, a part of the First Interstate system.

There have been seven men in recent memory who have carried the CEO title at First Interstate, each of them strong and able in different ways, leaders not only in financial circles, but also in the civic, cultural and social life of Portland and, indeed, the entire state.

What was known as the First National Bank of Portland was taken under the wing of the San Francisco-based Bank of America in 1930. At that time, E.B. MacNaughton was the voice of the bank, and a potent voice he was. Not only did he make his mark in the organization, he went on to head Blue Cross, the *Oregonian,* and later Reed College. Studious and humorless, MacNaughton had a low tolerance for anyone who disagreed with him, but was regarded as a very shrewd and effective businessman. In his day, "Mac" was the person to get on your side if you wanted to make a deal in the Rose City.

Frank Belgrano, an affable Italian immigrant, was next up to bat at First. He had come to Portland from San Francisco and the parent banking organization. He soon headed nearly every civic drive in the area, but was remembered most, perhaps, by having the most illegible signature that bank tellers ever had to decipher. Best that they knew, however, whose autograph it was at First National.

A native son, C.B. Stephenson, was the popular choice to succeed Belgrano when the latter was promoted to head the holding company. Stephenson was as people-oriented as MacNaughton was book-oriented. Because he had come up through the ranks, he was held in high regard both inside and outside the organization. Never one to throw his weight around, Stephenson became a community leader by example. He was intensely loyal to his friends. I vividly remember the time when an extortionist set off a bomb in a restroom at Meier & Frank, and Stephenson personally delivered the cash required in the note, never questioning the reason or asking for a receipt. The money was never delivered to the extortionist, who was later apprehended and jailed.

During the regime of Ralph Voss, who was sent to Portland from Los Angeles to succeed Stephenson, the institution became a wholly-owned affiliate of Western Bancorporation. Voss, a skilled professional, served for a number of years. He then went on to become head man in the corporate offices in California, only to return to retire in Portland, his first love.

Next in line was Robert Wallace, a large and imposing man, with a style as big and as all-encompassing as his presence. There was never any question where Wallace stood on an issue; he was a strong voice for his bank and for the city of Portland. He left First Interstate to join the National Westminster Bank in New York, where he now serves as head honcho.

Bill Wilke followed Wallace. Wilke was as laid-back and mild as Wallace was the opposite. Few knew Wilke well, but those who did found him to be not only a man of his word, but also a person who had little time for the trappings of importance.

Wilke's tenure was a building one for the fortunes of the bank. When he retired to enjoy a more leisurely life at his dream home in the San Juans, his imprint was cast indelibly in the annals of First Interstate Bank.

The present boss, Bruce Willison, is a young (thirty-nine), articulate and tremendously able banker from headquarters in Los Angeles. Although he has not been in the area long enough to be well-known by many, those who have worked with him have found him to be one of the most able and progressive bankers this community has seen in a long time.

Bruce and his wife Gretchen have already taken prominent positions in a number of civic causes, with particular effectiveness in the arts area. Most agree that Willison's career will one day move him into a prominent position in the banking arena on the national scene.

Next week we will trace the leadership at the U.S. National Bank of Oregon, with a cast of characters as colorful and varied as the state that it counts as home base.

Leadership of U.S. Bank constructive force in state

*L*ast week we traced the leadership of one of the major statewide banking organizations, First Interstate, recalling how its chief executive officers had contributed in such a major way to the progress of Portland and the entire state of Oregon.

This week we do the same for the other major bank, U.S. National Bank of Oregon, a unit of U.S. Bancorp, the largest banking organization in the Northwest.

It is fitting to begin the recent history of U.S. Bank with the career of Edward Sammons, one of the most colorful and influential citizens this state has ever produced. Sammons came to U.S. National from Iron Fireman, the furnace-control folks, where he was a close associate of civic leader T. Harry Banfield. However, before beginning his career as a business executive, Ed Sammons had come up the hard way, starting on the street corners of Portland, peddling the local newspapers.

Sammons was much sought after as a leader of community drives. Few folks in the city were able to say "no" to him, and he loved the opportunity to be a constructive and outspoken voice.

One of the most memorable battles that pitted Sammons against other members of the Portland establishment was in the late fifties, when funds were being raised to build the new Portland Hilton Hotel. The owners of the Benson and Multnomah hotels (at that time Western International) were very good customers of U.S. Bank, so it was only natural that Sammons would become a vocal opponent of plans for the new hotel. The acrimonious battle left deep scars, even after the hotel was finally opened.

Long in the extended shadow of Sammons, Edward J. Kolar took over with a much different style. Ed Kolar was every inch a kindly gentleman who seldom raised his voice and rarely became involved in controversy. His tenure at U.S. Bank was one of peace and calm on the outside but of quiet building and strengthening of personnel on the inside. Kolar enjoyed the confidence of the leaders of the community, and he had great skills as a banker.

One of Portland's soundest heads, who is still around to be helpful in a multitude of good causes, next occupied the corner office at U.S. Bank. LeRoy Staver, who had headed the bank's trust division for many years, brought the bank into modern times by expanding into a number of related financial service areas. Staver saw how the banking industry would change in the years to come and was able to position his organization to take advantage of those approaching trends.

The most prominent individual Staver put his arm around was a young Basque from Jordan Valley, John A.

Elorriaga. Elorriaga had worked himself up through the chairs at the bank from an early age. He left the bank for a short period to help straighten out the financial fortunes of several other local companies.

Elorriaga was then brought "back home" by Staver to become one of the most dynamic bankers in the history of our state. "Big John" was the ultimate in boundless enthusiasm and contagious charisma, and he guided the expansion of U.S. Bank into a major regional bank, operating in both Oregon and Washington.

Elorriaga was the perennial "cheerleader," lacing his meetings and speeches with a wide collection of stories and jokes. There was no joking, however, when it came to bottom-line performance at the bank. In that area, he was tough as nails.

Elorriaga recently retired, but before doing so he made certain that his successor, another in-house man, Roger L. Breezley, was properly schooled in the sound banking principles that had guided the locally controlled bank for so many years.

Breezley is widely respected as a star in asset management, and he has a well-deserved reputation for being very tightfisted when it comes to expense control. Not content just to run this major business, Breezley has become involved in several community projects where his presence is felt more behind the scenes than at center stage.

Of course, there are many other individuals at independent banks throughout the state who have also had a major influence in the banking life of Oregon. Names such as Doris Bounds of Hermiston and Bill Sweet of Coos Bay are examples of local leaders who have made deep and constructive imprints in their areas.

Oregonians can sleep well at night, knowing that the fortunes of their major financial institutions continue to be in the hands of such able practitioners.

FRIDAY SURPRISE

Americans learn lesson, tighten up purse strings

The restaurant Aureole in New York is magnificent. The service is polished and professional. The food is presented in a pleasing manner and is very tasty. The price tag is outrageous. They are bucking the trend.

Down Fifth Avenue, the high priest of snob appeal, Bijan, who thought he could conquer New York the way he soft-soaped the folks in Beverly Hills, sits behind a door marked "By Appointment Only," while a white-jacketed doorman stands guard. The truth of the matter is that you really don't need that appointment after all to shop in his men's boutique. He'd be glad to see any customers.

And just a couple of blocks east, the "Palace," the Helmsley Palace Hotel, ruled by the lady who advertises as "the only palace where the Queen stands guard," is having almost as much trouble filling high-priced hotel rooms as "the Queen" is having with the courts of New York. Leona Helmsley is on trial for all kinds of shenanigans with the tax authorities.

Although this scene is New York, where everything is supposedly bigger and better (and stranger) than anyplace else on earth, almost the same scenario could be played, with different characters, in just about every major city in the land. Opulence, extravagance, outdoing the next guy, has gone out of style. Way out of style. It's just about time.

For a while it seemed as though it was almost a game to see who could one-up his or her neighbor, business associate or former classmate. Swanky eating places, flashy imported cars, vacation homes in the desert or Hawaii, imported designer clothes were the current table topics.

At the same time the interest payments on over-used "plastic" were getting out of hand.

Suddenly all of this radically changed. The pricey restaurants are sick and many are dying; folks are now interested in healthy food, served in a casual manner, perhaps brought home from the appetizing gourmet take-out counters at the local Safeway or Fred Meyer.

Instead of staying in overpriced hotels, paying a dollar for every telephone call, and shelling out twelve bucks for a breakfast that isn't any better than those served at McDonald's or Wendy's, the smart traveler is taking the advice of Tom Bodett and his Motel Six radio spots.

Many are forgetting about motels or hotels altogether, and using a camper for a roof when they tour the country. The kids are partially anesthetized in the back seat with the latest Nintendo computer game.

When it comes to new clothes, outrageous price tags make the outlet and discount stores look more attractive all the time. Clothing prices have gone up at an alarming rate every season; it's no wonder the ready-to-wear business has been so poor.

It's no longer the "thing to do" to flaunt the designer label as a garment is casually placed over the back of a chair.

What has caused this almost complete reversal in the way Americans look at their life?

For one thing, the stock market crash in October 1987 scared the dickens out of a lot of people who thought that the economic glory balloon would never burst.

Tough economic times in many areas made a lot of others take a second look at what they were saving (not much) and what they were spending (more than they had).

The realization of what was necessary to keep in the bank to send the kids to school put a different spin on the satisfaction chart.

More recently, the example set by the president and the first lady of the land has undoubtedly had an influence. No longer are the motorcades a mile long, the designers staying at the White House, and the rhetoric oblivious of the economic pains suffered by so many.

The healthiest part of the whole picture is the effect that all of this has had on our young people.

They, more than their elders, sensed the need for change. The great majority of them, despite what we hear about the drug culture, know that they must get themselves properly prepared for a tough and competitive job market. They have come to realize the value of a dollar, and are not about to waste those hard-earned bucks in a senseless show of competitive, conspicuous consumption.

The easy days of "Big Brother will take care of you" are a thing of the past. And were they really so easy, remembering our current debt situation? The aftermath, a hell-bent-for-election spending spree, looks like it has also been relegated to the history books.

We are finally getting a lesson from our young people, underscoring the common sense of that ancient Chinese proverb: "Give a man a fish and you give him a meal; teach him how to fish, and you feed him for a lifetime."

Business tycoons often trip over their own egos

*W*hen a three-letter word gets in the way of sound business decisions, watch out.

That little word is "ego."

We have seen in recent times what ego has done to some great plans. And we are seeing it being played out again, with names that are familiar to many Oregonians.

It was not too long ago that an able and ambitious man, Richard Ferris, had a grand proposal for the travel and hospitality industry. He was positioned to combine some of the best names in America: United Airlines, Westin Hotels and Resorts, Hertz Rent-A-Car.

As chief executive officer of United, Ferris was a headstrong individual. I can remember sitting in with him on some tough bargaining sessions trying to get United Airlines to give Portland better schedules. A strong case was made for the Rose City, with its long history of support for United and the major part United plays in providing service for Oregonians.

All the facts and figures did not seem to sway Ferris in the least. He appeared disinterested in the Portland market. We had little success in convincing him of the opportunities that lay ahead if he could provide more wide-body service and some non-stop flights to major East Coast cities such as New York and Washington, D.C.

Another time I recall watching Ferris descend on the Plaza, then a Westin Hotel property in New York, with his retinue of aides and advisers. The manager of the hotel remarked afterward that it was like an invasion; there was little opportunity for give and take. Ferris had made up his mind what he wanted, and that was it.

"Allegis" was the name of the combined outfit that Ferris put together, hoping that it would become the major entity in the travel world. His dreams were short-lived. Labor problems at the airline, along with discontent that United was being sidetracked to provide funds for the rest of the conglomerate, grounded his project. The Allegis directors, in a most unusual action, dismissed Ferris. Although other reasons were given publicly, there was no question that the major problem with Ferris was the familiar three-letter word.

For some time now we have been hearing about more airline problems, this time with Texas Air, the parent of Eastern and Continental airlines. When all the accusations are cast aside, the same story seems to emerge: a good case of ego on the part of Frank Lorenzo, its headman. He has become the focal point of the problem, which is just as much a personality problem as a business problem.

It seems that the personal service areas are the most prone in attracting those individuals who are intent to leave their special mark, no matter what it does for the corporation or its workers. Don't forget hotel "Queen" Leona Helmsley. The hotel, airline and retailing areas are special victims of ego problems.

The latest, and perhaps the most fascinating, situation has just emerged with Robert Campeau, the chief executive officer of Toronto-based Campeau Corporation, as the star performer. About a year and a half ago, Campeau won a hotly contested battle with R.H. Macy & Company, the famed national retailer with major outlets in New York and California, to win the crown jewel of the retail world, Federated Department Stores.

Campeau seemed to have an insatiable appetite to assemble the largest string of retail pearls in the world. In late 1986, he bought Allied Stores, owner of Brooks Brothers, Ann Taylor, Jordan Marsh and others, and then added the luster of Lazarus in Ohio, Rich's in Atlanta, Burdines in Florida, Abraham and Straus in the New York and New Jersey areas and the *pièce de résistance*, New York-based Bloomingdale's.

Well, Campeau's ego was bigger than his thick wallet, and the pieces began to fall apart. A weak retailing market since 1986 has hurt cash flow in the industry, and now Campeau is forced to sell some of his jewels to meet cash needs.

Fortunately for the retail world in general, and Bloomie's, in particular, plans are afoot for Marvin Traub, the sixty-four-year-old president of Bloomingdale's, and one of the nation's best merchants, to put together a syndicate to buy his own firm. The price? Analysts are talking anywhere from $1.2 billion upward to the $2 billion Campeau says it is worth.

So Campeau's $10.1 billion retailing empire is disintegrating, just as did Ferris' travel behemoth. Caught in the cracks are thousands of employees who have faced the uncertainties of new management.

Heady stuff, this ego. Is self-interest really that important in the long-term scheme of things? The scoreboard seems to give the answer.

FRIDAY SURPRISE

Vision and service give Toys 'R' Us retail lead

Growing up in the department-store business, I had one secret ambition: to be the manager of the toy department. What red-blooded, young American boy is not fascinated by the model trains and the toy soldiers and everything else that makes this section of a retail store so fascinating?

I remember that I could hardly wait until the F.A.O. Schwarz catalog arrived each Christmas. The fabulous array of toys from this famous emporium in New York was almost more than a young man could grasp.

Well, this fascination has continued through the years. And though I was never assigned to the toy department by my father, who well knew what the consequences would be, I have watched with continued interest the ups and downs of the world's toy merchants.

A fascinating story is unfolding in New York where Toys 'R' Us, the nation's leading toy retailer, is embarking on the biggest gamble of its life. In the heart of Manhattan, almost next door to Macy's, the world's largest department store, a block that once housed the now defunct Korvette store has renewed problems. The reincarnation of this multi-storied building into a vertical shopping center, the Herald Center, has been a disaster. Even with the initial help of master retailer Stanley Marcus (of Neiman-Marcus fame), this ill-conceived project has been a big loser.

And who comes to the rescue? Toys 'R' Us. It has announced that it will open a major unit on the ground floor of this building in the heart of the city, a far cry from its usual policy of building in the suburbs, adjacent to large shopping centers.

The retailing world will be watching with special interest because this is one of the few stores that has the potential drawing capacity to turn around an unfavorable shopping pattern. As if this wasn't enough to draw attention to this area, A&S, a former unit of Federated Department Stores (now a part of the troubled Campeau organization), has just opened a huge new complex in the adjoining block.

With its well-publicized cash-flow problems, the timing of the A&S opening, just as the holiday season gets started, could hardly have been worse. What happens with these two developments will have a profound influence on the whole retailing picture.

Toys 'R' Us also has announced that it plans to open as many as one hundred new stores in Japan within the next ten years. And who will its partner be? None other than McDonald's Japan, Ltd. Our friends across the water will be able to buy their Big Macs and their big teddy bears under the same roof.

What has accounted for the enormous growth of a toy chain that, as of January 1989, operated 358 stores in the

United States and 74 more in Canada, Hong Kong, Malaysia, Singapore, Great Britain and West Germany?

Can it be technical expertise? Intelligence? Guts? Maybe money? All of those things may be important, but I prefer to say the major factor was "vision." It takes an extraordinary vision to foresee a better way of doing something, to devise and build a product to achieve it, market that product and ultimately be successful at selling it.

Charles Lazarus, the founder and chairman of Toys 'R' Us, is a shining example of the fact that you don't have to spend years tinkering in your garage, hold a patent or think up a new service niche to be an entrepreneur. You just have to have vision.

He took a competitive industry and dominated it with selection, price competition and customer service.

Since 1978, Toys 'R' Us sales have compounded at about 28 percent per year. The stores have a market share of better than 20 percent and do close to $4.8 billion worth of business a year. They are more profitable than Nordstrom or Walmart, two of retailing's most successful companies.

Charles Lazarus likes to win. The basic principle behind his stores is selling brand-name toys at discount prices. His company is able to do this by locating stores near shopping malls (but not in them), by servicing stores with distribution centers that are even larger than its warehouse-size showrooms, and by buying merchandise during the off-season when prices are lowest.

The message here is that there is room for growth out there for those with vision. There are few get-rich-quick schemes around. It is much better to spend some time in a field and learn how it can be improved. Maybe I should have pushed harder to get into that toy department after all.

FRIDAY SURPRISE

Icy life at South Pole station supports Antarctic science

*O*ver the past few weeks we have been reading about a meeting in Paris where delegates from thirty-nine nations discussed the almost unknown Antarctic Treaty of 1959. A great deal of attention was paid to this meeting by scientists and environmentalists the world over, for that continent contains more than 90 percent of the world's ice and a very large percentage of the fresh water of our planet.

Unfortunately, the conference adjourned before the delegates could agree on how to save that fragile environment. The mining potential of the area was one of the major areas of disagreement among the nations involved. They will come back together again next year for more deliberations.

I was particularly interested in this conference, because it brought back memories of one of the most interesting, educational and exciting experiences I have had during the past several decades.

My visit to Antarctica was no boondoggle, believe me. It was an oversight inspection of U.S. operations "on the ice" at McMurdo Station and at the South Pole.

Staging for the trip took place at Christchurch, New Zealand, where members of the party were outfitted with all sorts of cold weather gear. Although this was in December, it was actually the warmest time of the year in that area and the only time planes are able to land.

I was very proud of the parka that was given to me (an authentic explorer's garment) with a special patch that was a real status symbol. After all, how many people take a business trip to the Antarctic?

The plane trip was made on a trusty old Hercules, a craft fitted for troops, not tourists. Seating was on benches around the shell of the plane. Although I imagine most of my readers would agree that modern air travel leaves something to be desired in the comfort department, the Hercules would have to be placed near the bottom of any scale.

Landing on the ice after the eight-hour trip was a memorable experience. Although the aircraft was equipped with skis, I could not help but wonder how in the world the pilot could stop the plane. Obviously our pilot had done this several times before, as he made a perfectly normal landing on the ice-covered "runway."

The scene at the base, on a peninsula off Ross Island, conjured up visions of what the moon must look like, with ice taking the place of lunar rocks. There was no life or greenery anywhere in sight. It was awesome.

The strangest part of all was the twenty-four-hour daylight. It certainly mixed up the day (and night) to the extent that it was hard to know if you were supposed to be getting up, going to bed, eating breakfast or eating dinner.

My accommodations were at what was affectionately known as the "Antarctic Hilton," a group of barracks at McMurdo Station put together with no windows, sparse, hard-to-turn-around-in rooms and plumbing facilities the likes of which I had never seen (or used) before. Remember there is no way to get rid of waste in this icy land; everything must be burned.

The food was magnificent. Because there was little else to look forward to (most personnel stayed on the ice for nearly a year) every effort was made to provide first-class chow.

A side trip to the South Pole was made by chopper. Here U.S. personnel live in huts under the ice in cramped and close quarters. During the day they are working on various experiments both inside and outside; evenings are spent watching endless movies and writing.

To be properly initiated at this station, the newcomer must strip completely and run around an area determined to be the South Pole. If he is able to survive that outing, it is assumed that he will make the grade for the yearlong residency.

The penguins were about the only bit of natural life to be seen, and they were a show in themselves. In their natural habitat, they are proud and impressive creatures. The down side is that, despite their prim tuxedo-draped appearances, they are really not very well mannered.

Antarctica remains one of the more pure areas left on this globe. It is hoped that the nations of the world will be able to come to some agreement to ensure that this extremely unusual and valuable area for science studies will continue to be used for the betterment of all mankind.

FRIDAY SURPRISE

Imprisoned in own country, Czechs throw off shackles

There was a special significance to the news that ninety-two-year-old Cardinal Frantisek Tomasek, Archbishop of Prague, celebrated a mass last week in that tumultuous city before a quarter of a million people who filled the Cathedral of St. Vitus, and spilled out into the grounds near the government headquarters at Hradcany Castle.

Reports from the Czech capital indicated that the throng, joined by hundreds of thousands of other celebrants, went on to a huge open area along the banks of the Vltava River, because Wenceslas Square, the usual site for demonstrations, could not hold the immense crowd who wanted to show their support for freedom.

Less than a year ago, I had the pleasure of visiting with the cardinal in his quarters, not far from the site of these historic activities. But the mood of that cold and dreary wintry day was a far cry from the euphoria being shown in recent developments.

Cardinal Tomasek was a pathetic, lonely and disheartened man, as he sat in his ornate reception area, looking back on a lifetime as a symbol of faith and hope in a nation which, at that moment, seemed so far from individual liberty. Alert and informed even at this advanced age, the cardinal had stayed on past the usual retirement age of seventy-five because the powers of the country would not allow a successor to be named.

Not only were the authorities unwilling to receive a replacement for the cardinal, they would not even allow any new bishops or priests to be installed.

I had a feeling that the cardinal was almost a prisoner in his own home. He related that few folks now came to call, and he was especially delighted to get some firsthand news from Western visitors. Although the official appointment was for just a few minutes, the cardinal would not let us go. He literally held hands with his visitors as he guided us around his headquarters, so happy to have someone to talk to and someone who was interested in what he had to say about the real state of affairs in Czechoslovakia.

Little did we imagine what was going to happen less than a year later in the life of that brave religious leader, or in the lives of the small group of dissidents with whom we had coffee that same day in the seclusion of a "friend's" apartment.

The story that group of men and women told us, then in the strictest confidence, has now been retold many times in world headlines.

For example, we were told that the religious education of children and the number of future members of the clergy were strictly controlled. Unofficial gatherings (like prayer meetings or privately celebrated masses) were forbidden. Male religious orders had been banned since 1950, and most women's orders were barred from accepting new members. A priest's license could be revoked at any time, and without any explanation. Clergymen who continued to follow their calling after losing their licenses were subject to criminal sanctions.

The group consisted of a mixed lot. They were fifty-four-year-old Dana Nemcova, who was trained as a psychologist, and then worked as a cleaning woman; Thomas Hradilek, an engineer who lived in Northern Moravia; and Sasa Vondra, a young man who was trained in computer programming and was the editor of a journal called *Revolver Review*. The most vocal of the group was Jiri Dienstbier, who was a Communist Party member until the early 1970s and had worked as the Prague radio correspondent in the United States from 1968 to 1969. He was fired from the radio station upon his return to Czechoslovakia, served three years in prison (1979-82), and, although a talented writer, was working as a coal stoker for the Prague metro.

The examples of repression and intimidation were endless. Independent organizations were not permitted in the country. Membership in the state trade union (the "Revolutionary Workers' party") was virtually compulsory. Strikes and independent trade unions were forbidden.

Artists, writers and intellectuals (and there were several of them present) told tales of being organized into professional associations, under strict party control.

Particularly troubling was the record of divided families. Czechs who had fled their country through a neutral country, such as Austria, entered the United States as refugees. Their families were not allowed to emigrate to join them. Spouses and children had to wait at least five years before obtaining permission to come to the West.

The results were particularly tragic as wives filed for divorce so that they and their children would not be punished through loss of employment or denied permission to attend a university.

What a thrill it must have been last week for the cardinal, and the others who had labored for so long underground, to see the start of change. The mass that he celebrated on that momentous day underscored his long-standing belief that the tools of change were indeed in the hands of the people. And now those tools could really be put to work.

FRIDAY SURPRISE

Approval ratings shadow White House retirees

The other day a young friend, very interested in politics, told me of his disappointment in a recent contact with the office of former President Reagan. He had requested an autograph from Reagan. The answer had come back negative, due to office pressures and "because of the many requests for autographs." The boy's previous image of his hero had been quickly destroyed.

A small incident, to be sure. But a very important one to this individual who was anticipating that one day he would be able to take part in the political life of his country. He was having second thoughts.

When put in the context of several other events that have taken place since Mr. Reagan left office, the story does underscore how quickly public opinion about leaders can change.

Reagan left the White House with a 68 percent approval rating, a very respectable score for a man who had been in the most difficult decision seat in the world for eight years. Although there were numerous incidents during that time when the public was critical, the overall feeling was one of love and respect for a man who seemed to calm the turbulent waters and tell the folks at home what they wanted to hear...and do it in a very engaging manner.

The fact that the deficit became larger and larger seemed irrelevant. The decaying infrastructure of the country was forgotten. Housing problems for the poor, lack of adequate funding for medical research for cancer, AIDS and Alzheimer's disease, and serious environmental deficiencies played second fiddle to an all-pervasive need to keep the defense establishment extremely well funded.

In fairness, the point could well be made that the strong stand Reagan took versus Mikhail Gorbachev could have led to some of the positive moments we have seen in recent months throughout Eastern Europe.

It has been just a year since the Reagans left the big house on Pennsylvania Avenue for not-so-shoddy digs that friends helped them purchase in Bel-Air, California. What has happened to their place in history in just twelve short months is almost tragic. A recent article about the former first family described them at this moment as "the most unpopular first couple in history."

What has caused this roller-coaster ride? It seems that it hasn't been just one or two things, but a series of events that show poor judgment by those around the Reagans, as well as by the couple themselves.

The word in California is that the Reagan offices on the 34th floor of Fox Plaza in the Century City district of Los Angeles have been impenetrable to practically anyone except visiting heads of state or former staff members. Requests for small favors (like the autograph) or for appearances are ignored.

An all-expense-paid triumphant visit to Japan, with a $2 million goodie envelope for two twenty-minute speeches, has been well publicized and well criticized.

Then there was the former first lady's Phoenix House Center Association. This California treatment center for children with drug problems was to receive sizable funds from the Nancy Reagan Foundation and would eventually boast her name. Several large fund-raising events took place in Southern California. But after some neighbors of the chosen site began to complain about the new center, Nancy Reagan suddenly withdrew her support. Her actions left the institution $600,000 in debt and with a reported $5 million in donations in question.

At the same time, it was reported that she had turned down a request from the state of California to speak at a drug abuse conference, with an honorarium of $500. But a widely reported appearance for Toyota, with a handy check for $30,000, was accepted.

Then there was the former first lady's book, *My Turn.* Folks in the book publishing business couldn't help but be impressed with the hefty advance (reportedly about one million bucks), but also with the fact that for several weeks the volume was No. 1 on the *New York Times* best-seller list. Then the book died.

In a way all this is very sad, but it also points out how time can quickly change the public perception of people and events. Once thoroughly disgraced, former President Nixon has staged an unbelievable comeback, to the extent that even newspaper publishers gave him a standing ovation at a recent convention. Former President Carter, whose White House days were anything but happy ones, has conducted himself since leaving office in a manner that has underscored what a truly decent and caring person he really is.

Of course, it is much too early to speculate on what history will say about President Bush. But those who were early to criticize him for a lack of making tough decisions are taking a second look after events of the past several weeks. Time is not only a helpful healer, but also the provider of a broader and wiser perspective.

FRIDAY SURPRISE

Sweetland transformed Oregon political history

*I*t wasn't the Douglas fir or the lodgepole pine that the folks at Portland's World Forestry Center were talking about last week. It was a different tree, the Oregon twentieth century political-life tree.

The occasion was the birthday party of one of the most colorful individuals in the public life of our state in this century: Monroe Sweetland, political activist and newspaper publisher.

Before 1948, the governance of Oregon was solidly in the hands of the Republican establishment. The headquarters for the wheeling and dealing was the Arlington Club in Portland, where the power structure would decide who among their ranks would be candidates for various elective offices.

At that time, both United States senators from Oregon were Republicans, so were the four members of Congress, the governor, the secretary of state and practically all the leaders of the Oregon Legislature.

A trio of young "upstarts" felt that it was about time that the state returned to a two-party system. With a combination of guts, determination and sheer hard work, these three gentlemen built an organization against sizable obstacles.

Although they came from different backgrounds, Dick Neuberger, Howard Morgan and Monroe Sweetland had one thing in common: fire in their bellies.

Neuberger, who went on to become a distinguished United States senator, was a brilliant speaker and writer. Morgan was a tough political organizer, whereas Sweetland was the tireless detail man, putting together party meetings and cajoling national political figures in the Democratic party to come to the state with help.

The three men were eminently successful, although the road was not an easy one. By 1957, they had succeeded in electing two Democratic United States senators (Wayne Morse had switched parties), three members of the House of Representatives, a Democratic governor, a Democratic attorney general and had the leadership of the Oregon Legislature in their hands.

So when Sweetland's daughters wanted to celebrate a special eightieth birthday for their father, they thought that a surprise party was surely the appropriate vehicle. Sharp as ever, Sweetland soon found out about the plans, and the affair turned into a reunion. Dozens of folks, not only personal friends of the birthday boy but those who made the wheels of the state spin in the middle part of this century, came to pay tribute.

When Barbara Hanneman of Salem took the podium to read a letter of congratulations from Governor Neil Goldschmidt, she commented that she was seated at a table with three of her former bosses. It was not too shoddy a crew!

The first was Maurine Neuberger, wife of Dick Neuberger, and a former United States senator herself. I always have had a special place in my heart for this lady: as Maurine Brown, she was my English teacher at Lincoln High School.

Seated next to her was Bob Straub, a former Oregon state Democratic Party chief, state senator, state treasurer and governor. A respected and skilled businessman, Straub still devotes a majority of his time to worthwhile civic activities.

Hanneman's third boss at the table was Alf Corbett, for a number of years an Oregon state senator. He also is a brother-in-law of Howard Morgan.

Corbett is the scion of one of Oregon's most distinguished families. In the early decades of this century, the Corbett name was at the top of the list in the social, business and political life of our area. Henry W. Corbett (Alf's grandfather) was appointed a United States senator in 1897, but was never seated. Young Corbett strayed from his family's strong Republican roots to become a leading figure in the opposite party.

The political branches at the other tables included many familiar names. There was Travis Cross, for years considered one of the most talented political public relations men in the business. His career was capped by time with national figures, including George Romney and Barry Goldwater. It was a tribute to Cross that although his political stripes were of a different color than Sweetland's, he was considered a long-time friend.

Dorothy and Bob Thornton, Dan Goldy, Jebby and Sylvia Davidson, Keith Burns and Hans Linde are names that still are mentioned when the political junkies meet. They were all there, along with Ancil Payne (ex-KGW-TV station manager in Portland), now a resident of Seattle.

But the spotlight was on Sweetland himself. The quartet of speakers recalled how this "sports nut" (he came by this naturally as his father was a football coach at Willamette University), this caustic and assertive editorial writer, this champion of minorities (he was a strong critic of World War II Japanese internment camps), used his considerable talents to make a difference in the history of Oregon.

One speaker recalled that Sweetland's wife, Lil, was attracted to him because he was the only gentleman she knew who owned two tuxedos. Sweetland certainly kept those two garments in the closet for the years that he was out slugging in the muddy trenches for the under-recognized of his state.

Mayo Medical Center is masterpiece of logistics

*C*an you imagine the logistics involved in operating a medical center with more than 15,000 personnel? It boggles the mind to think of the organization necessary to make such a place function properly. But there is indeed such an institution, and I can tell you from firsthand experience that it is one of the outstanding examples in this country of superb management.

The place I am describing is the Mayo Medical Center in Rochester, Minnesota, a private group medical practice that includes the Mayo Clinic, St. Mary's Hospital and the Rochester Methodist Hospital. In the medical center, there are more than 900 staff physicians and medical scientists; nearly 1,400 medical students, fellows and trainees; and 7,000 paramedical personnel. The affiliated hospitals have another 6,000 people.

Rochester, Minnesota, *is* Mayo. The city literally lives and breathes by the clinic, and the life of the community reflects the worldwide reputation of the Mayo Center.

At present, downtown Rochester is undergoing major reconstruction, with new luxury hotels being planned or built to accommodate the people who come from around the world to seek advice and treatment. Last year, more than one million patients saw doctors at the center.

Although some patients are referred here by their own physicians, more than 80 percent make their own appointments. It is vital to make the appointments as far ahead as possible, as the center can handle only so many people, and examination times are booked weeks and months ahead in many cases. However, emergency patients are taken at once, and every effort is made to accommodate those who have an immediate or serious problem.

The fascinating part of the Mayo operation is the efficiency of the organization. With that many people on the staff, and with the thousands of people they see every week, you would wonder about the right test results getting to the right place and in the proper doctor's hands at the right time. Well, they do!

At the start, a patient is assigned to a specific area of the clinic that specializes in the problem that the person might have. In this area, the patient also is assigned a particular doctor, who serves as the contact person and the base for examination and treatment. Of course, this doctor has, at his or her beck and call, hundreds of experts in every field to whom the patient can be referred.

As you start at the clinic, you are given an envelope with your name and assigned physician. He or she will usually ask your medical history, give you a complete physical examination, and then prescribe the tests and exams that he or she feels necessary in line with your own physical condition. All of these tests are then programmed by a central computer that knows how many patients each department of the clinic can handle at a certain time.

The test results are available in amazingly short order. The latest equipment allows them to process hundreds of examinations quickly, and the distribution system gets the results back to the primary doctor in a matter of hours. A complete physical examination which I have done there every year, with practically every test available for evaluation, can be accomplished in less than six hours.

The Mayo education budget is sizable. Approximately a third of the medical staff are involved in some kind of research effort, and most of it is clinically oriented.

The combined assets of Mayo are nearly $2 billion. Because of its reputation and the demand for services, it was deemed desirable to open two satellite operations in different areas of the country. One is located in Jacksonville, Florida, and has a staff of nearly 500 people. The other is in Scottsdale, Arizona, in a facility that uses a satellite video communications system designed to give patients access to all of Mayo's resources in Rochester.

Little did Dr. W.W. Mayo dream what lay ahead when he established a medical practice in Rochester in 1864. A solid history of growth and expansion began, and in 1919 the Doctors Mayo (there were three family members) turned over all assets to establish the Mayo Foundation. In 1972, the Mayo Medical School opened and, in 1983, the Mayo Foundation was accredited to grant degrees. It is projected that during the next five years, expansion of the operation will result in capital expenditures of between $750 million and $1 billion.

It is comforting to know that in these days of bigness, there are organizations such as Mayo that are able to operate an absolutely first-class program and still maintain the individual care and attention that the U.S. public has a right to expect.

Play your kings, queens, Trump card is biggest deal

*T*he new president of Czechoslovakia is visiting the United States for the first time, our troop concentration in Japan is under discussion, German re-unification is on the front burner, but the headlines in the New York tabloids are all about Donald and Ivana Trump. The reason is not so difficult to come by: certain people have "star quality," and many folks are fascinated by their lives.

Probably no person in the past few years has so captured the interest of New Yorkers (and indeed millions of others around the nation) as has Donald Trump, business tycoon and man-about-town. His business exploits have been well documented; his fortune is estimated in the billions, the exact number depending on which list you read.

Personal lives aside, Donald and Ivana Trump have, in a way, shown that some people's American dream of great success in the marketplace is still possible. When the inefficient and sometimes corrupt city administration of New York was having a slow and expensive time fixing up the decaying Wollman Ice Rink in Central Park, Trump stepped in. In a matter of months, he had the place operating in first-class order.

Trump's real estate ventures in the Big Apple are legendary. He has been smart enough to grab the best property available, creating structures that are without peer in Manhattan. Trump Plaza and Trump Parc are highly desirable apartment complexes and Trump Tower is a "must see" by visitors to New York.

In the air, Trump bought the tacky, cattle-car operation known as the Eastern Air Shuttle (between Boston, New York and Washington), put his name on the planes and created a classy operation with sparkling new plane interiors and flight attendants who not only serve tasty snacks but actually smile while they're doing it.

At the Plaza, the grand dame of New York hotels, Trump has spent millions in refurbishing the old lady. He installed wife Ivana as president, brought back the public areas to their original beauty, upgraded the rooms and suites with period furniture and fine linens, and made the hotel's Edwardian dining room and legendary Palm Court the place to be.

The result? The hotel is doing better than it ever has, with a booming banquet and party business.

Last week, as I was having breakfast in the hotel's Edwardian Room, the staff was buzzing because "the Donald" was coming in to meet some friends. Soon the big man arrived; it was obvious that the star quality was shining brightly.

He could not have been more gracious to guests and help alike. He had a "good morning" greeting to the bus boys as well as to Marty Raynes and

Andrew Stein, both Big Apple bigwigs, who were dining at the table next to me. My long-time employee friends at the hotel think Trump is great. They admire his brains, his energy and his success. One thing is for sure: if the Trump name is on something, it is clean and efficient.

But the Trumps are not the only ones with that attention-getting magnetism. In Washington, a Capitol dining room or hearing room can be crowded with congressmen, senators, ambassadors and White House officials, but it takes the entry of personalities like Senator Ted Kennedy or former Secretary of State Henry Kissinger or evangelist Billy Graham to bring a hush to the room. These three gentlemen seem to cast a special aura over a gathering.

There is something unique about their place in modern U.S. life; they are indeed celebrities in different ways. Billy Graham is a majestic figure, having spoken in front of more human beings in his lifetime than probably anyone in history.

Any member of the Kennedy clan is newsworthy; the senator is probably the most visible.

Kissinger speaks with such authority that it is difficult not to be awed by his experiences and his savvy.

The halls of Congress see many stage, screen and television stars from time to time. No one has quite the same attention-gathering ability as Elizabeth Taylor, another person with a special kind of star attraction.

I can remember attending a national governor's conference some years ago when the chief executives of all of our states were present. Not much attention was paid to forty-nine of them, but one, Nelson Rockefeller, had the media and the galleries following his every word and his every step.

Whether it be sports, movie or political stars, the public will always be fascinated by those who possess that elusive something that sets them apart. Maybe one of these days some real live heroes and heroines with real life star quality, like President Vaclav Havel of Czechoslovakia, will emerge in our society. We need them.

FRIDAY SURPRISE

Prominent couples abound as Portland enters the 1990s

*C*ertainly one of the most memorable figures in Oregon politics was a maverick Republican turned Independent turned Democrat, named Wayne Morse.

This highly intelligent, combative loner was respected in the U.S. Senate for his keen knowledge of our parliamentary system, but was never an insider because of the difficulty he had with political relationships.

Even his Oregon contemporaries in Congress often had strained relationships with this gentleman who never was afraid to say what he thought, even if it was not the most politically correct thing to do.

I had a different kind of association with Morse because we shared an interest in horses and a mutual friendship with Glenn Jackson, who was probably the state's most influential private citizen during Morse's public years.

Morse and his family were familiar figures around horse shows, with the senator a dashing driver in the roadster classes. He was also an accomplished rider, and I can remember competing against him in horsemanship classes, although he was a generation older than I. There was no disgrace coming in second to this tough competitor; the one time I managed to snare the blue ribbon was a great moment in my equestrian career.

The crowning event in this relationship was when my father, unknown to me, decided that I had outgrown my favorite pony and sold (or gave, I'll never know) her to the Morse daughters. It was like losing a member of my family, but she had a great home at the Morse ranch in Eugene.

In those days, unlike today, it was not too common for a spouse of a prominent personality to be a top achiever in his or her own right, but Midge Morse was not an average lady. She was very much the organizer and the calming voice in the office of a man known to be full of ups and downs. Midge Morse ran the political side of the "Tiger's" business.

The Morse combination brings to mind prominent couples in today's Oregon, where one spouse is high profile, yet the other performs in his or her chosen field with equal competence, but perhaps without quite so much visibility.

One of these pairs is Elizabeth and Tom Vaughan, he the recently retired director of the Oregon Historical Society. Less well known is Elizabeth "Sherry" Vaughan, an outstanding Russian scholar and writer. She is also a much sought-after member of top-notch business boards of directors (First Interstate Bank and Nordstrom, for example).

John Storrs has long been recognized as one of our city's most talented architects, with Salishan Lodge at Gleneden Beach one of the prizes from his fertile drawing board. Equally talented, but in a completely different field, is his wife, Dr. Frances Storrs. She is known as one of the area's most able dermatologists and practices at the Oregon Health Sciences University.

Speaking of Salishan and OHSU brings to mind another couple who very much fit this mold. John Gray, a highly successful businessman who made Omark famous in the chain saw field, was the builder and continues to be the operator of the Salishan complex.

An extremely generous and environmentally conscious individual, Gray is at the forefront when current community leaders are mentioned. But not mentioned as often is Betty Gray, daughter of a former state attorney-general, herself one of the most effective community workers around.

She was a driving force as the chairwoman of the board of overseers of OHSU, taking an unusually active part in rebuilding the volunteer and financial base of this vital local institution.

Modern-day political families have their dual success stories, also. In Portland we hear "whoop, whoop" from our colorful Mayor Bud Clark. However, his partner, Sigrid, is a star achiever in her own right. Portland's first lady is not only an accomplished violinist with the Oregon Symphony, but also runs the Goose Hollow Inn.

Former Secretary of State Norma Paulus, now a candidate for state superintendent of public instruction, has made headlines for years as a strong voice in the Republican Party. Her mate, Salem lawyer Bill Paulus, is one of the city's most respected attorneys, having served as counsel for Salem schools for many years.

In the marketplace of the nineties, with so many family dual-wage earners, we will be seeing more examples of double achievers under one roof. Midge and Wayne Morse were just a little bit ahead of the times.

•

Visit to Ethiopian Emperor proves to be eye-opener

*T*he longest civil war in Africa is still going on in one of the poorest countries in the world: Ethiopia.

The war began twenty-eight years ago when an area known as Eritrea rebelled against an annexation by then Emperor Haile Selassie.

In the last month, the current president, Mengistu Haile Mariam, has declared that the country should move away from its failed Marxist economic policies.

Famine is the hard reality of life in this troubled nation. Nearly 5 million people in the northern provinces of Ethiopia are once again facing the hardships that go along with their nation's catastrophic agricultural policies.

The problem is a familiar one: the collective farms are not working, and grain production has fallen sharply.

Our country has worked with other nations around the world to try to relieve some of the suffering. We have delivered nearly 20,000 tons of food, and another 140,000 tons are planned to be delivered before mid-summer.

But getting the food to the needy is not easy in this ravaged land: distribution channels at best are inefficient; at worst there is wholesale corruption.

This is not the first time we have pitched in to help these suffering masses. Five years ago we, along with other Western nations, sent more than a bil-

lion dollars worth of aid to Ethiopia.

The same difficulties were in play then: large numbers of refugees, overpopulation, outdated economic planning and a backward educational system in the north. In the southern part of the country the situation is somewhat better. The farmers in this region used the help they received in the mid-eighties to revitalize their agricultural system.

I visited Ethiopia, a country of special interest to me, in 1968 on a mission to persuade Emperor Selassie to visit the United States and take part in the international Presidential Prayer Breakfast.

I stayed at first in Addis Ababa, the capital city, with our Ambassador William Hall, whose wife, Jayne, is the daughter of one of Oregon's most distinguished former governors, Jay Bowerman.

The Halls were highly respected in the ranks of the Foreign Service. After his assignment in Africa, the ambassador became director general of the Foreign Service, one of the most prestigious jobs in the State Department. A few years later he returned to Oregon and began teaching at Lewis and Clark College, only to pass away at the pinnacle of his productive life.

From Addis Ababa, I flew to Asmara, the Eritrean capital, the area engulfed in the current rebel offensive.

I then traveled to the historic city of Massawa on the Red Sea. It is there that the emperor had his vacation home, for he tried to escape the wicked heat by being near the water. It is said that Massawa is the hottest spot in the world in the summertime. The city has a distinctly European flavor because of the previous Italian occupation.

Upon arriving in Massawa, I went directly to the Red Sea Hotel, where I was to receive a call from the palace for my appointment with the emperor.

Finally the call came to go to the palace. A special car arrived, and I was taken along a country road with armed guards every few yards. The scene at the residence was straight out of the *Desert Song,* and the great music from the Broadway show was the only thing missing.

I was ushered into the residence and to the porch where the emperor sat alone in a large, cane-backed chair. He was a magnificent man, who looked as if he had just stepped out of the Bible. He was sitting erect, smiling, confident. Of course, in actual stature, he was very small, but this surely did not show as he held court.

He understood English very well, although he spoke in his native tongue most of the time. I can remember he caught me quickly when (through the interpreter) I used the words "country" and "nation" synonymously. In that part of the world, the two words have a very different meaning.

During the time we were talking, he had his constant companion, a small dog, at his side. I had the feeling he was much more interested in the dog than in his guest.

When the interview was over, there was a question about how I was going to get back to Asmara to get the plane to Addis Ababa.

Even in those days, because of the terrorist activity in the area, the road was closed after dusk. The emperor and his private secretary put me in a special police car, with a convoy of a jeep and five armed guards. I'll never forget that journey. And I'm happy that I succeeded in persuading the emperor to visit the United States.

Selassie was an unforgettable figure, a wise man who had a strong influence on the entire African continent. His experience and wisdom could certainly be used today in trying to do something about the turmoil in his country.

The area is fortunate, however, in having a wise (and sometimes underrated) former U.S. president, Jimmy Carter, stepping in to help mediate the longstanding hostilities.

FRIDAY SURPRISE

The ghost of Aunt Rosie still smiles on the Benson

*W*ord that Portland's venerable Benson Hotel is embarking on a $15.5 million modernization program brought back memories to many locals who recall the glory days of this historic landmark.

Since its opening in 1913, the hotel has served as a temporary or permanent home for numerous famous persons who came to the City of Roses for political, entertainment or business reasons. They found a charm and elegance that made it one of the most popular stops on the West Coast.

For many years in the early part of this century, one of the most fascinating personages at the Benson was a permanent guest who was known to hotel employees and legions of Portlanders simply as "Aunt Rosie."

Aunt Rosie was really Mrs. Isam White, widow of an early Portland merchant who died when his much younger bride was just entering the prime of her life. Rose White, not content to fade into the background, an accepted trend of widows of her time, carved out a special niche for herself in the life of the Benson Hotel and her community.

Left with comfortable financial resources, Rose White took a suite on the ninth floor of the hotel, where she was looked after personally by two daily companions, first Jessie Wilson and later Anne Roy Munro. In addition, of course, the hotel staff members were well aware of the Victorian queen in that corner apartment, and they were summoned many times to provide some assistance or information.

Aunt Rosie's active day began at the Broadway entrance of the hotel early in the morning, when her chauffeur picked up the two ladies and drove them to a different area in suburban Portland. In those days it did not take long to reach empty stretches of attractive open space.

The driver would let the ladies out of the car in a spot chosen by Aunt Rosie. He would then drive down the road for exactly three miles, where he would await the arrival of his charges. But this was not just an ordinary country stroll.

Aunt Rosie was an avid reader, and would note each day ten words that she was not familiar with. At the end of the day, she would look up the list of words in her dictionary, and write down the definitions in her careful script.

During her walk, she would have her piece of paper with words and meanings, and would memorize them for further personal use (for crossword puzzles) or, more important, for questioning her relatives and guests as they came to pay duty calls.

The grand old lady continued her daily walks even after her ninetieth birthday in the early 1940s. Her one hundredth birthday brought dozens of old-time Portlanders to her apartment to pay homage. Those who attended the command performance were treated to many stories of how life used to be in our fair city when proper ladies left calling cards when they visited their friends.

Rose White loved to entertain. Her suite was the scene of historic dinner parties, served by members of the Benson Hotel staff. Her favorite waiter was a long-time Benson fixture, known to everyone as just "Nick." Nick Flessas knew better than anyone how to put up with the demands of the hostess, who would tolerate nothing less than absolute perfection.

After the lengthy (and somewhat stuffy) dinner sessions, the ladies would adjourn to the living room, while the gentlemen would stay around the dining room table. That is, all the ladies except Aunt Rosie. She would stay with the men, enjoying a rousing game of poker. The men met their match with this colorful woman.

One of those familiar figures at the poker sessions was Julius Meier, one-time president of the department store that bore his family name, and later Oregon's first (and only) governor elected as an independent.

Meier was a fun-loving extrovert, who enjoyed the give-and-take with Aunt Rosie as much as the give-and-take in his political office. He knew that Rose White, in addition to the periodic poker games, loved to play the nickel slot machines. Of course, the one-armed bandits were not legal in Portland.

Through some connections which were never revealed, he secured one of these machines and had it delivered to Aunt Rosie's Benson Hotel parlor for her personal use. The sheer joy of hearing the periodic jingle of two cherries or three plums blanked out the fact that she had put many dollars into the machine before the small payoffs came her way.

Julius Meier loved to invite his poker-playing friend to his Columbia River Gorge retreat, Menucha. His aristocratic wife, Grace Meier, was horrified to have Aunt Rosie use the facilities where Julius Meier had installed a loud musical toilet seat.

When Aunt Rosie died at age 101, in April 1952, a colorful chapter in the life of Portland and the Benson Hotel passed into the history books.

FRIDAY SURPRISE

Luminaries pay tribute to son of immigrants

*A*nyone who thought that the legendary American dream of success was a thing of the past would have had second thoughts at a "Big Apple" gathering earlier this month. In the stately Terrace Room of Manhattan's Plaza Hotel, the crowd of 150 was noteworthy, even by sophisticated New York standards. Not many times in recent history had such a glittering array of well-known personalities from every avenue of U.S. life been together in one room.

There was one common denominator that brought all these personalities together: to help Senator Abraham Ribicoff celebrate his eightieth birthday. But there was one other thing that most of those in attendance had in common: they had achieved prominence in their chosen field by sheer hard work and determination. They were the epitome of "the local boy (or girl) who made good."

Although the scene was a continent away from our home state, there were several Oregon ties. Herb Siegel, who parlayed razor-sharp business acumen into a mega-fortune with his Chris-Craft and Warner connections, owns television station KPTV (12), among a number of other broadcasting properties. Tom Brokaw, the NBC news anchorman, who comes across in person as much younger and more laid back than he appears on the tube, was expecting to make more trips to the "Beaver State" if his daughter accepts a radio position in Eugene. Henry Kravits, of leverage-buyout KKR fame (Fred Meyer), almost was playing second fiddle to his wife, Carolyne Roehm, a top Seventh Avenue designer.

Besides Brokaw, the media world was well represented by its top achievers, several of whom now have lower visibility. Walter Cronkite, "the most trusted man in America," and David Brinkley, of Huntley-Brinkley fame, both having covered the guest of honor when he was a prominent political personality, came to pay their respects. These familiar faces came up the media ladder the hard way, one tough step at a time. Cronkite, in particular, is a charming and down-to-earth gentleman, completely unimpressed with his star quality.

From the newspaper world there was Kay Graham, head of the *Washington Post*; Abe Rosenthal who recently stepped down from the top desk at the *New York Times*; and Suzi, the *New York Post* columnist who "scooped" the rest of the world on the Trump separation.

The business world was especially well represented. Lew Wasserman, who made a fortune putting together a gigantic entertainment network in California; Jim Evans, who rose from a bank loan officer to become CEO of

Union Pacific; Estee Lauder, who parlayed her sense of beauty into one of the largest cosmetic businesses in the world. They were all paying homage to their friend Ribicoff.

From the political world there was a galaxy of superstars. Jack Danforth, respected senator from Missouri, and Ted Kennedy, the newsy senator from Massachusetts, never had to worry about where their next buck came from. Danforth's came from Ralston-Purina; Kennedy's had a decidedly Irish whiskey taste. But the rest of the political entities present had no such silver-platter starts. There was the ever-engaging Henry Kissinger, former secretary of state; Chris Dodd, the young senator from Connecticut, and his governor, Bill O'Neill; and Cy Vance, long a big wheel in the Washington power scene. Kennedy, as usual, was the center of attention.

But it was Ribicoff himself who proved that our nation like no place else provides the fertile soil that allows those with that special something to truly make a difference in the world around them.

The son of Polish-Russian immigrants, Ribicoff's career almost is without parallel in U.S. political history.

First a state legislator, beginning in 1937; then a state judge for several years; on to become a member of the House of Representatives for two terms; then Connecticut governor for six years; secretary of health, education and welfare in President Kennedy's Cabinet; finally finishing his spectacular career by serving three terms as a U.S. senator.

This classy gentleman, ably assisted by his savvy wife, Casey, was one of the first to climb aboard the John F. Kennedy for President bandwagon. Because of this early support, Kennedy offered Ribicoff his first choice of Cabinet jobs. Would he be attorney general? "No," said Ribicoff. "That belongs to your brother, Bobby, whom you counsel with more than anyone else. Let him come in the front door of the White House, not backstage."

The guests at that party knew they had a wise man in their midst.

Chief-of-Staff guards desk where buck stops in capital

*T*here are two administration office holders in Washington, D.C., who have a constituency of just one person to please: the vice-president of the United States, and the chief of staff to the president. While the vice-president's position is pretty high profile, the demanding job of running the staff of the White House is usually held by someone whose name is not a household word unless he gets into trouble.

Serving as chief of staff to the most important man in the world is a multifaceted position. Loyalty and trust are the basic qualifications. Not only does this person have the daily responsibility of seeing that the big house on Pennsylvania Avenue runs smoothly and efficiently, he (so far, there has never been a woman serving in the job) must ensure that the proper papers get into the president's office, that suitable action is taken on the papers coming out of the office, that the boss sees the "right" people (and doesn't see the "wrong" ones), and that Cabinet members are kept in line with their actions and statements.

Most occupants of the job will say that they are not in the policy loop, although few would really believe that they do not influence major decisions. Examples of those who certainly did add their voices when it came to major items on the agenda included Hamilton Jordan, who was President Carter's

right-hand man; James Baker (now secretary of state) in the Reagan years; and the current holder of that important corner office, former New Hampshire Governor John Sununu.

A president should come across as a "nice" guy at all times; that is how the approval ratings stay high. Disciplining staff members, firing personnel and all those nasty little housekeeping chores are usually left to the chief of staff. A memorable example of this was after the 1972 election when Richard Nixon called a meeting of his crew to thank them for their support in the election. Shortly after the love feast, H.R. Haldeman (his chief of staff) asked everyone in the room to submit their resignation letters.

John Kennedy and Lyndon Johnson did not have anyone serving officially in the position of head White House honcho. They wanted to run the show personally. Johnson, especially, who had years of experience in the usual ways of the nation's capital, liked to pull all the strings himself. When it came to a real political operative, Johnson was without equal.

In the Gerald Ford years, two men occupied the gatekeeper office: Donald Rumsfeld and Richard Cheney. Cheney is now serving in the sensitive and tough job of secretary of defense in the Bush Cabinet.

The early days of the Reagan administration were unique in that three men formed the top operating crew at 1600 Pennsylvania Avenue. Although Baker had the official chief of staff title, Ed Meese and Mike Deaver shared the power and prestige of running the show. But having a three-headed hierarchy didn't work. In later years, Reagan settled on one master: Donald Regan, then Howard Baker, Jr., then Ken Duberstein.

Donald Regan got in trouble with the first lady, always a fatal thing to do. Howard Baker, who had built a splendid reputation in his years in the Senate, was perceived more as a pacifier than an activist in the office, and Duberstein was a caretaker.

In recent days, John Sununu has become more of a household word. The national press takes delight in analyzing the influence of a chief of staff, and there has been no shortage of opinions of the person some have called the "pit bull" of the administration. Sununu, who made a record as an outstanding governor, came to Bush's attention during the presidential campaign because of his tough, effective efforts on behalf of the candidate.

Of course Sununu's influence in this regard is not looked upon with favor by some members of the environmental community. The president lets him take the heat on some matters when he himself probably agrees with Sununu, but feels it is more politic for his chief of staff to be out in front.

Unlike some others in his position, Sununu does not take a prominent position in the foreign policy area. In the Reagan years, Baker would be close at hand during summit conferences. His interest in this area no doubt led to his placement in his current job. Sununu prefers to make his influence felt in domestic matters, and he is not afraid to get involved in face-to-face confrontations with his adversaries. Around Washington, D.C., the word is well understood: if you are going to get into a discussion with Governor Sununu, you darn well better be prepared with all the correct facts.

In the status-conscious world of the White House, some try to keep on the good side of Sununu because he controls the keys to the White House tennis courts and the coveted "mess" (dining room). But those with a slightly broader perspective know that their pet projects have scant chance of presidential attention or action if the "pit bull" chews them up before they reach the desk where the buck stops.

FRIDAY SURPRISE

One man's foresight leads to vibrant east side activity

*I*t would seem highly unlikely that a California geologist could have a profound effect on the growth of our city, but indeed that is true. The geologist, Ralph Lloyd, was a fascinating, early twentieth century character who saw the potential of an area that was to become almost the heart of his beloved city.

Lloyd was always vitally interested in the land around him after he and his family moved from Missouri to Ventura, California, in 1886, and bought what is now the Hampton Canyon Ranch. Not only was Lloyd astute in valuing real estate, and what lay underneath it, he also was a farmer and cattle rancher.

In many ways he was way ahead of his time. He ventured into the oil business in Southern California before others really understood the value of the resource in that area, and later made millions from leasing the family holdings to the Associated Oil Company.

Because of a knee-cap injury in his youth, he could not compete as actively as he would have liked in athletic events. But still he was an accomplished sportsman, a runner and a pole-vaulter, even though one leg was two and a half inches shorter than the other.

More than anything, Lloyd wanted a son to carry on the family business tradition. But no luck. He and his wife had four daughters, the last of whom they nicknamed "little Ralph."

She in reality was Lulu May, later to become Mrs. Richard von Hagen, a lady who had a great influence on the character of the area that bore her father's name.

Lloyd's dream was a complex not too unlike what is now developing on Portland's near east side.

He thought the land around what was to become Lloyd Center would be a spectacular site for office buildings, a golf course, a stadium, apartments, retail stores and a great hotel, modeled after one he admired in Chicago.

A false start was made on a $2 million, twenty-one-story hotel at the time of the Depression in the 1930s; after that, the ground lay relatively quiet until the early 1950s, when plans began to develop for the retail giant to be called the Lloyd Center.

Ralph Lloyd died in 1953, before he had a chance to see his dreams become a reality, although he did review the development blueprints before his death. The four daughters, Eleanor Dees, Ida Crotty, Edna Davis and Lulu May von Hagen, carried out their father's hopes and ambitions.

Lulu May von Hagen, an avid naturalist and environmentalist long before the terms became so popular, insisted that the center include colorful paintings, an outdoor ice rink, and an open feel in keeping with the beauty of the

Northwest.

Downtown Portland retailers were faced with a very difficult decision when plans for the shopping mall were presented to them. In distance and travel time, the Lloyd properties were not far from the hub of the established business district, even though there was a river in between. The big question was: can we afford to go into a new development so close to the site of our major buildings?

The real question was: could we dare not to, because of the competitive situation that would naturally develop with others coming into the territory?

The verdict from most of the forward-looking entrepreneurs of the city was to go ahead, and on August 1, 1960, one of the largest shopping centers in the world opened in Portland with fanfare, glitz, and the release of 700 pigeons. At the time, the center boasted over one million square feet, putting it in competition with the size of giant Ala Moana Center in Honolulu.

Much has happened in recent years. The entire area now has over 15,000 workers involved in 450 businesses and a number of government organizations. There are nearly 2,000 hotel rooms in the district, and with the opening of the Oregon Convention Center in September, we will see additional activity.

Melvin Simon and Associates, one of the nation's leading shopping center operators, now owns the Lloyd Center itself. As recent visitors know only too well, the area is almost under siege with construction.

A huge cinema complex is up and running, the Red Lion Hotel is being modernized, a new Bonneville Power building is in use, and, after some difficult moments, it looks as if a new State Office Building will be a reality.

It is difficult to imagine that the area where Ralph Lloyd built a two-story garage at the corner of Union and Wasco in 1910 is now one of the busiest places in the Pacific Northwest.

Portland is much the richer because of the foresight of this Horatio Alger geologist. With a unique downtown that really extends to both sides of the river, we can look forward to progress and convenience unlike any other metropolitan area in the nation.

FRIDAY SURPRISE

Efforts of former governor revealed during trip to coast

Through the years, I have found one of the most enjoyable Sunday activities is to spend time with individuals who have played an important role in the history and development of the state.

Before oral histories became popular, personal conversations were just about the only way to get a firsthand view of some of the fascinating episodes that eventually would fill the pages of our history books.

Sadly, there has been one major problem with these visits. Perhaps I have waited too long to call on these legends, for some of them have passed away shortly after our conversations. I now almost feel guilty visiting older folks who have so much to relate from their early years.

I can remember fascinating hours with Charles Pray, the first superintendent of the Oregon State Police, a man appointed by my great-uncle, Julius Meier, when he was governor.

Then there were visits with Elmo Smith and Charles Sprague, both of whom served our state as governor, and Judge Hall Lusk, who for a short period was a United States senator from Oregon.

But the one visit I will never forget was with Os West, also a former governor, and one of the most colorful leaders Oregon has ever produced. He was a man of strong words and lots of action. He never hesitated to let one know exactly how he felt about most any issue.

Os West came to mind recently as I spent time in one of the most beautiful and scenic parts of America, the southwestern coast of Oregon, Coos and Curry counties. We have the late Governor West to thank for his remarkable foresight and unswerving dedication in making sure that the great majority (about 90 percent) of the Oregon coast will be forever in public hands.

One of these days, a major airport will be in operation in this region, and then watch out! When travelers experience what has been one of the best-kept secrets in America, the area will never be the same.

Coos Bay has always been looked upon as a bustling port, and indeed it is. But there is much more to this dynamic community that is now seeing a resurgence in activity.

It will be easier to travel through the city as two new, one-way streets are being prepared along the waterfront.

There are a number of comfortable motels in the community; one of the best is a new one, the Edgewater Inn, owned and operated by local folks. It is giving the aging Red Lion a run for its money.

North Bend, a sister city of Coos Bay, is not nearly as well-known, yet it is one of the most picturesque places on the coast. Charleston, twelve miles to the southwest, boasts some great fishing right off the docks and offers the visitor the opportunity to catch crabs or dig clams in the adjoining bay. It looks like the Cape Cod of the West.

But the real secret of the area, and truly the jewel of the Oregon parks system, is Shore Acres, located just outside Charleston.

Three state parks that encompass nearly 750 acres await the explorer. Sunset Bay and Cape Arago parks are magnificent, but it is Shore Acres that you will never forget. It was once the estate of an Oregon lumber baron, Louis Simpson, who developed the property in the first decade of this century as a summer home for his wife.

Tragedy and neglect took its toll on the mansion, which included an indoor swimming pool and a large ballroom that was the social center of the region in the second decade of this century. A fire leveled the first home in 1921; a second structure was not looked after and was razed when the state acquired the site in 1942.

Visitors to Shore Acres can stand at the site of the original mansion, now housing a shelter where the awesome 180-degree view unfolds.

The state has restored the formal Oriental and rose gardens. After years of work examining old pictures, work that began in 1971 was completed in 1975.

More than 100 different species of rhododendrons, azaleas, and rare trees and shrubs that were planted as far back as 1906 are on show.

After touring this "secret" gem, hop in the car and head south toward Bandon, a city that has seen its share of tragedy. A huge fire engulfed the community in September 1936, but the spirit and determination of its citizens have rebuilt it into one of the most charming communities on the coast.

The coastal air will probably bring on some hunger pangs. No worry. Stop for dinner at the new Lord Bennett's restaurant, owned and operated by chefs Rich Iverson and Don Salonen. Named after George Bennett, a Bandon, Ireland, native who came to the Oregon coast and founded Bandon, Oregon, in 1873, the restaurant (overlooking the mighty Pacific) serves some of the tastiest fresh seafood in the state. Rumor has it that Bennett was not really a lord; it was just a nickname given to him by Bandon friends.

George Bennett died in Bandon on October 15, 1900. His lifelong wish was to be buried on a hill overlooking the bay, a view that thrills thousands of visitors and is a tribute to a real lord of the Oregon coast, Os West.

FRIDAY SURPRISE

Library dedication speaks volumes about presidency

*T*here never had been a head table quite like that one, although in Lincoln's day there also were five living presidents. Last week, in Yorba Linda, California, four men who have occupied the most important job in the world met together to pay tribute to one of their own in this small town of Nixon's birthplace that he once called home. The occasion, of course, was the dedication of the $21 million Richard Nixon Library.

The only one missing from this distinguished group was former President Carter, who has received more rave reviews from his post-presidential activities than from his troubled economic times in the White House. Carter was invited to participate in the event, but indicated that he had scheduling problems. For history, this was too bad, as his presence would have been significant, adding a bipartisan touch to the program.

At a time like this, one cannot help but compare the backgrounds, personalities and accomplishments of these national leaders. Yes, they are all white, Protestant, Republican, Anglo-Saxon males, but their life stories reflect quite different niches in the mosaic of U.S. history.

It is probably natural that our evaluations are based on personal memories or experiences. I have had the privilege, at one time or another, of meeting each

of these presidents under quite different circumstances.

Former President Gerald Ford could be looked upon as somewhat of a professional politician, having spent a sizable part of his pre-White House life in Congress. He was certainly a low-key, likable individual, who probably was the right one to restore calm and confidence after the Nixon resignation.

I was struck by the man's intense loyalty to those with whom he worked. Edith Green, who will go down in Oregon history books as one of our most effective legislators in Washington, was known in the House of Representatives as "Mrs. Education." In that capacity, she worked closely with Ford during his leadership years. The bond that grew between them, even though they represented different political parties, was a strong and respected one. Green was an outspoken supporter of Ford, and many times he responded to her invitations for help when it came to Oregon visits or Oregon projects.

My most vivid memory of former President Ronald Reagan was the evening of his first inaugural at the White House. Watching the participants at that historic time, I was so impressed with the youthful vigor and enthusiasm of this man. He was like a youngster who was exploring the wonders of a newly discovered castle.

In the years that followed, surely one

of his greatest accomplishments was to convey that spirit of hope and positive thinking to a nation that had become pretty discouraged with itself.

History will decide what influence this man had in the significant events in Eastern Europe that followed his Pennsylvania Avenue watch. Some say he was not one who was really involved in the "process," but there can be no question about the fact that he was an eloquent cheerleader for our nation's basic values.

It would be difficult to imagine a more down-home couple than the twosome presently residing in the most important house in the land. Many times, one looks on President George Bush and First Lady Barbara Bush as a team. Not, surely, in the political sense, because the first lady shies away from public positions on the divisive and complex problems of the day.

Instead, it is in the "decency" area that these two shine.

Certainly the Nixon years were some of the most fascinating (and turbulent) in our nation's history. I still can vividly remember the day he departed Washington in disgrace. I also can remember visiting with an outwardly proud, but broken, man in San Clemente some time afterwards. And years later, I recall the goosebump standing ovation that the American Newspaper Publishers (including some of his most vehement critics) gave him after a stirring foreign policy speech. What a complex, talented man.

But the big news of last week's event was not in the speeches or the fanfare or the opening of the new facility. It was the historic occasion represented by four former leaders of a major world power gathered together on the same platform...the reason for the gathering far less important than the symbolism of the unity shown.

Doesn't this say something pretty great about the continuity and strength of the U.S. presidency? Won't it be a rather unique and significant line in tomorrow's history pages?

FRIDAY SURPRISE

Downtown buyers fill up shopping bags and Saks

*O*nce upon a time, Portland was known as a department-store town. This was in the first half of the century, before the retailing world was changed forever by urban sprawl and the establishment of shopping malls.

At the time, the majority of the volume in soft (clothing) and hard (appliances) goods was done in three major locations downtown: Meier & Frank, Lipman Wolfe, and Olds Wortman and King. All three of these full-line department stores were family operations started in the nineteenth century when Oregonians looked forward to a real happening: coming downtown to see the bright city lights and ride those novel escalators.

As succeeding family members took over, the ownership situation changed also. Olds & King became Rhodes and finally disappeared, to be reincarnated in its former home by the Naito brothers as the Galleria. Lipman's was bought from National Department Stores by Roberts Brothers; then the building became the Oregon flagship for Seattle-based Frederick & Nelson. Finally it expired and remains boarded up today.

The only one of the three still remaining in the same location and under the same name (but different ownership) is Meier & Frank, now a division of May Department Stores, based in St. Louis.

In those days, the small specialty shops had a difficult time competing with these giant stores in depth and selection of merchandise, in price, and in the variety of services offered. In the personal attention area, however, they excelled, and many smaller, owner-operated stores were able to build fine businesses. Carl Greve (jewelry), Rosenblatts (men's clothing), Charles F. Berg (women's clothing), and Harold Kelley (appliances) were all outstanding examples.

One of the better operations to move into the Portland area in the mid-part of the century was Nordstrom, originally a bustling shoe store based in Seattle. Through outstanding management by family members, Nordstrom built a specialty operation that dominated the men's and women's shoe field in their area. When Nordstrom arrived in the City of Roses, the shoe operations in the existing department stores knew that they were facing some real professionals.

The rest is familiar. "Nordies" moved into the clothing field, and by emphasizing the service aspect of its business, an area long dominated by the old-line department stores, it became a major player not just in the Pacific Northwest but also in California, Washington, D.C., and, now, in other selected sites around the country.

Local eyes and pocketbooks are once

again focused on the retail players in the community, as we have seen two major openings in the past several weeks. Nordstrom has a new Lloyd Center store, destined to be a major draw in that district.

The biggest news is the advent of the new Saks Fifth Avenue store in Pioneer Place in downtown Portland. This is the first Northwest venture for this Kuwaiti-owned national chain, long a major player in the high end of the nation's fashion business.

In the highly competitive retail world of New York, Saks has been one of the few outfits that knows what its market is, and has stuck to the area that it does best.

Now folks here are saying that it is going to be a battle royale between Nordstrom and its new downtown neighbor. Not really. Nordies is a culture, a happy shopping ground for the young and young-at-heart who like to roam around aisles crowded with merchandise.

That is not the Saks' culture. It has brought in a manager from Chicago, well-versed in its method of operation, who can pass along the special ambiance to the local crew. The new store is understated, with classy appointments letting the upscale merchandise, such as Australian Coogi sweaters for men and trendy DKNY items for women, be the focal part of the shopping experience. At the start, it is well-stocked with quality goods at prices that you would expect from a top-of-the-line retailer.

The challenge for Saks will not be wooing away the Nordstrom or Helen's "Of Course" customer, but keeping the locals who can afford the price of going to California or New York to buy their fashion goods. Fortunately, the entire Pioneer Place complex is so well-done that many upscale shoppers now make this a premier destination.

Whether we realize it or not, shopping has become entertainment. Just as downtown was the destination for our forefathers, present downtown operators realize that they must continue to provide excitement if they are going to be competitive with the ice rinks and food malls in the suburbs.

Some warning signals are in order for those who want to ensure that downtown remains the eye of the shopping world. Parking availability must be close, conveniently laid out and cheap. Inexpensive mass transportation is a must. The crime and drug scene must be controlled. City planners must be realistic on the mix of open space and building space, never forgetting that part of our charm is greenery and running water, but it is the floor space that pays the rent and taxes.

If nothing else, Saks has refocused our attention on one of the most livable downtowns in the nation.

Tiny town pours its heart into an artistry in bronze

Tiny Joseph, at the heart of this Switzerland of America in our state's northeastern corner, would seem an unlikely place for a bustling art community. Magnificent Wallowa County has been better known for lumbering and skiing and backpacking than sculptures, but now something new and exciting is happening.

About eight years ago, David Manuel, a local professional artist, had an inspiration and embarked with Glenn Anderson, a local businessman, upon a novel enterprise for their community: a fine arts casting foundry. Soon the fame of Valley Bronze spread across the world, and today it is one of the top-ranking foundries in existence.

Perhaps because of the dramatic setting of their homes, or because of the attraction of talented neighbors or because of the draw of Valley Bronze, two hundred individuals now have art-related jobs in Wallowa County, mainly in the Joseph-Enterprise area. More than thirty professional artists are living in these communities, and Joseph itself has six fine art galleries that would do justice to any metropolitan area in the country.

Wallowa County is now the home of four full or partial foundries. In addition to Valley Bronze, we find Parks Bronze in Enterprise and Parmenter Bronze and Joseph Art Castings in Joseph.

Because of the sophisticated interests of so many of the area's residents, other aspects of the arts world flourish, even in a county that boasts just 7,500 residents. There is a writer's conference, a major jazz festival, performances by the Eugene Ballet and Montana Repertory Theater and the Wallowa Valley Festival of Arts, one of the state's best local art shows.

Magnificent original works from artists in China, Mexico, Canada and the United States are reproduced at Valley Bronze, using the lost-wax casting process that allows production of limited editions of fine pieces.

At least seventy talented artisans, the majority of whom are native to the community, have been trained by an experienced staff and hands-on management, to produce some of the finest small bronzes and huge monumental sculptures available anywhere.

A fabulous depiction of a bald eagle in flight, cast in bronze, enhanced with a silver-plated head and tail, and gold-plated eyes, beak and feet, commands a price tag of $30,000. It is the work of Chester Fields, an artist who grew up in the ranch country of the Canadian and U.S. Pacific Northwest. He won national acclaim with his work *Splashdown*, a dramatic piece showing the strength of a bald eagle snatching German brown trout from a stream.

For the visitors to the area, Valley

Bronze offers tours, complete with craftsmen in Space Age silvered suits pouring hot bronze.

Across the street, one can marvel at the works of Ramon Parmenter, a native of Eugene, who is talented in many areas of artistic expression: music, dance, sculpting, writing and painting. He shows pieces grand enough to have caught the eye of commercial buyers such as Nike and Fred Meyer, in addition to such sportsmen as Olympic diver Greg Louganis and Alberto Salazar, a world-record marathoner.

One of Parmenter's pieces, a graceful ballet dancer who twirls in motion on her pedestal, will be on display at the opening of Portland's new convention center this month.

The drive from La Grande into this Oregon paradise is worth the trip. Even for those who are not caught up in the art scene, there are numerous other areas of activity to keep every member of the family busy.

A night or two at the rustic Wallowa Lake Lodge near Joseph is a special treat. Thirty rooms and suites, some looking out on the clear blue lake and others facing the Wallowa forests, have been redecorated with comfortable furnishings and antiques. It is an ideal place for a family vacation. Since 1920, the lodge has been a favorite headquarters for those who want to hike the Eagle Cap Wilderness.

The Mount Howard Tramway can take you 8,000 feet above sea level for never-to-be-forgotten views of the Wilderness Peaks and Idaho's Seven Devils.

A day trip to Hells Canyon, North America's deepest gorge, a rafting or jetboat trip on the scenic Snake River or a horseback journey to nearby lakes are special vacation ideas. Wallowa Lake and adjoining streams offer great trout and steelhead fishing.

The story of how this remote community pulled itself up by the castings is an exciting one. Tensions exist, of course, between the old-time logging and agricultural interests and their new artistic neighbors. But once again innovation wins out, especially when those involved are determined to make their operations the best available.

"Made in Joseph, Oregon" is quickly becoming a signature of distinction in the world of art.

FRIDAY SURPRISE

For Kam Sang Kwan, it's always year of work horse

From humble beginnings as a busboy in the Ruby Restaurant in Macao to proprietor of one of the largest Chinese restaurants in Oregon might seem like an impossible jump for some people. But not for diminutive Kam Sang Kwan, a fifty-four-year-old entrepreneur, who knows how to spell "work" in more languages than his native Chinese. As a matter of fact, this human dynamo took exactly three-and-a half days off last year, mainly to attend food seminars.

Kwan was born in Canton, China. He came to the Portuguese colony of Macao when he was just two years old. In his early teens, he went to work in the food business, taking English lessons on the side, knowing that some day he would need this training to become a truly successful businessman.

At the restaurant in Macao and later at a branch in Hong Kong, he learned how to cook, mix drinks, bake and wait tables. Finally, he was named a captain. While serving this apprenticeship, he caught the eye of a nearby shopkeeper, Jimmy Coe, one of the more prosperous Hong Kong businessmen. Coe soon realized that Kwan was a special person, and when the opportunity opened for a job in Oregon, Kwan was recommended as his first choice.

Stepping off the plane in Salem in 1969, Kwan was a lonely and somewhat bewildered young man. He had left his wife of five years and his first daughter in Hong Kong, in the hope he could bring them to this country at the earliest opportunity.

For five years, this enterprising young man worked hard and watched with more than passing interest what was happening in the food business.

He saved his money, and by the time his apprenticeship in a private home was over, he launched his own career: first to Idaho to work in a restaurant operation; then to Gold Beach, Oregon; and finally to Palo Alto, California. Each stop afforded him the opportunity to learn another phase of the business, the American way.

Upon his return to Salem, where he had decided he wanted to live, he went to work in the Canton Gardens, then leased the eating facilities at the Civic Center in Salem, operating that business successfully for eight years. His reputation spread. He was asked to become an instructor at Chemeketa Community College, and he soon became a local celebrity, conducting special cooking schools.

By the early eighties, he knew that it was time to strike out on his own. Kwan had saved his bucks wisely, in the hope that one day these funds could be used to make his dreams come true. He bought a vacant building on the south side of Salem, put into action the ideas he had collected through the years, and supervised the creation of a restaurant that seated 350 people. The real story here is that he did not borrow one cent to make all of this a reality.

Kwan's mind is as busy as his legs; he regularly puts in sixteen-hour days. Not satisfied in just having a Chinese restaurant, Kwan began to incorporate all the latest ideas in modern restaurant operation. First he installed a computerized bar, so that drinks could be measured and the profit margin insured.

Next came a state-of-the-art computer system that allowed management to know what tables were occupied and who was serving them so that the best use could be made of the help on duty.

A complete water purification system followed: the restaurant could advertise that there were no impurities in the drinks served.

Sensing the movement to more healthy edibles, Kwan was one of the first to present a nutrition analysis menu: no sodium, no oil, no sugar. Realizing that he had a real selling point here, he contacted the Oregon Heart Association, and the association soon recognized him.

Kwan realized the value of having children not only work, but also see how a restaurant really operates. He arranged tours and cooking exhibitions for the local schools; more than 6,000 youths have toured the Kwan Original Cuisine restaurant. This has paid off handsomely, as his place has become a family-type restaurant, with price and selections attractive to all members of the family.

You can imagine the pride that Kwan has when he looks out and sees Governor Neil Goldschmidt standing at the take-out counter getting an evening meal for himself, or the thrill of serving as host for a Chinese delegation visiting Willamette University for an educational conference.

And what has happened? Kwan employs forty people, serves 12,000 meals a month and has become a local TV star in the area of international cooking. He is finishing a modernization and expansion project that will give him 450 seats.

Oh yes, the time off. This year he plans to take two days' vacation: Thanksgiving and Christmas.

FRIDAY SURPRISE

Glenn Jackson led effort to add commuter airline

Some years ago, a group of civic-minded Oregon boosters decided that one of the most pressing needs for our area was a reliable commuter airline service. Frustrated with the reluctance of the major companies to provide adequate flights not just to our larger cities but to smaller ones as well, a call went out for private funds to put an intrastate system together.

The sparkplug for the effort was none other than the late Glenn Jackson, certainly the most effective voice at the time for the economic health of our state. "Say, coach," he would greet his multitude of contacts over the speaker-phone in his office, "we need your help for a little project we are working on." The "little project" meant that a number of us were asked to put up funds to expand Air Oregon, formerly just a courier service, into a full-fledged operation to serve various cities throughout the state.

Jackson himself found this an exciting new challenge. He was able to persuade individuals like Bob Booth in Eugene, Bill Sweet in Coos Bay, Dick Parker in Portland and others to come aboard. Most of them knew full well that the possibilities of the venture turning profitable were slim at best. But when the master persuader worked you over, who could possibly say "no?"

The first years were not easy. There were major decisions to be made, including which communities would be served. Portland, Salem, Eugene, North Bend-Coos Bay, Bend-Redmond, Medford, Klamath Falls and Pendleton (and some other smaller ports) were tried with varying degrees of success.

One thing was not lacking, and that was spirit and enthusiasm. The Air Oregon people would load up community boosters and take them on rides in the new craft they were buying.

On weekends, Jackson himself could be found at the Medford airport (he had a home in this southern Oregon town) shoveling luggage on and off the local flights, buoying the spirits of the staff at the terminal and loving every one of the astonished looks of passengers who watched this multimillionaire baggage handler.

Soon it became obvious that the pockets of the original investors did indeed have bottoms, and eventually a sale was consummated to Horizon Air, another regional outfit run as a one-man show by an exceptionally energetic entrepreneur, Milt Kuolt.

Kuolt was not of the Jackson mold. His very effective cheerleading was more of the flamboyant variety. He was a savvy operator, and under his direction the system expanded into a major entity in the Pacific Northwest, with significant service in the Portland-Seattle corridor.

But like so much of the recent history of the industry, another buyout took place. This time it was Alaska Airlines, a very healthy West Coast and Alaska operator, which became the parent company of Horizon. Alaska did not change the name but integrated the smaller network into its system. As it stands today, most major markets in Oregon are served by the company.

There are several interesting and significant corollary stories in Oregon aviation history. The individuals and the companies involved have had varied degrees of success in their endeavors.

Dave Hinson, a Portlander who successfully operated the private air service, Flightcraft, at Portland International Airport, left the local skies to take on much bigger challenges as chief executive officer of Midway Airlines in Chicago. Operating out of a much smaller airport that is a more convenient but under-utilized neighbor to booming O'Hare, Hinson has had his problems in competing with some of the better-financed, larger outfits.

Although his company has received high marks for service, Hinson has felt the pinch of over-expansion, and recently he had to abandon his dream of a Philadelphia hub to the tune of a $33 million loss. Rumors continue to circulate that one day Midway may be gobbled up by one of the major carriers.

In McMinnville, Del Smith's Evergreen International Aviation keeps a low profile but is a significant player in the cargo business. I can remember being impressed some years ago in far-away Nepal, when I learned that the helicopter I was flying in was being operated by this Oregon company.

Then there is the never-ending hope that more of the bounty of Boeing from our northern sister city of Seattle might spread southward. We do have a healthy Boeing of Oregon in Portland that employs more than 2,000 workers, but with the massive order file of the company, the dream remains that we might see a bit more of that green stuff and the resulting jobs.

We have come a long way since the days when local recreation included a trip to Swan Island to watch what was then our state's major airport. But thank goodness we haven't become so big that a fellow like Glenn Jackson can't still make a significant difference in what is regarded as an industry of the giants.

FRIDAY SURPRISE

Historian rubs shoulders with colorful governors

*F*ew people have had more celebrations in their honor in the state Capitol in Salem than Cecil Edwards. One of the reasons is that Edwards has spent more time in that building than most Oregonians; the other reason is that he remains one of the most fascinating characters in our state government's history.

The party occasion last week was Edwards' eighty-fourth birthday. The roasters and toasters included such legislative cronies as E.D. "Debbs" Potts of Grants Pass, Harry Boivin from Klamath Falls, former Governor Bob Straub, State Treasurer Tony Meeker, Justices Ed Fadeley and Wally Carson, State Superintendent of Public Instruction Norma Paulus and the most "memorable" of them all, historian Tom Vaughan.

Edwards' duties and hobbies included historian (for twenty years) of the Oregon Senate, member of the Oregon Racing Commission, counselor to numerous Oregon governors during a half-century period, army officer, horseman and collector of memorabilia unmatched by any other state official with the possible exception of Travis Cross, a former state employee and now a trustee of the Meyer Memorial Trust.

Listening to the speakers reminded me of my personal recollections of some of Oregon's more colorful governors.

The first governor that I had a close

personal knowledge of was a relative, my great-uncle, Julius Meier. Little did he think in his business years at the helm of the family department store that someday he would be a political candidate. But fate had something else in store for him. His close friend and attorney, George Joseph, the Republican nominee for governor in 1930, died between the primary and general elections. Many folks were not pleased with the choice of Phil Metschan to fill Joseph's spot and prevailed upon Uncle Julius to run as an independent in the general election.

He was easily elected as Oregon's first independent governor.

Personally, Meier was a fun-loving extrovert who liked nothing better than playing jokes on his visitors.

General Charles Martin, a Democrat, followed Meier. Martin was a straight-laced, tough-talking military officer, who had little time for those who strayed from the mainstream. He ran a tight ship and was responsible for getting rid of the "goon" squads of the late thirties.

The next occupant of the state house was a Salem native, Republican Charles A. Sprague, editor and publisher of the Salem daily, the *Oregon Statesman.* Sprague was a true intellectual, writing a daily column called "It Seems to Me" that was must reading for the intelligentsia of the state. He found it difficult to make small talk; visitors to his office were often aghast at his habit of not looking up from his desk to greet them or not offering them a seat.

I can remember being in a barber shop in Seaside when candidate Sprague was making a round of public appearances. My lasting mental picture was of Sprague's white, stiffly starched collar and equally starched demeanor. He was incapable of finding any common ground for discussion with a group of loggers waiting in the shop.

On the other hand, Earl Snell, a Republican, was a consummate politician, being twice elected governor, but serving only four and three-quarter years. On October 28, 1947, a plane accident changed the course of Oregon's political history. Killed in that crash were Snell, Secretary of State Robert Farrell, Jr., and Senate President Marshall Cornett. That effectively wiped out the Republican leadership of the state.

The political dreams of the party were thrown into disarray, and a relative unknown, John Hall, a Republican who was then speaker of the House, assumed the governorship.

Another Salemite, a Republican, and former mayor of the capital city, Douglas McKay, was elected in 1948. He and his wife, Mabel, were a great pair. Mabel McKay would prompt her husband with constituents' names, and McKay, the genial salesman, would charm them with his stories. He was re-elected in 1950, then resigned to become secretary of the interior in President Eisenhower's Cabinet.

In 1952, Paul Patterson, Republican Senate President, succeeded McKay and was elected in his own right in 1954. He died in office in 1956, and was followed by U.S. Representative Denny Smith's

father, Elmo, who also had been a Republican Senate president.

Historian Edwards would be the first to brag that during these years there was never even a hint of major scandal in state government. What better words could this historian record?

FRIDAY SURPRISE

1991's the year to display Bernard Baruch-type sense

*W*e replace the kitchen calendar on Tuesday with anticipation, fear, hope and determination. Although the immediate concern will be to get back in shape after splurging on all those good things that go with holiday celebrations, the long-term problems and opportunities facing us as individuals and members of society really occupy center stage.

Faithful readers of this weekly corner may remember that one of my all-time heroes was the late Bernard Baruch, counselor to presidents and one of our nation's most sought-after voices in times of economic and political distress.

His genius was being able to push aside the trimmings on a platter of problems and concentrate on the main course. He had common sense in abundance.

One of the greatest thrills of my life was being able to absorb a bit of his philosophy in a visit years ago, not on his famed New York Central Park bench, but in his Waldorf Towers apartment, shortly before he died.

I wonder what he would think about our current predicament in the Persian Gulf? What kind of advice would he be giving George Bush today in the Oval Office?

My suspicion is that he would be as horrified as many of us are at the possibility of losing thousands of our best young generation in the desert sands of Kuwait and Saudi Arabia and Iraq. I imagine he would counsel our president to call on the wisest, most experienced minds available to explore every considerable opportunity for a peaceful settlement before we undertake any action that could have terrifying worldwide ramifications for decades to come.

Might he suggest that "tough old hands" like former Presidents Jimmy Carter and Richard Nixon, or former Secretary of State George Shultz be brought from the sidelines to take advantage of their previous activities and contacts?

Carter did pretty well at Camp David; no one on the world scene can compare with Nixon when it comes to the dicey game of international politics; Shultz was one of the coolest and most respected heads we ever had as secretary of state. Why let those talents be wasted?

Baruch might then take a look at our domestic economic situation, one that has been on a roller coaster for years with little stability and even less long-term foundation building. It would be my guess that the wise old man would put his finger right on one of the hot buttons: the opportunities, incentives and training of our labor force.

He would point out the dangers we are facing with the kind (or better, the lack) of educational opportunities for sizable minority segments of our labor force. It takes no genius to see how other industrialized nations are running circles around us in the training department. We just don't have the necessary long-term plans for upgrading our labor force to match the needs of the twenty-first century. Although Baruch probably would not be familiar with our Oregon scene, he could certainly relate to concerns about the employment picture in our natural resource areas.

Unless I miss my guess, this figure-wise gentleman would take a close look at the tremendous disparity in wage and benefit scales between the haves and have-nots. Should there not be more incentives for the men and women at the lower end of the scale? And haven't salaries and extra-compensation packages at the top end of the ladder reached almost obscene levels in many cases? Do we realize the social implications of the trends we are witnessing?

Then Baruch might well address himself to the health crises of the nineties. He would probably point out that we have almost completely failed in trying to bring health costs under control. We have seen commercial health insurance premiums rise by as much as 20 percent just in the past year. Hospital, doctor and medicine costs continue to escalate. Aren't some kinds of controls a necessity? At the same time, we seem unable to focus on two of the major unsolved medical problems of our time: cancer and AIDS. With the enormous talent available in this nation, why aren't we able to find some answers here?

Baruch might offer the uncomplicated thought that we bring together, in one place under one roof, with adequate funding, the best brains of the nation. Lock them in their labs, where they can work hour-by-hour next to others who share their genius until they come up with some answers.

Haven't we done this successfully in other complex tasks, as when our founding fathers pieced together our Constitution? As we did in the early stages of the space program? As we did in effectively eliminating polio?

Then his focus might be on the status and health of the U.S. political machine. Is it perhaps time to do a little long-overdue repair? How about the length of campaigns? Need it be a never-ending activity? Can't those we have elected to office get about their business of doing something in office rather than continually campaigning?

Bernard Baruch might suggest, as a start, some simple solutions–such as limiting campaign periods and setting realistic spending limits. Such as fewer presidential primaries. Such as campaigns emphasizing the issues, not the personalities.

My hero was an optimist. Despite the problems, he would see the opportunities. As we hang that fresh 1991 calendar on the refrigerator door, how about unlocking a little bit of that common sense that is stored up? Bernard Baruch surely had no monopoly on that prized ingredient.

FRIDAY SURPRISE

We've lots of bright stars to lead Oregon's future

*W*ashington, D.C., is a city full of big shots. Some of them indeed occupy very important jobs, and many do not hesitate to let you know that: by not being available on the telephone without an extensive inquisition from a bevy of protectors or by not returning phone calls; by appearing at meetings with a herd of assistants and note-takers.

So it is unusual and especially pleasant when someone who does carry major responsibilities and does have a full schedule of appointments and a bewildering backlog of problems to deal with, presents himself as a normal human being and really does seem to care about the person with whom he is talking.

Such was the case in Washington offices when a youngish Oregonian, who served as secretary of transportation in the Jimmy Carter administration, came to call.

Receptionists and secretaries were flabbergasted when Neil Goldschmidt would arrive without an entourage and would chat informally with those in the outside office.

But it was not just the worker bees who were taken with this lack of pretense, this razor sharp wit and inquiring mind. Dyed-in-the-wool conservative Republicans, who ran most of the big outfits Goldschmidt had to work with, were equally impressed with this Western breath of fresh air.

Jim Evans, chief executive of Union Pacific during this period, recounts that Goldschmidt was one of the fastest studies he ever encountered. Ford Motor Company executives were equally lavish in their praise of the fairness and integrity of this young politician.

To them it was obvious that bigger things were in the offing.

Indeed, that was the case. Major responsibilities with Nike in Canada and an energetic term as governor of Oregon were to follow.

What some believed was a path that would lead to national office was detoured by personal considerations. Neil Goldschmidt, who like most successful politicians has an uncanny sense of timing, will now re-enter the private sector. For how long will be a hot topic of conversation for months to come.

Last Saturday evening, 800 friends, supporters, co-workers and family gathered for an evening of fun and tribute expertly orchestrated by Kathleen Dotten.

The affair included a first-class banquet served at the Hilton, a spectacular multiscreen Oregon video presentation, a spoof movie of the guest of honor's life, and tributes by Governor-elect Barbara Roberts, Tri-Met's Tom Walsh and Baker City's irrepressible Peggy Timm.

A number of those present had a

vital stake in the career of the honoree. They had mixed emotions: proud of what had been accomplished, sad that the era was ending.

Included in this group were folks like Mildred Schwab, a team player with Goldschmidt when he was a Portland council member and later mayor; Jerry Bidwell, Portland stockbroker and close personal friend; Ruth Ann and Mark Dodson, she a loyal assistant in a variety of capacities in Washington and Salem, he a trusted confidant; Tom Imeson, able, low-key chief of staff in the governor's office; Bob Ames, Bill Scott, Dick Reiten, Don Frisbee, Paul Bragdon and dozens of others who volunteered their time and resources for a multitude of causes.

It was also a time for many to look ahead, to speculate on who were going to be the Goldschmidts of tomorrow.

Who were the young, and some not-so-young, emerging stars whose special charisma sets them apart?

Any such listing would have to include individuals like Brett Wilcox from Portland and The Dalles, who almost singlehandedly put together the immensely successful Northwest Aluminum Company; Ted Kulongoski, popular and skilled former head of the Department of Insurance and legislator with high credibility; Tony Meeker, our respected state treasurer; and Larry Campbell, new speaker of the House; John Kitzhaber, an unassuming and talented physician who is president of the Senate; and scions of well-known Oregon families like Salem automobile dealer Scott Casebeer, whose grandfather (by marriage) was former Governor Doug McKay, and Glenn Ford, international commerce expert at the Department of Economic Development and grandson of the late civic leader,

Glenn Jackson.

Others who come to mind include prominent political names like Earl Blumenauer and Vera Katz; State Superintendent of Public Instruction Norma Paulus; Secretary of State in-waiting Phil Keisling; and Jenna Dorn, a native Oregonian who now serves as Elizabeth Dole's top assistant at the American Red Cross in Washington.

The fascinating part of the political stage is that never-ending cast of new faces; in Oregon, we have been and are blessed with an impressive group of actors waiting in the wings.

FRIDAY SURPRISE

Conflict in Gulf produces impact throughout world

S idelights of the Persian Gulf conflict continue to dazzle us:

Pride: Americans everywhere are standing a bit taller, as our fighting men and women show outstanding courage and ability in every phase of their assignments. This pride extends to the technical genius apparent on our production lines, as the little computer chip leads the array of technological advances that have given us such superiority in the air war. Many are looking forward to the day when this same talent can be diverted to our needs at home, and once again America can take her rightful place at the forefront, developing those goods for better living that we have recently been buying from abroad.

Politics: Political eyes are very much focused on President Bush, watching the polls as the conflict hardens. If we continue to be as successful as we have at the start, and if this is a relatively short war, the president will be a heads-on favorite for a second term. Many in Washington are wondering why we haven't heard more from former Presidents Nixon, Ford, Carter and Reagan. Each of them certainly could provide a unique perspective from their wartime experiences.

Position: When the current conflict ends, the one Middle East principal (other than Saddam Hussein) who stands to lose the most is Jordan's King Hussein. Trying to position himself as a friend to both sides, he has succeeded only in alienating leaders in both the Arab and Western worlds. When he next comes to Washington to plead for more money and arms, he will find a pretty chilly reception.

On the other hand, the winner will be President Hosni Mubarak of Egypt. Even with some rather intense criticism from some of his Arab brothers, Mubarak has steadfastly maintained a close working relationship with our country and the European Community. Another favorite will be Turkey, whose countryfolk (both Turks and Kurds) are practically all Muslim.

Palestinians: Unfortunately, the Palestinians are facing more sad days ahead. At a time when it looked as if there might be some chance for talks leading to a settlement with the Israelis, the current conflict has again ignited strong feelings on both sides. In addition, a number of Palestinians who worked in the Gulf States have lost their jobs and their homes, the tense situation in Israel has complicated their economic plight, and now the closed money chests of the oil monarchs mean dried up subsidies for Palestinian causes. Nowhere is this more troubling than Jordan, where Hussein faces an increasingly hostile Palestinian presence.

Protection: Security precautions

have been reviewed across our country, and nowhere is this more apparent than in the nation's capital, considered one of the prime targets for possible terrorist activities. Streets around the capital have been closed, screening procedures have been intensified, and an increased presence of police security is apparent. Bomb-sniffing dogs are at work around the Capitol and the White House.

Travelers will notice a tightening of inspection operations at airports, as we have (for the first time) reached level-four security precautions. Signs are posted asking that ticket holders indicate whether someone else packed their bags, if they have any packages given to them by others, and whether there are any recently repaired electronic items or clocks in their luggage. Bags are taped and sealed in front of the traveler. It is a good idea these days to arrive at airports well in advance of departure time.

Many hotels and transportation facilities are feeling the impact of uncertainty and higher energy costs.

Prestige: It is comforting to note that some business firms and government agencies are already planning for the return of Persian Gulf war veterans and taking immediate steps to help families whose individual members are now in combat positions. Surely this is the time to make certain that returning service men and women do not face the kind of brush-off accorded many Vietnam veterans.

Peace: Just at the time it seemed like true peace in our generation was possible, one madman temporarily changed the script. But hopefully as a result of this present conflict, no one, not even a madman of the world, will dare threaten the security of free nations. The consequences of trying will surely be indelibly written in the pages of our history books.

FRIDAY SURPRISE

Fear stalks neighborhoods as America shrinks inward

I ran across a startling statistic the other day: the number of private security guards in the United States exceeds the number of public police officers.

Undoubtedly, one of the reasons for this shift is the overall fear of crime that reaches into every household, every neighborhood, every business. The high visibility of robberies, assaults and other violent crimes has sent shock waves throughout our nation.

But there are other serious, more long-term concerns that can be read into this statistic. Quite simply, the concepts of community that have set America apart through the years, that have made us just a little bit different from any other country on Earth, are changing. Are we becoming less concerned with the overall health of our cities and becoming more concerned with the smaller orbit that each of us lives and works in?

The city of New York provides, possibly, the most dramatic illustration of the trend. For decades the genius of this pulsating metropolis was its diversity. There was the black culture of Harlem. There was the "silk stocking" district on the Upper East Side. The Germans centered in Yorkville. Little Italy and Chinatown were unique. The Lower East Side provided the background for the continuation of a Jewish heritage that waves of immigrants brought to this country.

The overall strength of the community was as strong as the diversity of the neighborhoods. Residents and visitors alike took advantage of the extraordinary bargain shopping opportunities in lower Manhattan. The intermingling of French, Italian, Japanese, Chinese and dozens of other cuisines made for some of the most enjoyable taste treats that are found in any city in the world.

No place had bread as good as New York City. Why? Because of Old World bakers from Germany and Austria and Italy and Hungary. The arts were alive with exciting talent. There were superb painters and artists of dance, song and script from all over the world who worked together to provide an unequaled cultural climate.

But all of this has been changing, perhaps so slowly that many do not perceive what is happening to the strength of America. Where we were, by necessity, a nation that brought almost everyone together for the common good, the movements in the latter part of the twentieth century have been going in the opposite direction. And disturbingly so.

Today, many New York buildings are almost like armed camps.

No longer do people feel comfortable strolling around their city, using the subway to save time and money, entering into an informal touch-football game at the corner park. Sidewalks, even in the better neighborhoods, serve as shelters for the homeless shivering in cardboard caverns. The parks and the subways are no place for the unaccompanied woman or the elderly. Youngsters must content themselves to stare endlessly at the tube for their recreation.

What is happening in the city of New York translates to just about every other city, including those in Oregon. The scale is different, of course. The signs are not quite as apparent. But the trend for "exclusion" rather than "inclusion" is nonetheless a fact of life.

What are the by-products in Oregon? Because of budget problems and crime concerns, public parks and playgrounds continue to deteriorate. It is not that our officials condone the trend; they don't have the money to provide the amenities that we had all taken for granted. At one time Oregon was known for the finest highway and park network in the nation. It still has certainly one of the best, but signs of wear and tear and lack of maintenance are all too obvious.

Walls are being built around us. Neighborhoods are providing their own security forces. More and more homes have alarm systems. Factories have their own security forces, as do schools and hotels and stores. Residential communities are providing their own (and mostly exclusive) parks and swimming pools.

Private health clubs are springing up everywhere, with equipment that used to be provided for (and heavily used by) the general public. Private golf courses are building in a number of areas; crowded public courses are practically impossible to use during weekends.

For those with the means to take advantage of the new facilities, life is good. But what about those less fortunate? The United Way campaigns are having tough times nearly everywhere as more and more private organizations inch onto their fund-raising turf. Public schools are struggling to maintain their quality as private institutions compete for the limited resources of a few wealthy donors and for money from a short list of foundations.

I'm glad my parents sent me to Portland public schools for the first twelve years of my education. It allowed me to gain a sense of the importance of community diversity at an early age. Is tomorrow's generation going to have to live in a much narrower and more restricted world?

FRIDAY SURPRISE

Thatcher's 'iron fist' proves right technique for the time

*B*arbara Walters has become one of the most popular interviewers on television today. Her tenacity in chasing down some of the world's most interesting personalities has given her a wide audience among those who enjoy watching a famous individual react to very penetrating questions.

But the other evening Walters met her match, and then some. Seated next to her was Margaret Thatcher, former British prime minister, cool and composed, articulate, strong and very opinionated. Thatcher made her hostess look like the second string had been brought in.

The discussion between the two women covered a wide range of subjects of personal and world interest. What came across in spades was the fierce devotion Thatcher has to her country and to a system that she felt would strengthen the underpinnings of the British economy. Equally impressive was her support for her husband, Dennis, to whom she gave great credit for her opportunity to serve her nation.

Mixed in with all of this was an appealing sense of humor, an informed recall of history and an obvious willingness to take the consequences of what she felt were correct, though unpopular, decisions.

Margaret Thatcher was really reflecting as much about the British personality as her own. Having lived in that country for three years, observing the words and actions of her countrymen and women, it seems to me that many of the points she emphasized are built into the psyche of the Brits.

I remember the tough days in that country after World War II. Food was in short supply, as was fuel for cars and gas and electricity for heating homes and buildings. Shelves in stores were low in consumer goods, and both government regulations and tight times made travel and recreation extremely difficult.

All of this did not seem to bother the ordinary citizen. One would see long lines to get a meat ration or some firewood. No one would think of complaining or trying to squeeze in ahead of someone else.

Their dry sense of humor was alive and kicking, even if there wasn't much to laugh about. I recall students pulling off a massive hoax at Cambridge by dressing up one of their own as a visiting foreign dignitary and bringing the entire city and university community to a state of great excitement with a parade and banquet and all the trappings of a royal occasion.

British brothers and sisters are hearty souls, too. The college chaplain took this Yankee student and a group of classmates to his retreat in the highlands of Scotland, near Kinloch Rannoch, during a vacation period. In bitter cold weather, we were up at five in the morning, climbing up and down what seemed to be huge mountains (but probably were not), gathering wood for the immense fireplace in the lodge, then returning for a breakfast of haggis.

With all her strength and wisdom, Margaret Thatcher was brought down by an ill-conceived and grossly unfair and unpopular poll tax. Even the best of politicians sometimes misread the reactions of their constituents.

In the interview with Walters, she was asked if she thought there would be a comeback for her. She doubted that would happen, although like any good politician, she did not rule out anything.

What she was saying is that there is a time and place for everybody and everything. Certainly British history has confirmed that, providing imaginative and gutsy leadership when the times demanded it.

But things have changed dramatically in the past half century. Where Great Britain was once a key world power, with interests in faraway places like Africa and the Middle and Far East, today it is a much more compact force.

On the scene comes John Major, relatively unknown to us, but an individual who seems to have a good share of traditional British grit. He was our strong ally in the Persian Gulf conflict. He has recognized the necessity of doing away with Thatcher's unpopular tax. And he is showing needed flexibility in Britain's association with the other eleven powers in the European Economic Community, scheduled to become viable in 1993.

Gone is the Thatcher hard line concerning cooperation in defense and monetary and agricultural matters. Now there is more infighting among the other members of the group than with their British neighbors.

Our ties remain constant. Just last week, President Bush met in a mutual admiration session with Major. And, Britain's Princess Margaret came to Washington, D.C., to strengthen cultural ties. (Alas, unlike her sister, Queen Elizabeth, or her mother, she was a totally unimpressive figure.)

Thatcher will probably go down in history as the needed iron fist at the right time. Only time will tell if Major will become, like so many of his predecessors, a major player on the world stage.

Good as we know we are, we know we can be better

*M*ost of us have personal "wish lists" that I suspect could be expanded to include our city and state.

We are blessed with many advantages that others would like to have in their home territory. But that doesn't mean that we can't think about some additional pleasures to add to our state where things certainly do "look different."

One of the great joys of spring and summer in our area is the opportunity to satisfy both the stomach and the senses in a manner unequaled in the country.

Not far from the center of our city we have fields growing great fruits, vegetables and nuts. The sweet corn, peaches, peas, beans and strawberries, just to name a few, take top place in grocers' bins everywhere. Our wine industry has become nationally recognized.

At the same time, our flowers, plants and trees are acclaimed around the nation for their beauty.

Although we do have numerous stands and stores throughout the region, there is no major Farmer's Market where our growers can bring their wares.

Witness the popularity of parked trucks selling fresh items direct from the farm. A companion marketplace for flowers and plants could add to the draw.

We are developing a number of specialized museums that underscore the diversity, interests and history of Oregon.

The Columbia River Maritime Museum in Astoria; the Oregon Coast Aquarium; the Oregon Trail Interpretive Centers; the new OMSI facility in Portland; the Pacific Institute of Natural Sciences in Ashland (all to be operational within the next few years); and the Oregon High Desert Museum in Bend are just a few examples of what we have to offer.

Some of these institutions already have (or soon will have) world-class pieces. Donny Kerr's rapidly expanding Oregon High Desert Museum will house the outstanding Indian collection of Doris Bounds of Hermiston. The Oregon Historical Society Center in Portland is a treasure-trove of early Oregon history; periodic shows highlight some fascinating aspects of Oregon pioneer life.

Can we package an "Oregon Treasure Tour" or whatever we want to call it, to give residents and visitors alike the opportunity to see, in an organized way, the fine museums of our state?

We have heard a great deal in recent years about a "children's agenda." This was a favorite of former Governor Neil Goldschmidt, and is an area in which he continues to show interest and support.

Oregon symbolizes opportunity for

youth. We are a young state, relatively, in years and outlook. Can we underscore this concern for our most valuable asset by becoming the national leader in facilities and activities for our young folks?

We have made a beginning. We have a great zoo and some fine children's museums, but there is more we can do. Focus on the finest educational opportunities, both public and private. Create the best medical facilities in the nation for children. Expand recreational opportunities for families with young ones; add parks and playgrounds and attractions (with private money involved) aimed just at the small fry.

In the adult medical area, we have made great progress in developing nationally recognized programs in a number of areas, among them heart, cancer, sight and hearing, bio-medical research and neuro-services.

What is most needed is proper coordination to insure that we continue to pursue excellence. We have fine hospitals, but we cannot afford the luxury of duplication and competition between them. Close and constant cooperation among civic leaders and the medical community would insure that we put our efforts and our resources where they are going to mean the most.

In the transportation area, expanded plans for Portland International Airport mean that we will continue to have a convenient and modern facility. Overseas flights are increasing; Delta has found that Portland is a natural Pacific hub. How about a Portland hub for West Coast-Europe flights so that Portland can take its rightful place with other major West Coast cities?

We can all add much more to this list.

No one expects all of these things to come to pass overnight. However, it is exciting to contemplate what might be in store for a region that already provides so much in the way of a good life for its residents.

FRIDAY SURPRISE

Senate holds strengths, weaknesses of humanity

*U*nited States senators, former and present, were in the national headlines last week. Sadness and tragedy touched the lives of John Tower, the former senator from Texas; Senator John Heinz of Pennsylvania; and Senator Edward M. Kennedy of Massachusetts. Air accidents took the lives of the first two; Kennedy once again was embroiled in controversy.

The series of events points up that what has been called the "most exclusive club in the world" is really no different than thousands of other organizations. Whenever individuals are banded together in a social setting, a business or government, the overriding human element always is present.

When I first joined the staff of the Senate some twenty-five years ago, I, like most Americans at that time, looked upon that body as one composed of superior individuals. They had to be, so it seemed, in order to be a part of that highly influential institution.

But I soon learned that the Senate was really not that much different from many other organizations. There were the great and the not-so-great. There were stellar performers in their role as debaters or foreign policy-makers. There were those who were really concerned with the plight of the minorities, the poor, the elderly and the infirm. But there also were those who seemed to be in over their heads in an institution that exerted so much influence on our daily lives. Some were more concerned with their position than with their obligations.

During this quarter of a century, a few members of the establishment made a particularly strong impression on me, albeit for different reasons.

At one time the Senate was a great debating society. We can remember reading about Senators Henry Clay and Daniel Webster in historic discussions on vital national issues. Today it is rare for such exchanges to take place; most of the Senate action takes place in committee. The recent floor debate on United States entrance into the Persian Gulf War was an exception to the current trend and it showed the Senate in its best light.

One of the star debaters of recent history was the senior senator from Oregon, Wayne Morse. Morse was a master of words. He knew the Senate rules like no one else. He had a fabulous memory to buttress his eloquence and expertise, plus a strong motivation to express his feelings, no matter how lonely he might be in his position.

Courtesy among the members has been a hallmark of the Senate for decades. Members still refer to each other as the "distinguished member from such-and-such a state," even if they really don't believe that. But a few former members did, indeed, embody senatorial courtesy at the very highest level. Senator John Stennis of Mississippi was one. And Senator Clifford Hansen of Wyoming stands out as one of the finest gentlemen I had the privilege of knowing. Unfailingly, be it with a peer or a staff member, Hansen was polite, interested, compassionate.

On the other hand, the late Senator Jacob Javits of New York did not enjoy that kind of reputation. No one questioned the superior intelligence of this hard-working gentleman, but he had little time for day-to-day courtesies. It always amused me that Javits was exceedingly polite whenever we would meet in the halls of the Washington, D.C., apartment house where we both lived. But in the halls of the Senate, he didn't know me.

A real favorite with his contemporaries was Senator Mike Mansfield of Montana. Mansfield capped his public career by serving as U.S. ambassador to Japan. His concise answers to questions, his no-nonsense handling of floor business as majority leader, and his overflowing common sense made him one of the most respected members of the Senate.

A Northwesterner, the late Senator Henry M. "Scoop" Jackson of Washington, was another favorite. He was as down-to-earth as an old shoe. But that human quality did not prevent him from exhibiting strong leadership on issues that affected his home state. Yes, he was sometimes called "the senator from Boeing," but no one doubted that he was really motivated by an intense loyalty to the people and the state that allowed him to serve for so many years.

I always had a warm spot in my heart for Senator Barry Goldwater of Arizona. Maybe it was because some family stories had my great-grandfather associated with his relatives in the early 1800s in Arizona, but I suspect more because he was never afraid to say exactly what he thought.

FRIDAY SURPRISE

Memories of Liz Taylor: always the star of the show

*T*he hottest ticket in the nation's capital today is not for a sports event or for the Kennedy Center. The Queen of England is coming to town in mid-May; politicos and residents alike are pulling every string at their disposal to attend one of the "royal" events.

My hot ticket arrived some years back when I was a Cambridge University student. At that time our ambassador to the Court of St. James was Lewis Douglas, a prominent businessman in Arizona before being appointed to this post.

The Douglases were an attractive family. The ambassador enjoyed the respect of top British officials. His wife, Peggy, was a charming and unflappable supporter of most every worthwhile cause. Their daughter, Sharman, was very much in the news at the time as a close companion of Princess Margaret.

So when an invitation arrived from these friends to a dinner "to meet Their Royal Highnesses, Princess Elizabeth, Princess Margaret and Prince Phillip," I looked forward to this once-in-a-lifetime opportunity.

The first step was to find out "the rules of the game" for such an occasion. That was not too difficult, as my university classmates were full of suggestions and advice. They were also quite miffed that a Yankee interloper was getting this opportunity! After all, it was their royal

family, and shouldn't they be the ones to have that kind of experience?

Yes, you do shake hands. "But by all means, Frank, watch your handshake. You have been known to practically tear a person's hand off with your less-than-gentle shake. No, don't start a discussion. Let them set the stage. And don't call them Liz, Maggie or Phil!"

Properly instructed, groomed and excited, I arrived at the home of our ambassador in London exactly at the appointed hour. Evidently everyone else had the same idea, for it seemed that all of the guests (about fifty) came at the same time.

Our ambassador's residence is in St. John's Woods. It is a fine old building, attractive in those days but not as fancy as it is today. Walter Annenberg, a later ambassador, spent a fortune (of his own) redoing the place during his term of office.

Peggy Douglas, the perfect hostess, made sure that everyone had the opportunity to meet all three of the guests of honor personally. First impressions? Princess Elizabeth (she was not queen at the time) was the more staid of the crew, perfectly mannered, with real political eye contact. Her husband seemed like a regular fellow, not stuffy or impressed with his station in life, happy to be in the background.

But as excited as everyone was to meet royalty, it was someone else who really stole the evening! That person was none other than Elizabeth Taylor, at that time married to Nicky Hilton, son of hotel magnate Conrad Hilton. She looked as if she had been carved out of marble, a classic beauty if there ever was one. She was probably the most relaxed of any of the guests, wandering around the royal occasion in her stocking feet.

The next time I saw her in person was on inaugural night of President Reagan's first term. No one within hearing distance could miss the intemperate exchange between Taylor and then-husband Senator John Warner of Virginia. She obviously was a lady with a mind of her own, by that time a little less glamorous and a number of pounds heavier.

However, Elizabeth Taylor was still a superstar. A year or two later at a State of the Union Address in the House of Representatives chamber, I recall watching as she entered to take her seat as a senator's wife. There were more eyes on her than on the president.

All of these incidents were brought to mind again recently. One afternoon I was engrossed in a telephone conversation in my office in Washington when I looked up and couldn't believe my eyes. In front of my desk stood Elizabeth Taylor, in person. Bang went the phone. I didn't explain, or say goodbye.

She looked great. She was making the rounds of offices on Capitol Hill lobbying for her current interest, more money for AIDS research.

One has to admire this lady who has been a superstar most of her life. Whether or not one agrees with her lifestyle, she has certainly captured the attention of generations of Americans, male and female.

There are sure to be any number of those who have "arrived," or think they have arrived, at the gatherings for the Queen. But I betcha if Taylor is among the guests, she will again be the star of the show, title or not.

Oh, yes, if the person to whom I was talking on the phone at the time when I was so rude happens to be reading this column, I apologize. I hope he or she understands what the priorities were at that moment.

Echoes from the past still ring at 'Little Grey Home'

*S*unset Magazine, in its first edition, called it the "Little Grey Home in the West." Horse lovers spent many an hour there witnessing some of the most colorful local equestrian competitions in the country on its grounds. And for over a half century, thousands of Oregonians enjoyed numerous charity and social events held on the spacious estate.

Garden Home Farm, where I was raised, was built in the 1920s on property adjoined on three sides by the Portland Golf Club, what was then known as the Nicol Riding Academy (now Bishop Dagwell Hall) and the Portland Riding Academy, in the backyard of a then tiny crossroads community, Garden Home, in Washington County.

This particular site was chosen because of its adjacency to the tracks of the Oregon Electric Railway, long since a part of local history books. As a matter of fact, a special spur off the main railroad track was built on the property so that horses could be loaded for journeys to major shows around the nation.

It was my father's love for horses that dictated the desire for such a home. The original thirty-five acres consisted of facilities mainly used for the breeding, housing and training of fine show horses: not just pleasure horses, but the cream of the competitive crop from England and America, hackney harness ponies and hackney harness horses, thoroughbred hunters and jumpers, roadsters and American saddlebred horses.

Luscious green pastures stretched over a major part of the grounds, allowing mares and their foals to romp and play to their hearts' content. A special brood mare barn housed facilities for mothers-to-be. A full-time professional farrier made sure that each of the horses had the proper shoes.

A covered ring of competition size, with a gallery area allowing hundreds of spectators to watch the goings-on, was made of huge Oregon timbers. An eighth-of-a-mile outdoor track, surrounded by immaculately groomed hedges, provided an area for schooling.

Horses were not given just "any" water to drink. It is said that they found Bull Run water too pure for their desires, so a well was dug on the premises that provided them with the real thing. In addition, that well water provided the necessary ingredient for a fully integrated fire system that covered the entire grounds. As fate would have it, that fire system turned out to be in the wrong area.

The showpiece of the estate was the magnificent barn. On the first level were fourteen oversized stalls, each with a special bin of food and water. On the door of each stall was a brass nameplate for proper identification of the occupant.

On the stable floor was a maroon carpet, in keeping with the maroon and red colors of the stable. Some of those who looked after the horses, like George Rankin of Garden Home, joked that the horses were "house-broken."

In the tack room, only first place blue ribbons and trophies won by the horses in competitions around the United States were displayed.

Upstairs in the barn were private accommodations for the personnel.

But fate was not to be good to these beautiful animals. In the early 1930s, a tragic fire swept the grounds of the Oakland, California, horse show. A number of this string of horses, along with those of the Carnation Farms and Why Worry Farms (owned by Lurline Matson Roth of the famed shipping family) died in the blaze.

In addition to the animals, dozens of hansom cabs, roadster carts and English-made Houghton viceroy buggies were destroyed. As if by fate, the historic brass and oak fire buckets were not burned; they had been left at home.

That same year, many of the horses that did survive the first tragedy were killed en route to the Madison Square Garden Horse Show in New York. My father, Aaron Frank, was devastated. He felt that he was not meant to have horses. For the rest of his life, the estate was used to accommodate events for various charities and as a private residence.

And now the grounds that hold so many memories for those who visited and played among its trees and pastures take on a new life. Apartments built by a developer are being rented on the former Frank estate at Garden Home. The dozens of pheasants which also called the wooded paradise "home" during the years will have new neighbors; I hope they stay around to enjoy them.

FRIDAY SURPRISE

Great White Way lassoes American folk hero

Ziegfeld has come back to life on Broadway. Only this time his spotlight is on an unlikely personage of the past, the great American humorist, Will Rogers. The vehicle is the *Will Rogers Follies, A Life in Revue,* which just opened on the Great White Way in New York.

The setting is the historic Palace Theater, a grand building set in the midst of the gaudy signs, the tacky souvenir shops and the girlie shows of Manhattan's Times Square. The area was once the pride of the city; now drugs and crime have become commonplace. Finally the property owners and city fathers have embarked on a plan to clean up these famous blocks. It's about time.

The history of the Palace goes back to a gala opening of 1913; for the next twenty years the cast of performers in this magnificent structure included Ethel Barrymore, Eddie Cantor, W.C. Fields, Mae West, Fanny Brice, Harry Houdini, Sophie Tucker and, yes, even Will Rogers himself.

Three of America's greatest comedians broke into the big time at this showhouse. Jack Benny was unknown until his Palace appearances, and Burns and Allen shared top billing with a new show every season.

Later on, when vaudeville faded from the scene, movies took over the house. Then came another reincarna-tion. This time the Nederlander brothers converted the Palace into a legitimate theater, and it became the home of such famous productions as *George M!, Applause, Oklahoma* and *La Cage aux Follies.*

And now, renovated again, the grand old lady is hostess to one of the strangest attempts imaginable to combine history and humor in a sophisticated spectacle about a very unsophisticated man.

It almost works. The stage settings are magnificent. Moving stairs provide the background for a number of the scenes, with the leading characters appearing from the roof of the stage on ropes and imaginary moons.

The music, composed and arranged by Cy Coleman, is catchy and boisterous, but not memorable. However, Broadway's longest-running creative partnership in theater history, Betty Comden and Adolph Green, have written some fun lyrics that do not seem too out-of-place for a takeoff on the life story of a person who "never met a man I didn't like." That phrase is even the name of the musical number of the grand finale!

Keith Carradine, a veteran of the Broadway stage, movies and television, plays the lead role. He comes from a well-known entertainment family. He worked with his father, John Carradine, in productions of *Tobacco Road.* His wife is actress Sandra Will, and his daughter, Martha Plimpton, is a rising stage star.

There are the what-you-would-expect touches in any production that has a Ziegfeld connection. Beautiful, scantily clad chorus girls, performing outstanding numbers choreographed by Broadway's master, Tommy Tune. A dog act, complete with the little black poodle who hides in a barrel. A black light scene. Tears and troubles at the time of the Great Depression.

Carradine does a passable job with Will Rogers' famous rope, but it takes a real professional, Vince Bruce, to bring down the house with a fabulous interlude of the classiest rope-twirling that side of the Pendleton Round-up!

The voice of Mr. Ziegfeld periodically booms out over the house to give instructions to the struggling actor Rogers. And whose voice is used? None other than Gregory Peck's!

With a top ticket price of $55, the orchestra and front mezzanine seats are sellouts, but the lower-priced high balcony goes begging.

Those who splurge on an evening with Rogers will wonder what in the world Peter Stone (who did the book) saw in the lives of Rogers and his wife, Betty, that would connect them with a Ziegfeld extravaganza. But they will go away reminded how one "common man" with so much common sense captured the hearts and minds of generations of Americans.

Sitting in the Palace, I thought about the Portland connections of many of the great stars who had performed on that stage. Sophie Tucker, one of my favorite entertainers, was a regular visitor to the Rose City when Mary and George Amato operated their supper club in downtown Portland. This "last

of the red-hot mamas" would charm young and old alike with musical stories of her adventures.

Jack Benny came to town to help us raise funds for what was then the Portland Symphony. He hardly looked (or acted) like the penny-pinching character of his show, as he sat in his Benson Hotel suite recalling his early show biz days. His supporting singing group, the Sportsmen Quartet, were frequent visitors; Bob Garsen, the lead, was a popular Portland TV star some years ago. Charles Correll (Andy of Amos 'n' Andy fame) was our master of ceremonies for one of the Rose Festival shows held in the Civic Stadium.

One wonders if we will ever again have headline personalities with talent like Rogers and Ziegfeld and Benny and Tucker. What is that magic ingredient missing in today's lineup?

When playing world stage, character rules everything

*W*hat do Boris Yeltsin, James Baker III and Fidel Castro have in common? Not much, you say. One is a robust, hard-driving Soviet individualist; the second a button-down, establishment conformist; the third a bearded revolutionary.

And how about Kurt Waldheim, John Sununu, Paul Wellstone and John Major? Are they an unlikely foursome, without any common bond? The first an imperious Austrian president; the second a brilliant, tough White House political pol; the third a populist senator from Minnesota; the latter a freshman British prime minister.

All seven of these gentlemen have been in the news in the past week, all doing different things, in different forums, with different reactions.

Yeltsin took the East Coast power centers by storm. While Mikhail Gorbachev was at home trying to balance his checkbook, with predictable results, Yeltsin, the newly elected president of Russia, was out shaking hands with Yankees, charming United States senators, paying a call on President Bush, speaking to students at New York University and even visiting the Big Apple garment district to see how "the other half" works.

It was a different kind of visit than Yeltsin's previous trip to the United States when he was not allowed in the Oval Office, and when he consumed stuff much stronger than the just plain water he asked for this time at a dinner in his honor.

Here was a Russian paying homage to the kings of capitalism, visiting the canyons and corner offices of Wall Street and the Federal Reserve Board, to learn how a free market society really operates.

There was James Baker, our secretary of state, addressing a tumultuous crowd of more than 300,000 in the main square of Tirana, Albania, the small Eastern European nation that, for more than forty years, had shunned ties with the rest of the world.

The amazing part of the Baker episode: it was a completely spontaneous event. There were no advance men, no organized buses to bring in the country folk, no posters or newspaper ads or radio announcements and no free lunch for those in attendance. They were the common folk of this poor and sad country, where a temporary government is running things in preparation for historic multiparty elections to be held next year.

Baker took full political advantage of his forum, bringing hopeful words from the world's strongest democracy to a country so backward that there really is only one fax machine in the entire nation! (Is that REALLY so backward?)

Fidel Castro, the longest-playing actor on the communist stage, was receiving bad news from his Soviet sponsors. He was learning that Soviet aid may be cut by as much as 50 percent from the approximately $4 billion a year he has been receiving. Even though thousands of his countrymen continue to flee the country, Castro still is the man in charge, with seemingly no real opposition.

But how about that Waldheim-Sununu-Wellstone-Major foursome? Sensing that his time was up, Waldheim announced last week that he was not going to seek a second, six-year term as president of Austria. Tarnished by reported ties to Nazis during World War II, Waldheim has been an embarrassment to his country.

Air Sununu has been flying in turbulent skies for several weeks now, but finally both the president and his chief of staff have said "enough is enough." It looks as if Sununu may be using a new travel agent in the future.

In the Senate, an institution where mavericks get more attention in the press than in the power halls, Paul Wellstone has certainly not become an insider in the world's most exclusive club. Even on the outside, he has seen his approval rating in his native state drop to 35 percent.

Pity John Major. Following in the controversial, but respected, shadow of Iron Lady Margaret Thatcher would not be easy for anyone. But Major has been criticized (not openly) by his former mentor. The Laborites have taken advantage of his rather bland style and manner, and recent polls show that the Conservatives will face an uphill battle at the next election.

So what is the common denominator of these two groups of headliners? Political style or political class, call it whatever you want. Some have it and some don't.

Yeltsin and Baker and Castro have it in spades, playing with different decks. They are the survivors.

On the other hand, Waldheim, Sununu, Wellstone and Major flunk the test. Their political instincts, that intangible something that sets apart winners from losers, places them in the latter category.

Ambitious politicians, take note. How is your P.S. or P.C. working?

Surprise! It's Friday already, and time for page in history

I have been asked many times by the scores of people who were either former employees or customers of the institution that gave birth to the title of this weekly column to recall the early history of the store.

Aaron Meier, the founding father, was born in the Bavarian village of Ellerstadt in 1831, came to America at age twenty-four and went to work in his older brother's store in Downeyville, California. History books relate that "its shelves were piled high with cigars, playing cards, miner's tools, revolving pistols and cans of fruit. Best of all, on the counter was the scale that weighed the gold dust."

In 1857, Meier decided to open his own general store in Portland: it was a 35-by-50-foot establishment at 137 Front Street, near Yamhill. Early bills were paid with eggs, potatoes, pickles, salmon and fur.

At that time, Portland was a village of just over a thousand hardy souls, but the city already had forty-two dry goods and grocery stores. (And Oregon was not even a state yet. It was admitted to the Union in 1859.)

Bad luck came when Meier's partner bankrupted the store in 1863. Recovering, Meier then saw his establishment wiped out by the great fire of Portland in 1873.

Still, the store grew, and as additional hands were needed, Aaron's wife (the former Jeanette Hirsch) brought over relatives from Germany. During the great flood of 1894, the newcomers helped paddle customers around the counters in small boats.

Some of the relatives soon left to form their own businesses. One was a pioneer wholesale drug company, Blumauer-Frank. Another was the White Stag Company, named for partners Hirsch and Weis. They started making canvas sails and tents for Alaskan gold prospectors, but changed with the times to become one of the nation's leading manufacturers of sportswear and skiwear.

The one untypical thing in Aaron's life, and for thirty-six years after he died in 1889, was his wife. She was the most important force in building the store and preventing its destruction by the normal ambitions and rivalries of a growing family.

"Shannet," as she was called, was a short, stout, heavy-bosomed and firm-jawed lady, eleven years younger than her husband. She was, from the beginning, the one who was in charge. She went to the store every day of her life, and although she never had an office or a title, every package boy and ribbon clerk know she was the boss. Her cane pounded the floor to give emphasis to her every word.

She and she alone determined which marriages were suitable and which were not. Her husband, on a buying trip to San Francisco in 1872, met a recently arrived German music teacher by the name of Sigmund Frank. Meier offered him a clerking job, and after Shannet certified that Frank would make a proper spouse for her oldest daughter, Fannie, Frank became a partner in the business and the name was changed to Meier & Frank. Fannie and Sigmund would become my grandparents.

The history of the store and the city was interwoven. In 1878, the first telephones were installed. In later years, the store's switchboard was the largest and the busiest private operation in the West. Over a dozen operators took orders for everything from girdles to groceries, all of which were delivered first by horse-drawn rigs and then by the familiar green trucks.

In 1885, a two-story building was constructed on Taylor Street between First and Second avenues.

The first "Friday Surprise" sale was held on Friday, April 29, 1887. It was to become one of the most famous weekly merchandising events in the nation. Specially priced goods, obtained from prime sources all over the country, were reduced in price just for this one day. Thousands of customers, eagerly awaiting the surprises (no prices were advertised) lined up at the store doors on Friday mornings.

More growth and expansion came in 1889, 1891 and 1897. The latter years brought the momentous move uptown to an elegant five-story building on Fifth Avenue between Alder and Morrison, a store that had sixty-eight times more floor space than Aaron Meier's original establishment.

In 1930, the store's president, Julius Meier, became Oregon's first (and only) governor elected as an Independent.

During the Great Depression, Murphy and Finnegan (as it was affectionately called) ran a one-word ad:
"CONFIDENCE."
Portlanders by the hundreds brought their savings to the store for safekeeping.

The tradition of a Meier or Frank family member as president continued until 1965, when the business was sold to a national chain, the May Company. Thousands of Oregonians from Clark Gable (who sold neckties) to Judi Hofer, who rose from stock-girl to president of the store today, have contributed to making the Friday Surprise store a unique institution in merchandising history.

One of Meier & Frank's early homes welcomes customers on Front Street in Portland (1887).

The original Oregon American Automobile Association clubhouse on the Sandy River, where high jinks were reputed to be a popular pastime in the early decades of the twentieth century.

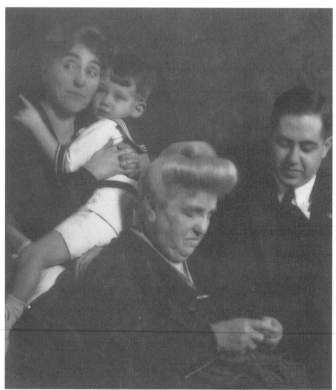

Four M&F generations: family matriarch Jeanette (Shanett) Hirsch Meier, daughter Fannie Meier Frank, grandson M. Lloyd Frank, and great-grandson Frederick Frank (1921).

Mrs. Isam White (Aunt Rosie), dowager queen of the Benson Hotel, holds court in the thirties.

Dorothy McCullough Lee, the first woman mayor of Portland (1949-1952), was not afraid to take on the establishment.

A family gathering at Gearhart, Oregon (1930) includes Gerry and his parents, Ruth and Aaron Frank.

The downtown Portland Meier & Frank store is decked in bunting for the Independence Day celebration in 1929.

Aaron Frank on downtown M&F's new mid-century escalator. He personally supervised its construction each evening.

The first disaster relief truck in the nation, named in honor of Portland Fire Chief Jay W. Stevens, was given to the city by Aaron Frank in 1939.

Cadet Commander Gerry Frank (fourth from right) and some of his troops in the Army Specialized Training Program, Loyola University of Los Angeles (1943).

"Papa Bud" (Aaron Frank) with sons Dick and Gerry at the groundbreaking of the Salem Meier & Frank store (1954).

Two colorful Oregon statesmen, Mark Hatfield and Tom McCall, exchange greetings at Hatfield's fiftieth birthday party (1972).

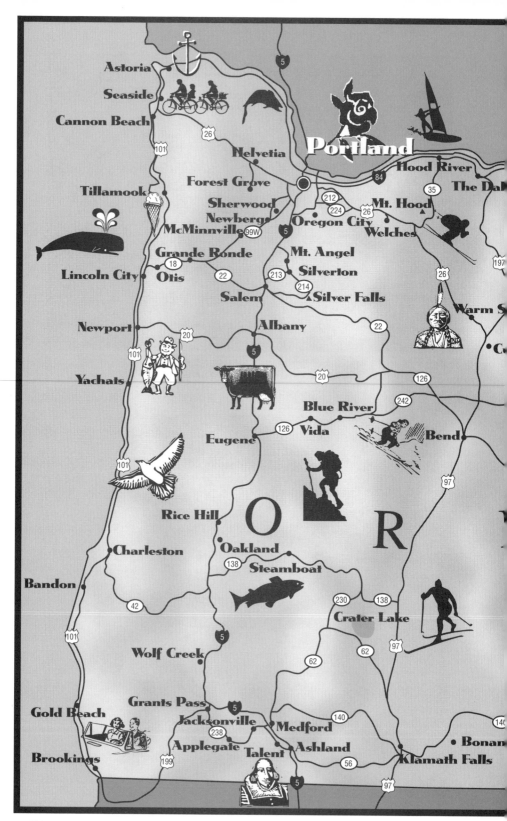

Astoria
Seaside
Cannon Beach
Helvetia
Portland
Hood River
The Dal
Tillamook
Forest Grove
Sherwood
Newberg
McMinnville
Oregon City
Mt. Hood
Welches
Grande Ronde
Mt. Angel
Silverton
Lincoln City
Otis
Salem
Silver Falls
Newport
Albany
Warm S
Yachats
Blue River
Bend
Eugene
Vida
Rice Hill
O
R
Charleston
Oakland
Steamboat
Bandon
Crater Lake
Wolf Creek
Gold Beach
Grants Pass
Jacksonville
Medford
Bonan
Brookings
Applegate
Talent
Ashland
Klamath Falls

101
5
26
84
35
212
224
26
99W
5
18
22
213
214
26
197
20
101
126
242
97
138
230
138
42
101
5
62
97
62
140
140
5
238
199
56
97

124

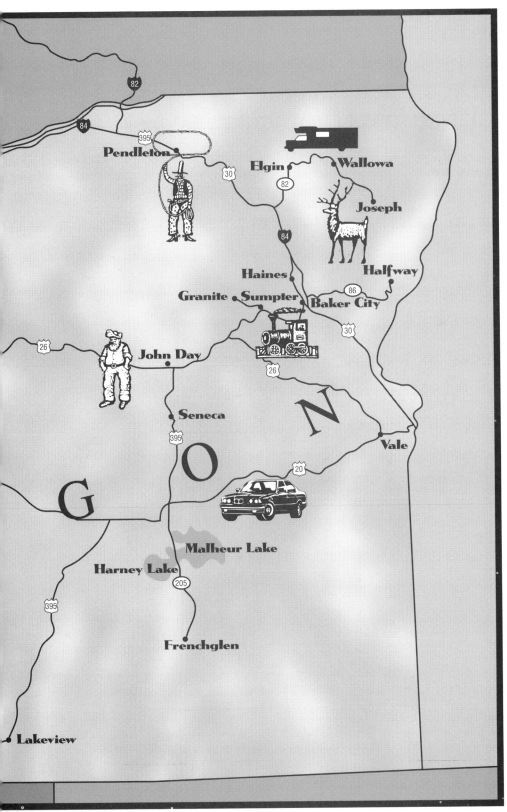

Pendleton

84

82

395

30

Elgin

82

Wallowa

Joseph

84

Haines

Halfway

Granite • Sumpter • Baker City

86

John Day

26

30

O R E G O N

26

Seneca

395

Vale

20

Malheur Lake

Harney Lake

205

395

Frenchglen

Lakeview

The Best of Oregon
Destination Attractions
Places to visit, eat, and more

Albany	Novak's Restaurant, Hungarian goodies
Applegate	River Ranch House, riverside grill
Ashland	Antique Rose Inn, Victorian B&B splendor
	Monet, classic French meals
	Natural History Museum, education center
	Shakespeare at his best
Astoria	Josephson's, best seafood
	Museum, maritime history
Baker City	Oregon Trail Interpretive Center, spectacular site
Bandon	Cheese factory, creamy cheddar
	Old City, fascinating galleries
Bend	High Desert Museum, nationally acclaimed
	Rock Springs Guest Ranch, dude's delight
Blue River	Holiday Farm, McKenzie River retreat
Bonanza	Historic ghost town
Brookings	Mama's, authentic pizzas
Cannon Beach	Stephanie Inn, oceanside luxury
Charleston	Shore Acres Park, awesome views
Crater Lake	Lodge, blue-ribbon digs
Culver	Beetle Bailey's, 12 great milkshake flavors
Elgin	Opera House, restored elegance
Eugene	Saturday Market, colorful
	Chanterelle, delicious dishes
	Campbell House, a city inn
Frenchglen	Hotel, rustic charm
Gold Beach	Jerry's Rogue Jets, fabulous whitewater experiences
	Tu Tu Tun Lodge, Oregon's premier hideaway
Grande Ronde	Strawberry Patch, mouth-watering shortcakes (seasonal)
	Spirit Mountain Resort, big time gaming
Granite	Historic ghost town

Oregon's best, continued…

Grants Pass	Flanagan House, superb Yankee pot roast
Haines	Steak House, hearty appetites
Halfway	Pine Valley Lodge, candlelit dining rooms
Helvetia	Tavern, outrageous burgers
Hood River	Windsurfers' paradise
Jacksonville	Jacksonville Inn, memorable meals, beautiful bedrooms Peter Britt Festival, music under the stars Old Stage Inn, sensational B&B
John Day	Kam Wah Chung Museum, Chinese history Fossil beds
Joseph	Foundries, nation's best Wallowa Lake, breathtaking tramway
Klamath Falls	Baldwin Hotel, fascinating museum
Lakeview	Schminck Museum, pioneer life
Lincoln City	Bay House, romantic dinners
Malheur County	Wildlife refuge
McMinnville	Nick's, Italian family fare
Medford	Under the Greenwood Tree B&B, ancient trees, modern luxury
Mt. Angel	Library, architectural showpiece
Mt. Hood	Timberline Lodge, rustic rooms, gourmet dining
Newberg	Rex Hill Vineyards, superb wines
Newport	Aquarium, whale of a time Canyon Way, great food Sylvia Beach Hotel, spend the night with an author
Oakland	Tolly's, charming food, antique treats
Oregon City	Interpretive Center, end-of-the-Oregon-Trail
Otis	Cafe, hearty breakfast value
Pendleton	Underground, bawdy days recalled Working Girls Old Town Hotel, memories Raphael's, Northwest dining, Queen Anne ambiance

Oregon's best, continued…

Portland	Marsee Baking, fabulous pastries
	Grand Central Bakery, best Italian bread
	Oregon History Center, Oregon on exhibit
	OMSI, space-age excitement
	Pittock Mansion, historic home
	Powell's, miles of books
	Rose Garden, sports palace
	Alexander's, a feast for the eyes and stomach
	Huber's, best turkey
	Zefiro, four-star dining
	Avalon, riverside gourmet treats
	Jake's, world-famous crawfish
	Candy Basket Factory, a chocolate waterfall!
Rice Hill	Quickie's, Umpqua ice-cream bargains
Salem	Willamette University, Goudy Commons, good lunches
	Gilbert House, enchanting children's museum
	Kwan's, authentic Chinese cuisine
	Konditorei, extravagant cakes
Seneca	Ponderosa Cattle Company, working ranch
Sherwood	Sleighbells, Christmas fairyland
Silver Falls	State Park, Oregon premier showpiece
Silverton	Oregon Garden, floral showcase (being planned)
Steamboat	Steamboat Inn, gourmet paradise, fishing
Sumpter	Railroad, steam-powered train
Talent	New Sammy's Bistro, unpretentious fine dining
The Dalles	Oregon Trail Interpretive Center, picturesque
Tillamook	Creamery, sensational ice cream
	Blue Heron Cheese Company, wonderful samples
Vida	Eagle Rock Lodge, McKenzie riverfront splendor
Warm Springs	Museum, Native American artifacts
Welches	Resort at the Mountain, best Sunday buffet
Wolf Creek	Tavern, historic accommodations
Yachats	Coastal B&B headquarters, many special retreats
	La Serre, refined dining

Dynamic Oregon leader Glenn L. Jackson (1902-1980), a power company executive, rancher, newspaper chain owner, and chair of the Oregon State Highway Commission.

The author (fourth from right) at the entrance to the chilly accommodations at the South Pole (1970).

President Richard Nixon expounds his views at a private dinner at the Hatfield residence in Georgetown.

President Ronald Reagan tries out some novelty specs at a family dinner at the Hatfield home. (1982)

Lady Margaret Thatcher, former British prime minister, is a visionary who is never afraid to take a controversial position.

Vice-President George Bush was the genial host at a Washington, D.C., reception for Portlanders Esther Jantzen and Richard Moore. (1985).

Former Governor (1987-1991) Neil Goldschmidt remains one of the century's most eloquent and energetic Oregon citizens.

Here comes 'da chocolate cake judge' (since 1959) at the Oregon State Fair.

The Salem Boys & Girls Club's 'kid's night out' gives the author the honor of playing 'foster Dad' for an evening.

Dear Gerry Frank.
God love you for the
love you share through
the help you give
to our sisters
God bless you
Mother Teresa me

The 'Saint of Calcutta', Mother Teresa, shares her humanitarian work with all who are interested.

FRIDAY SURPRISE

Putting best face forward, growth industry of the '90s

*H*ow will it play in Peoria? But it isn't just Peoria that people who mold your opinions think about; it's you and me in Portland and Scio and Washington, D.C., and Amman and all points in between.

And it isn't just in the political world that this spin takes place. It goes on in business, in the restaurant scene, in social circles and just about everywhere else you can imagine.

No place is this more evident than in the Middle East, where what we read and what they read is very different indeed. We have watched, with some disgust, the on-again, off-again love affair that King Hussein of Jordan has with our country. His Majesty has not had the intestinal fortitude to stand up against what he knows would be unpopular winds in his own country. Thus, for internal consumption, he rails against our participation in Desert Storm. On the other side of the Atlantic, the news intended for the breakfast tables of the boys and girls in Congress who are going to dole out his next welfare check reads very differently: "I love America."

In Washington, D.C., there are masters in the coloring of the events of the day in just about every nook and cranny of our governmental bureaucracy. The nation shuddered a bit to learn that President Bush had a mild weakness bout several months ago. But the White House disc jockeys lost little time in trumpeting the news of presidential golf games, boat trips and horseshoe contests to reassure the American public that the president was right back in shape and doing everything (with gusto) that he had been doing before.

The other day, Richard Darman, who balances the checkbook at the White House, allowed that there had been a slight mistake in one of the entries in his register...not too serious, mind you, just about an $180 billion oversight that really wouldn't make that much difference in the whole federal deficit scheme of things. Voluminous figures were produced to show that this "small" amount was really just a drop in the bucket when one considers the red ink that continues to flow out of the nation's capital. (The latest total debt figure for fiscal 1992 is estimated at $4.3 trillion, yes, trillion.)

American business has learned from the politicians. What we know of many of our major consumer-goods firms, financial houses, airlines and just about any other outfit that has contact with the public, is presented, naturally, with the best possible twist. If an outfit that has a listed stock is expecting a bad quarter, many times we read about it before the official earnings announcement. This can calm the nerves of some of the analysts, prevent a selling spree and make the later news sound less damaging.

Some financial houses have been tarnished of late by the problems that have plagued the savings and loan industry. Unfortunately, sometimes the brush is used too broadly. There is no question that some businesses are, indeed, having their problems. But many others are well and happy, thank you. It is the job of the public relations gurus who handle the affairs of these healthy entities to let the public know how their bank or insurance company or whatever differs from the industry perception.

Even palaces have staffs that ensure that their royal occupants are properly presented. Well, almost. These retainers were royally upset recently when Queen Elizabeth's lectern was too high for one of her Washington appearances. All the television audience could see was her hat bobbing over the microphones.

At the G-7 conference in London, the royal spin merchants got even. In the seating for pictures of the heads of state with Her Majesty, they made sure that she was front and center. All participants were carefully assigned not only seating for this photo, but marked places on platforms for other group pictures.

It even happens in restaurants. A reviewer may savagely assault an eating establishment with a very uncomplimentary piece, but the dining house will carefully extract one flattering comment ("the caesar salad was exceptional") and that will become the feature line in an ad extolling that particular place.

We have seen broadsides promoting new movies or stage shows. Many times the writer's original feelings are lost in the two or three word bites that sound like that particular production is the best thing since *Gone With the Wind*. You have to go back and re-read the whole review to see where the few complimentary words were mentioned.

An entire industry has grown up around us to make sure that we see the best side of people, places and things. That isn't all bad, I guess. But we do have to wonder if we are not all smart enough to make our own evaluations without having this constant coloring of the scenes in tones which sometimes are not really too accurate.

John Hancocks document history and personalities

*C*ollecting autographs can be like a treasure hunt: it takes a lot of time, a bit of luck, some ingenuity, but most of all being in the right place at the right time.

My participation in this hobby started at an early age, when my father got me interested by securing pictures and signatures of some of the more prominent individuals of his time. These centered on his own hobbies: sports, horses and comedy.

Early pieces included the great boxer Jack Dempsey, track star Jesse Owens, comedians Jack Benny and Olsen and Johnson, New York Mayor Fiorello La Guardia, and screen star Spencer Tracy.

The one picture and inscription I prize the most of this era is that of Charlie Chaplin, one of the most famous (and controversial) of the early performers. Although my father was a serious individual, he did have a light side that many people did not recognize. His favorite recreation at horse show gatherings was to mimic Chaplin.

In recent years, activities in Washington, D.C., and overseas have allowed me to add to my collection in several fields, with a particular emphasis on history and political personalities of our time.

Perhaps the single toughest, but most satisfying, task was collecting signatures of the fourteen gentlemen who served as presidents of the Continental Congress in the period 1774-1789.

There are not many complete autographed collections of these individuals, and single documents are difficult to come by. The presidents did not stay in power long. The list begins with Peyton Randolph (who served only a month and a half the first time he was in the office) on through such little-known names as Elias Boudinot, Nathaniel Gorham, Cyrus Griffin, Henry Laurens, Thomas McKean, Thomas Miffin and Arthur St. Clair.

Better-known presidents were John Hancock (who served twice), John Jay and Richard Henry Lee. Naturally, the John Hancock signature was the easiest to find; some of the rest took years of searching in out-of-the-way antique stores, at auctions, in used book stores, and through networking with others interested in history.

Nathaniel Gorham was the most elusive; I finally ran across a deed signed March 16, 1789.

Another early piece that I am particularly proud of is a letter dated September 30, 1886, signed by Jefferson Davis. In language uncommon in those days, he writes, "I recently sent a rather long letter to the *Baltimore Sun,* being a notice of the executive document published by the U.S. Senate in which that chief of liars, W.T. Sherman, had renewed his assault on me."

My collection includes documents or

pictures signed by all the presidents of the United States; the more recent ones have been collected personally, the older ones were part of a magnificent volume put together by a member of the Crocker banking family of San Francisco. The Nixon piece is framed with undistributed tickets for his impeachment hearings signed by then House doorkeeper, "Fishbait" Miller.

Some of the more interesting current items include a copy of the Camp David agreement, signed by Menachem Begin, Anwar Sadat and Jimmy Carter.

An especially significant (to me) letter is written on plain, lined paper, the kind we might use for kitchen notes. How fitting that the message is handwritten by one of the saints of our time, Mother Teresa. No formal stationery, no secretary. It was written as a result of a day spent with her in Calcutta, visiting her home for abandoned infants and her leper colony in the outskirts of the city; it is signed simply "M. Teresa." (See photo, page 132.)

During the first Reagan inaugural in 1980, my assignment was to get the members of the original Cabinet organized to take their proper places on the platform. This exciting opportunity allowed me to secure the autographs of all the members of that group.

Other documents that bring back particular memories include a letter from park-bench philosopher Bernard Baruch, a steely-eyed picture and accompanying letter after a visit with King Faisal of Saudi Arabia, and a signed snapshot from a breakfast with Emperor Haile Selassie of Ethiopia.

Handwriting experts tell us that a signature reveals a great deal about the person; that is, if you can read it. On the local scene, I bet such experts would have a field day examining the autograph of prominent Portland businessman Sam Naito.

FRIDAY SURPRISE

Chocolate cake contest tests judge's stamina

*I*t was chocolate cake time again at the Oregon State Fair recently, and for the thirty-second year I was the judge of this classic caloric contest.

Fifty-nine young and old bakers, men and women, from all parts of the state, lugged their rich renditions to the home economics section of the fair. Here Janet Lee, the department boss, Don Hillman, the fair manager, Orville Roth, the fair commission chairman, and nearly 500 spectators watched this annual outrageously delicious ritual.

As always, I judged the cakes for both appearance and taste, taking into account that a number of them slid around in cars getting there, and several suffered minor hemorrhaging during the judging period.

One family has dominated the winner's circle for the past several years. Whether they have found the secret recipe key to this fellow's chocolate heart or whether they are just awfully artful in the kitchen, I don't know. Daryl Kihs won first place for three years, so this year he was not eligible to compete. However, two daughters did not let the family down: Tammy and Kristina Kihs of Jefferson won third and fourth place awards.

First-place honors this year went to a lady who had never won a prize before. Susan Tompkins of Salem, a teacher, made a masterpiece that would easily persuade me to be teacher's pet in her class anytime.

To keep the audience amused for the two-and-a-half-hour show (I take two bites of each entry), I try to assemble as many chocolate "facts" as I can. These include: chocolate does not cause cavities (according to Boston's Forsyth Dental Clinic); chocolate isn't loaded with caffeine (a one-ounce bar has only six milligrams); the average American eats 18.7 pounds of chocolate a year.

In previous years, I was able to have members of the audience share in the tasting fun. But strict new insurance rules don't allow me to offer pieces of the homemade beauties to the spectators, so I brought along professional cakes from my Konditorei as rewards for those who come to the platform to be put through some rigorous chocolate questioning.

The youngsters are the most fun. One little girl was so awed by the sight of all those treats that she was not able to tell the audience her name or what school she went to.

How does one prepare for 118 bites of cake? I asked my doctor what he would recommend; after careful research he couldn't suggest a routine. But I have found my own answer: plain old Pepto-Bismol. A hefty swig before, another large shot afterward. This Pepto-chocolate stomach sandwich seems to take care of any unpleasant after-effects.

For your baking and tasting pleasure, the recipe from this year's winning state fair entry:

BEST FUDGE CAKE
3 squares unsweetened chocolate
1/2 cup butter, at room temperature
2 1/4 cups brown sugar
3 eggs
1 1/2 teaspoons vanilla
2 teaspoons baking soda
1/2 teaspoon salt
2 1/4 cups cake flour
1 cup dairy sour cream
1 cup boiling water

Melt chocolate in small saucepan over very low heat. Set aside. Grease and flour two 9-inch layer cake pans.

Beat butter until smooth in large bowl with electric mixer. Add brown sugar and eggs. Beat on high speed until light and fluffy about 5 minutes. Beat in vanilla and melted chocolate with mixer on low speed, then add baking soda and salt.

Add flour alternately with sour cream, beating on low speed until smooth. Pour in boiling water; stir with spoon until well-blended. Pour into prepared pans. Bake at 350 degrees for 35 minutes. Cool in pans on rack 10 minutes. Remove from pans, cool completely.

CHOCOLATE BUTTERCREAM FROSTING
1 cup powered sugar
1/3 cup unsweetened cocoa
3 tablespoons butter, softened
2 tablespoons milk
1/2 teaspoon vanilla
1 tablespoon light corn syrup (optional)

In small bowl, combine sugar with cocoa. Cream butter and half of the sugar/cocoa mixture in a small mixer bowl. Add remaining cocoa mixture, milk, and vanilla; beat to spreading consistency. For glossier texture, add one tablespoon of light corn syrup.

FRIDAY SURPRISE

Called piddling, this pond has some very big fish

S ome social snobs like to comment about the youth of our city and state, asserting that we do not have much history compared to communities of the South and New England. Well, that may be true, but in the relatively short span of years since Oregon became a state in 1859, we have produced more than our share of talented and colorful individuals who left indelible marks on their community.

Pioneering Leadership for Women: Dorothy McCulloch Lee, who served as mayor of Portland from 1949-1952, was one of the first women to become chief executive of a major city. Tough as nails, never afraid to be controversial, she took a strong stand on law and order in the Rose City.

She would be pleased to see so many women now serving as mayors throughout the state and would be one of those fighting for more recognition of women in top business and industry positions. (See photo, page 120.)

Undergirding the Young Generation: G.H. Oberteuffer was a legendary outdoors hero to thousands of young men in Portland when he served as chief Scout executive of the local council from 1925-1958.

A living example of the Scout oath, "Obie" was the kind of father figure who influenced young lives in a most positive manner.

With the bruising battle today between those who use our forests and streams for recreation and those who make a living from our great reservoir of natural resources, one wonders if a man like this might not have been the ideal mediator for modern politicos to turn to.

Performing the "Best Sport": No one in recent memory had a more significant role in building a strong sports base for our area than the late James J. "Jimmy" Richardson.

Serving as head honcho of the Multnomah Athletic Club from 1928-1948, Richardson was the man most responsible for building that great institution into one of the leading clubs in the nation.

In addition, he gave strong support and encouragement to those associated with him. Jack Cody, trainer of the "Cody Kids," produced some of the finest swimmers in the country when he served as head coach.

A number of members of his team, such as Brenda Helser, Nancy Merki and Susan Zimmerman, distinguished themselves at the London Olympic Games in the summer of 1948.

On the national scene, Richardson was a strong voice in the Amateur Athletic Union, bringing major sports events to our city.

A Rose for You: One of the most engaging personalities of Portland in the young years of this century was a peripatetic ball of fire known to all as Tommy Luke.

Never without a rose in his buttonhole, and forever selling his native city to visitors and conventioneers, he probably did more than anyone to make the slogan "for you a rose in Portland grows" a local rallying cry.

On the business side, Flowers by Tommy Luke (established in 1907 and still in existence) provided the first corsage for many a prom date.

Building a Record: Portland was never known as one of the nation's major manufacturing regions, but one man changed that perception very quickly during the early days of World War II.

Edgar Kaiser, son of industrial giant Henry J. Kaiser, came to the Northwest to build more Liberty and Victory ships in his Portland and Vancouver facilities than any other yard in the nation. Not only did he establish records for the short amount of time it took for construction of these vessels, he is credited with training a superior labor force that allowed the metropolitan area to attract a number of other businesses.

Despite his wealth and national prominence, Kaiser endeared himself to his adopted city as one of the most generous and constructive citizens we have ever had.

Baker's Dozen: An individual who served as our daily eyes and ears had his finger on the pulse of our city like no one else. San Francisco had (and still has) Herb Caen, but we had a street-smart and gutsy columnist who wasn't afraid to call 'em as he saw 'em.

Doug Baker of *Oregon Journal* days will be remembered as one of Portland's most influential citizens of the twentieth century.

FRIDAY SURPRISE

Miss Arbuckle great story; her desk another column

A larger-than-life lady, who touched the lives of thousands of young Oregonians, passed away last week. Ruth Arbuckle, an English teacher and counselor at Lincoln High School in Portland for thirty-four years, was the embodiment of loyalty and support for the school she served and the students she inspired.

Possessed of an infectious sense of humor, a consistently inquisitive mind and a fabulous memory, she seemed to know everyone in town. Miss ("just call me Ruth") Arbuckle kept up to date with many of her former students. She knew who married whom, what they were doing, where they were living, and how many possible new Lincoln students there might be in the new families.

Stories abound about life in her classes. Most of her former students can relate amusing, and many times touching, stories of their memories of this one-of-a-kind mentor. There is one facet of her operation that no one forgets: her desk. We have all seen messy desk operators, but this lady's work station was a classic. However, as you would expect, she could find anything she wanted among those piles. Surely no one else could.

Other people's desks always have intrigued me, as I admit, unashamedly, that I am the consummate "clean desk" operator. It bothers the dickens out of me to have piles of stuff on my work station, and I have a personal pledge not to leave my office in the evening until every piece of paper is taken care of.

Much to the annoyance and amusement of some of my co-workers, I have tried to pass along my own work habits. It is a source of constant kidding that "you better get your desk cleaned up, Gerry will be around soon."

There are all sorts of disorganized desk operators. One of my friends in the real estate management business in Salem, Rob Ray, has a rather unusual style. An immaculate person and a highly successful businessman, his office is a disaster. Not only is his desk overflowing with papers, the floor around his work area is piled high with folders and other assorted material. Predictably, when asked how in the world he operates in this den of disarray, he claims he knows (just like Miss Arbuckle) where everything is resting.

But my favorite story about work station habits concerns a man who came to work in Washington, D.C., at a young age, full of ideas and energy, and with an incredibly able mind to go with it. It was obvious that he was going to go places, and he has.

His name is Tom Imeson. You may remember hearing about him, as he has taken his place in the top ranks of PacifiCorp, and before that as chief aide to former Governor Neil Goldschmidt. Imeson accurately has a reputation as one of the savviest political operators in our state.

You should have seen his desk as he started his public career. I'd talk to him about it daily. I'd turn the other way when I passed his area. It did no good. Finally, in desperation one day, while Imeson was out to lunch, I gathered up everything on his desk and locked it in an office storage area. When he returned to find everything gone, he was furious. He knew full well what had happened. He didn't speak to me for days.

Well, you can imagine my delight when, years later, as the fellow responsible for keeping the desk in the gov's office in working shape, Imeson called me to ask if I would speak at a seminar for his staff about efficient paper management. I'm sure it was a tough call for him; however, he had been converted to this mode of operation, and he wanted to share the reincarnation. It has been a source of many laughs since.

The desk as we have known it through the years is in for a lot of changes. Many already have taken place. The dictionary is no longer needed; we now have a miniscule computer program that gives all the data we need on spelling and definitions. Some even announce the information verbally.

A set of encyclopedias is a thing of the past. Another program that just came on the market is a self-contained storehouse of factual information on every subject imaginable. The data is easily retrievable by just inputting a name, a place, an event or what-have-you.

It is the telephone, however, that has become, in my opinion, more of an annoyance than a pleasure. I long for the days when you could dial one phone company and get all the service you needed. And wasn't it great when you could call someone and get a real live person on the other end instead of "after the tone, please leave..." How did we live before we were given a whole menu of recorded choices: "press one for Betsy, press two for..." One could even enjoy a quiet dinner without the interruption of one of those computerized sales pitches.

Thanks, Miss Arbuckle. You were a charming individualist. Is automation robbing us of this opportunity today?

FRIDAY SURPRISE

Got your bellhop caps on?
It's a quiz on historic hotels

*R*eady for a quick quiz on historic Oregon hotels? Few aspects of our state's colorful past touch more lives than some of the great rooming houses that were the focal points in many communities in the latter part of the nineteenth century and the early years of the twentieth century.

1. What hotel was the headquarters for movie workers during the filming of the classic Paramount film *Paint Your Wagon?*

2. Where was the hotel originally known as the Golf Hotel?

3. What former Oregon governor was the driving force behind plans for a large Oregon oceanside hotel?

4. What Oregon hotel landmark had the first TV west of the Rocky Mountains?

5. What Oregon coast lodging house featured a putting green on its front lawn in the early 1920s?

6. What city's major hotel was twice destroyed by fire in the 1920s?

7. Which Oregon city has a hotel that took every penny of an immigrant Finnish baker to build?

8. And finally, what hotel served as a resting place for six U.S. presidents, and which one was the best tipper?

If you can answer all of these correctly, you have done your homework for Oregon Hotel History 101.

1. The ten-story Hotel Baker (Baker City) opened in 1929, featured a top floor octagonal observation center, and was the home of the Hollywood movie crew.

2. Gearhart's Golf Hotel, so named because at that time the resort's golf course ran right up to the building, was built in 1921 by D.R. Schroeder. The place was renamed Ocean House in 1929, after the Lombard House next door was purchased by the owner and an addition was constructed between the two buildings. Mrs. Schroeder, a lady with an infectious motherly presence, was known to generations of beach lovers for her Sunday night dinners.

Clatsop County on the north Oregon coast was the scene of several memorable buildings and events relating to the state's early hotels.

3. (and 6.) Another area legend, the Gearhart Hotel, twice destroyed by fire in the second decade of this century, had close ties to my family. Former Governor Julius Meier (a great-uncle)

was the driving force to build a new hotel with the same name in 1920. Better at running a department store than a resort, the Meier & Frank ownership period was not a financial success. My father never forgave my brother and me for helping to put out a fire at the Gearhart Hotel in the late 1930s. We were so proud of "saving the grand old lady," but he wondered if a fire might have ended the fiscal problems.

4. A landmark known for years as the John Jacob Astor Hotel opened unofficially as the Astoria Hotel on New Year's Day 1924. Despite attractions like the first TV in a hotel west of the Rocky Mountains, and a succession of operators (including John Osburn, who also ran the Gearhart Hotel for a period), it had a series of financial upheavals.

5. The Grimes-Moore-Seasider Hotel in Seaside (1901-1983) was the site of the original boardwalk (later the prom), and also was the home of a magnificent putting green in the front yard.

Similar problems plagued a number of other communities. The Tioga Hotel in downtown Coos Bay, started in 1927, not finished until 1938, was finally occupied in 1942.

7. A Finnish immigrant baker, Jacob Hirvi, used every cent he had to build the Winema Hotel in Klamath Falls. As newer area motels sprung up, this popular gathering place turned a number of rooms into senior apartments.

(Portland has had its share of well-known hotels: the Heathman, the Mallory, Imperial, Benson and Multnomah all bring back fond memories for locals and visitors alike. But the old Portland Hotel was the real city charmer. I can remember the anguish that my father went through in the decision to tear down the old beauty (M&F owned the property in later years. It was necessary to do so because of the fire hazard.)

8. Of the six presidents who signed the Portland Hotel's guest register, it was said that Teddy Roosevelt was the best tipper. I imagine veteran headwaiter Iverson Burnett and longtime manager H. C. Bowers would be pleased that the site of once-famous courtyard concerts has given way to the more boisterous music of the nineties.

FRIDAY SURPRISE

Whom do folks admire most? Those who make life better

On Christmas Eve at a friend's home, while everyone else was occupied in opening and examining their gifts, one of those present seemed to be much more concerned about the sounds that were coming from a beeper attached to his belt.

Greg Keller is a firefighter and paramedic by profession, and although not on call at the moment, he found the goings-on at 9-1-1 headquarters much more significant than the goings-on under the holiday tree.

It is no wonder because he, and thousands more like him, are firefighters and paramedics, the two occupations that Americans most admire. They bring a sense of caring, security, sincerity to every aspect of their chosen work. Men and women in this field many times risk their own lives in attempting to save the lives of others; the reward must come from the satisfaction that they are, indeed, making a difference.

Following these two professions on the list of occupations that Americans admire the most are, in order: farmers, pharmacists, grade school teachers, mail carriers, Catholic priests, housekeepers, babysitters, college professors, airline pilots, rabbis, scientists, chef/cooks, flight attendants, dentists, engineers, accountants, Protestant ministers and medical doctors.

On the other end of the list, going from the bottom up: drug dealers, organized crime bosses, TV evangelists, prostitutes, street peddlers, local politicians, members of Congress, car salespeople, rock and roll stars, insurance salespersons, labor union leaders, Wall Street executives, lawyers, soap opera stars and investment brokers.

If there is any common thread about these admittedly unscientific rankings, it is that the first group is bringing us life-enhancing activities, while the latter group is perceived as destroying a decent and productive standard of living.

Some thoughts come to mind as we look forward with hope and concern to a year when we are going to need all the positive actions that can be mustered to enhance the quality of life in this country.

Where do we start? Well, one place seems to be pretty obvious. That is in prioritizing the expenditure of our tax money. We are still hearing that our national defense budget will be in the neighborhood of $300 billion this year. We are told that it will still be necessary to keep at least two full divisions in Europe until at least 1995. We are looking for new places to build military facilities in southeast Asia to take the place of those abandoned in the Philippines.

What in the world are they thinking about? Just who is the enemy today? Few question an adequate defense capability, but how much is adequate? Ask the farmer or the pharmacist or the grade school teacher what their priorities are.

The farmer might tell us that he needs an even (as well as a fertile) playing field in order to produce what we need to eat. He must be able to compete fairly in world markets without discriminatory subsidies and penalties. He must be able to harvest his crops at a cost that will wipe away the all-too-prevalent hunger in our midst. He must be able to entice his sons and daughters to enter a noble field that is slowly being deserted.

The pharmacist might tell us that we must do something about reducing the costs of proper medical care for the average citizen, before we go broke as individuals (and as a nation) trying to provide necessary facilities and care for our people. We need crash programs for cancer and AIDS and heart disorders and dozens of other problems and a Food and Drug Administration that is a facilitator rather than an obstacle. It is staggering to realize that the FDA approved only about twenty-five new drugs last year, which in itself was a 25 percent increase from the previous year.

The grade school teacher might tell us that he/she faces almost insurmountable tasks these days. The size of the class is increasing. The pay is not keeping up with other professions that take an equal amount of training. Drugs are being peddled in schoolyards. The teachers are expected to take the place of parents in child discipline, and then many times get blamed when they do. In the meantime, they see funds being expended for increased layers of administrators, for bricks and mortar, for extraneous activities that bear little relation to the three Rs.

It could well be that some of those on the bottom list would disappear with a reallocation of our resources and our priorities. The drug dealers, the organized crime bosses, some of the TV evangelists and the street peddlers would have fewer customers. Some local politicians and members of Congress might once again hold their heads high in a profession that should be at the top of the most admired.

Maybe what we really need is an expansion of the "9-1-1" philosophy beyond the caring individuals who now operate a service that does make a difference.

It's time to chew the fat over life as a food critic

*D*o you sometimes have visions that being a restaurant critic would be the greatest job? All that fun eating out in dozens of new and exciting places. Tasting all those marvelous (and rich) new dishes and trying the most exotic wines. Hold on, it's not all that it's cracked up to be.

Although I certainly do not regard myself as a gourmet, I do a lot of restaurant eating and reviewing in my travels and in my capacity as author of *Where to Find It, Buy It, Eat It in New York.* As a matter of fact, at last count I think I have eaten in nearly 1,500 restaurants in New York of every kind and description, pricey and inexpensive.

The most influential person in the eating-out scene in this country is Bryan Miller, the restaurant critic for the *New York Times.* When Miller comments, restaurateurs and diners listen. And well they better, for if the review is a good one, their establishment could be launched as a winner. Conversely, if the write-up is not so hot, it will not necessarily destroy a restaurant, but it sure will set it back, sometimes irretrievably.

Take the case of the operations run by Harry Cipriani in New York, the Harry of Harry's Bar fame in Italy. A well-patronized society spot where people went to see and be seen, rather than eat great food, was prospering in the Sherry Netherlands Hotel in Manhattan under the name of Harry Cipriani.

Miller had given this place a less than glowing tribute (as I had in my volume). Cipriani was not pleased, but the unfavorable words did not seem to affect the attraction for his well-heeled patrons.

Because of the success of this spot, Cipriani opened another Manhattan operation called "Bellini," catering to much the same clientele. Evidently the Sherry Netherland folks did not look too favorably on this branch operation, and on a quiet Monday afternoon several years ago they closed the restaurant under Cipriani's ownership, and by dinner time the same place opened up with a new name, new menu and new personnel. (The restaurant has since reopened with the original name.)

The next challenge as far as Miller was concerned was to review the new Bellini's. Cipriani did not want this to happen; when Miller and friends arrived for a meal, he would not seat them. Being a true newsman, Miller was not to be out-smarted. He grew a beard.

Fortunately, he was not recognized in his new look. He went back several times, as is his normal practice. The resulting review was devastating, to say the least. Cipriani was not the least amused. This time he took out a large ad in Miller's paper to say some uncomplimentary things about the critic. This was prime grist for the foodie gossipers in New York for weeks; of course, the public loved it.

I have gotten to know Miller through our mutual interests in evaluating restaurants, and I find that doing a critique for the *New York Times* and for a New York guide book or just for a hobby are not all that different. The routine is much the same. You have your choice of literally hundreds of places to go, but you choose the ones that you have heard the most about, are new or are "in" at the moment. You make reservations in someone else's name, you arrive in clothes to fit the occasion, and you come with a number of guests in the party. Each orders a different starter, entree and dessert. Notes are scribbled during the process, the bill is paid in cash, and you take along a copy of the restaurant menu for reference.

Before you decide that this is a great hobby or a wonderful way to make a living, be forewarned. Eating out every night, after awhile, is a pain in the neck. The bills can be high, and who is going to bankroll the operation?

But the worst is what it does to your health. Marian Burros, Miller's predecessor, gave it up after she saw what it had done to the "weighty" lady who preceded her, the famous critic Mimi Sheraton.

My problem is a little bit different. I don't do it so often that the calories have become a problem, and I walk around Manhattan a great deal in between meals. My difficulty is right here at home, with my friends. They have this mistaken image that I'm rating every lunch or dinner I have with them, and it isn't true. And besides, they always seem to include a dense chocolate dessert, knowing that I am a confirmed chocoholic.

This brings me around to my Portland restaurant choice of the week. The finest French cuisine in town is at the tiny La Mirabelle, 1126 S.W. 18th Avenue, open only for dinner Wednesday through Saturday. Owner and chef Robert Kincaid presents a superb table; the chocolate box dessert would be a memorable feast for Miller or anyone else.

FRIDAY SURPRISE

Studies of bias in schools lead to look at leaders

*D*o girls take second place in educational opportunities in our schools? Do boys get a better start in preschool and continue to be shown favoritism through their high school education?

A recent study commissioned by the American Association of University Women came to this conclusion, and the results have prompted a closer look at what has been going on in our schools.

On Wednesday, some of the leading educators of our state and others interested in this problem took part in a forum in Salem where the issues of gender stereotyping were discussed; many suggestions were put forth to try and remedy the apparent bias that has been unfairly shown to young women. It was my job to serve as moderator of this event, which turned out to be a very educational experience in itself.

It is significant to note that the AAUW study found that it was not only in the schools that bias was shown. In the marketplace and even in the home more attention has been paid to the young men of the family.

Despite this disturbing trend, it is worthwhile to take a look around our state and see the opportunities that exist for women and how a number of them, special achievers in one way or another, are making their mark in so many areas of Oregon life outside of politics.

These women have many times bat-tled the odds against them and have come out on top. They should serve as role models for the youngsters of today.

A number of Oregon women have been prominent in family businesses, carrying on traditions of their fathers or working with their husbands in a joint effort. Some of the more dynamic businesswomen include Helen Jo Copeland (Copeland Lumber), who runs a highly competitive business with a special flair and competence. Irene Ellicott (Easy Street fashions) takes second place to no one when it comes to energy and merchandising talent. She is an author, besides. Joan Austin (A-DEC dental equipment) of Newberg is another influential woman who has played a major role in the success of the business she and her husband run. Linda Shelk (Ochoco Lumber) of Prineville is one of Central Oregon's most accomplished leaders.

Sometimes highly successful parents leave their offspring in the shadows, with both sons and daughters feeling that they can never quite equal the mark made by their elders. When we consider that some of Oregon's leading entrepreneurs have daughters who are showing that they have what it takes, it should give the current generation renewed hope. Cynthia Jackson Ford of Southern Oregon and Portland has carved out her own niche in educational administration at Southern Oregon State

College, besides serving on the Oregon Transportation Commission which her father (Glenn Jackson) once headed. Patsy Smullin of Medford is one of the hardest working people in the state's television industry and has taken the place of her father, William Smullin, in civic and business affairs. She has just been elected president of the Oregon Association of Broadcasters.

Dynamos Marilyn Eichinger (OMSI) and Sherry Sheng (Washington Park Zoo) are living proof that running major community institutions can be a woman's field. In Newport, Phyllis Bell, who comes from a merchandising background, has been the driving force behind the soon-to-be-opened Oregon Coast Aquarium.

A number of prominent women have raised families as well as climbing the ladder of responsibility in their chosen profession. Barbara Mahoney of Salem has been the point person in Willamette University's very detailed (and successful) 150th anniversary celebration and fund-raising. Super-executive Jill Thorne of Pendleton, who received special training in the corridors of the statehouse under Governor Neil Goldschmidt, is now leading the wagoneers who are preparing the path for our 1993 Oregon Trail sesquicentennial celebration. Brenda Penner of Astoria, besides being deeply involved raising two small children, finds time to use her nursing background in work for the Clatsop County home health services and the Red Cross.

Of course, there are countless others. Arlene Schnitzer (the arts), Gertrude Boyle (Columbia Sportswear), Harriet Drake (exterior lighting), Elizabeth Crownhart-Vaughan (Russian scholar) Laurie Van Zante (Tu Tu Tun lodge operator), university presidents Judith Ramaley (PSU) and Nancy Wilgenbusch (Marylhurst), Ethel Simon-McWilliams (health interests), Judi Hofer (M&F), Marsha Congdon (US West) and Carolyn Chambers (television) are a few special achievers who come to mind.

When a woman is picked out of the crowd who most exemplifies achievement in family, community and nation, I nominate Mabel Livingstone Bishop of Portland. Here is an environmentalist (you can find her out on the river fishing in the toughest weather) and involved mother and grandmother, one who even finds time to serve as head regent for the organization that takes care of George Washington's Mount Vernon home.

FRIDAY SURPRISE

Speaking of farms, phones, more phones, and stress

*W*ho Keeps Them Down on the Farm? Indiana's Senator Richard Lugar recently pointed out that in 1932, the Department of Agriculture had 32,000 individuals on its payroll to serve a nation in which one of every four Americans lived on a farm.

Today, the same department employs about 110,000 people, while fewer than 2 percent of our citizens are farm residents. The ratio: in 1932, 1 employee for every 1,000 farm residents; today, 1 for every 45.

Can't say our farm friends don't have enough bureaucrats to call.

Who's Minding the Store? It seems inconceivable that some of America's top execs who serve on the United Way of America board sat silently by with their hands folded and let their president, William Aramony, get away with a $463,000 yearly salary plus a whole host of perks. Trying to explain to local United Way givers (many of whom are on payroll deduction plans) why the head honcho of a charitable outfit found it necessary to take the Concorde to Europe might be just a bit difficult come campaign time.

A Corta Distancia? (Walking distance?) One of the newest wrinkles in the never-ending telephone service battle is a language line service interpreter, provided by AT&T, that is especially handy for travelers. A skilled Spanish, Japanese, French, or German linguist will relay your messages or questions to the proper parties until your communication needs are completed.

Who Has the Key to the Restroom? An international advertising agency office in Hong Kong has the normal two washrooms. However, their use is not quite so normal. Instead of posting "men" and "women" signs on the door, this outfit decrees that one of the units is for the use of senior execs, and the other for "lesser employees." Quite democratic one would think, but that is really not the case. There is only one senior exec, the managing director himself.

Who Said Small Luxuries Have to be Expensive? Try croissants (instead of toast), cloth napkins (instead of the paper variety), gourmet coffee (instead of the regular brands), a new wild tie (instead of a new suit), a classy Oregon Trail mug (instead of a paper cup), a real fountain pen (instead of the disposable jobs), a Sunday picnic hike through the Silver Falls State Park waterfall trails (near Stayton).

Who Would Have a Leg-up on the Next Election? Some candidate who would spell things out in the simplest of terms: (1) do something about reducing the national debt, now amounting to over

$51,000 for every American family, and (2) do something to make the tax code as simple as humanly possible, like the seemingly not-complex-enough idea of having a flat X percent tax for everyone, no deductions, period.

Who's Wanted on the Phone? Speaking of new phone wrinkles, in some parts of the country you can now have your phone programmed with three different ring patterns. You are given three numbers to give out to frequent callers, and happily the kids can have their own calling signal handled electronically on just one single line into your home. You could even give a distinctive number to the boss, and be able to answer him/her each time with a special sunny smile in your voice.

Where am I? To complete the array of interesting new phone items for today, Phone Home (available in some discount and variety stores for $19.95) is an automatic dialing device that allows lost children or elderly or disabled people to call their homes even if they don't know their telephone number. A "home" button is pressed, activating a system whereby up to sixteen digits can be dialed.

Do You Have Desk Stress? Someone with not too much to do figured that by the year 2000, U.S. businesses will file 120 billion pieces of paper a year. The things that don't get filed (returned phone messages, dog-eared business cards, last month's newsletters) are what give the average deskworker daily Excedrin headaches. A management outfit suggests a four-D solution: do it (Nike take note), date it, delegate it, discard it. And now there is even a Clean-off-your-desk day.

Do Your Kids Have Hunger Pangs? Twenty-three years ago, Guss Dussin (whose family has been in the restaurant business in Portland for over seventy years) opened his first Old Spaghetti Factory in Portland. It is still going strong here, and in twenty-nine other locations in the states and overseas, serving some of the tastiest food available for both kids and mom and pop. What is probably Portland's best food bargain is presented in a nostalgic atmosphere at 0715 S.W. Bancroft Street (John's Landing).

FRIDAY SURPRISE

In shadows of headlines lurk real legislative issues

*T*he taxi drivers and souvenir peddlers and hotel bellmen all have smiles on their faces these days in the nation's capital. Visitors are arriving in droves, and more are expected as spring break for the schools is in the offing, and the cherry blossoms are looking as if they might to come to life a bit earlier than usual.

While everyone is delighted to see the families and play host to the children, who find the Air and Space Museum much more interesting than the National Archives, it is really the horde of association and group representatives, lobbyists and activists for one cause or another who put the sizzle into the local economy.

Why are they crowding the corridors of power in such big numbers these days? Simple. Money. There is no shortage of worthwhile (and perhaps some not so vital) needs, and members of Congress are almost "on tilt" as their ears are being bent to hear why one particular cause just has to be funded over another. It is not easy for the elected representatives to say "no" to their constituents, so the usual scenario these days includes a great deal of listening and a lot less promising.

It used to be that visiting groups would host lavish receptions at local hotels and restaurants to put their representatives and senators in a good mood, but now the entertaining is on a much reduced scale. Cheese and crackers have replaced oysters on the half shell.

In addition, those who were paying the bills finally woke up to the reality that the guests they wanted (elected officials) were skipping these predictable affairs, and their invitations were being passed to office interns who were delighted to have a free meal to ease their own budget crunch.

One has to remember that Capitol Hill is an island unto itself. What is big news over the coffee cups in the enclave's cafeterias is not necessarily what is bothering the folks on Main Street, USA. For years, different rules and activities have governed the inhabitants of these august buildings. The members of the establishment pretty well did things the way they wanted, and no one seemed to pay much attention.

Thus, you had the unique banking operation in the House, special rates for stays in some of the national parks, a tight rein on new members by House and Senate leadership, absolute power by committee chairmen. All of this has changed drastically in the past few years. Perks are being questioned. House Speaker Tom Foley and Senate Majority Leader George Mitchell have a much more unruly constituency.

Away from the glare of the big headlines about bad checks and presidential name-calling, happily there still are some who are thinking about…and working on…the more vital issues of our time.

• Like an understanding in the Middle East. Behind all the posturing that we read about, Secretary of State James Baker and his crew continue to struggle to keep some kind of conversation going. There are high-powered and low-visibility sessions being held on a continual basis. The recent visit of King Hussein of Jordan to the White House received much publicity; the King of Saudi Arabia was in this country a short time ago, and if there was any coverage of the trip, I surely missed it.

• Like the best possible educational opportunities for our youngsters. Our classes are too big; our teachers are being asked to assume responsibilities that belong in the home. If homework time and classroom time are considered equal (and outside reading ignored), 12 years of Japanese education are equivalent, in terms of time spent, to 22.3 years of U.S. education. If there ever was a need for a Mr. (or Mrs. or Ms.) Education, it's right now.

• Like our fiscal mess. It is estimated that the gross federal debt for fiscal 1992 will be a little more than $4 trillion. For fiscal 1991, it was $3.5 trillion; in 1976 it was $629 billion. Remember, too, that $313 billion of receipts and $249 billion of outlays are considered "off-budget." It does not take an economics professor to point out the dangers. The related interest payments undercut savings and take away funds which could and should be used more productively beefing up our infrastructure, providing new manufacturing facilities and equipment and providing much needed funds for research and development.

• Like adequate health care for all. A large number of people in the United States (91 percent) believe we are in a health-care crisis, and most of them say we need some kind of reform. Long-term nursing care and the costs of everyday medicine are high on the list of concerns. A need for real leadership on the national level is apparent.

The question I hear asked the most is, "What can I do?" Probably not much that is going to change things overnight. but we all can take out our stationery and pour out our feelings to those who are in charge. In an election year, their eyesight is much better.

FRIDAY SURPRISE

There's really no show biz like store biz, even on Broadway

Sometimes what goes on behind the scenes is far more fascinating than what appears in front. I was reminded of this the other evening sitting in the audience of the new Broadway hit *Crazy for You.*

The show is a redo of the famous vehicle of years ago, *Girl Crazy.* Some of the same great Gershwin tunes are included, along with others that had been forgotten over several decades. The musical comedy is colorful and entertaining. There are no outstanding stars in the cast; the choreography is probably the show's high point.

But it was the technical side of the production that fascinated me. I was sitting where I could watch some of the activities backstage: the instant movement of the various settings was a tribute to modern electronics; the dance scene where the chorus girls were outlined in the shape of fiddles was a miracle of superb lighting.

All of this reminded me of some of my behind-the-scenes experiences at Meier & Frank. Merchandising is very much like the theater; the attraction of audiences (and buyers) is similar. You must capture their attention, provide a good product, then make the setting and ambiance as exciting and inviting as possible.

One of the most popular events years ago was "Oregon Products Week," when local producers and man-ufacturers were invited to display their wares in high-traffic locations in the downtown Portland store. The idea was to familiarize the public with the quality and variety of things made right here at home. It was a forerunner to the current rage for encouraging the purchase of American-made goods.

One of my first assignments at the family store was planning and executing this yearly event. With the help of our display manager, Bill Palmer, a genius at getting apparently impossible things done, we did some highly unusual things in the store windows that attracted such crowds that they spilled off the sidewalks into the streets around the store.

The Hamley people from Pendleton had some of their expert leather craftsmen hand-tooling saddles and belts. From Langlois in southwest Oregon we had cheesemakers showing the public how this delectable commodity was made.

The space, heat, lighting and ventilation requirements, such as handling potent smells from live penguins and cheese, made unusual arrangements necessary.

The "purple" cow promoting dairy products sweated so much that the harmless dye on its hide began to run off, and the store's switchboard was besieged by worried callers. Some smaller animals escaped from their strange window habitats and had flash-light-carrying display workers searching the store aisles after closing for the adventurous little critters.

A nest brought in with a tree to be used for display purposes suddenly produced new life. The men's underwear department salespeople had a new musical background provided by young chicks, while their mother was frantically flying around the main floor (looking for bargains?).

Rube Adams, the store's guiding merchandising genius, was a strong supporter of lavish shows to promote top names in fashion. Twice a year the 10th-floor auditorium was used for a week to present not just clothes but real entertainment to thousands of Oregonians. There was singing and dancing and blacklight scenes, simulated rain and all the rest of the gimmicks. But it was an ice-skating scene that taxed the store crew to the ultimate. Keeping the ice from melting in a room occupied by several thousand warm bodies took the ingenuity of all of Palmer's talented helpers.

Then there was the time that some promoter thought it would be a great publicity stunt to have Roy Rogers bring his horse into the store and ride him into my father's carpeted office on the 12th floor. Fortunately for all concerned, the steed had perfect manners in the store's elevators and in the executive suite. Unbeknown to my startled father, provisions had been made in case the opposite had been true.

In Salem, there were elaborate plans for a community dinner in the store's Oregon Room the night before opening to show off the new dining area. The morning of the event the supplier of the table tops informed us that there had been production problems and the pieces wouldn't arrive for another ten days. What to do when 160 people are coming to dinner? Plywood substitutes were fashioned at the last minute; no one knew what was really under those white linen tablecloths. To add to the confusion, a grease fire broke out in the kitchen one hour before the guests were to arrive.

Ah yes, there is no business like show business.

FRIDAY SURPRISE

'Detectives' sift through treasure trove in archives

*A*ll of the sound and fury over the new Oregon State Archives building in Salem is beginning to subside a bit, and the passing of a local school bond measure for new facilities has given hope that a temporary classroom across the street from the marble edifice will soon be a thing of the past. The adjacency of the two structures, with such a stark contrast in the amenities offered, gave rise to strong feelings about expenditure priorities.

If nothing else, the level of interest in archives has certainly been raised; I found myself taking a closer look at the massive National Archives structure on Pennsylvania Avenue, in the nation's capital, every time I passed by. So last week I called my former associate, Jim Hemphill, who is now deputy assistant to the archivist of the United States, and asked if I could come over and see what really goes on behind the scenes of such an imposing facade.

The answer is plenty. There are four District of Columbia holding facilities, six other district offices, and twelve regional archives scattered around the country. (Seattle is the closest one to us.) A huge, new 6.8-acre building (dubbed Archives II) is being built in College Park, Maryland, with a capacity of 2 million cubic feet of storage area.

To put this all into perspective, the present holdings include more than 4 million paper documents, 5.3 million still photos, 286,000 motion pictures and videos, 1.8 million maps and charts and 7 million aerial photographs. It is not just the size of the inventory that is mind-boggling, it is the fact that the material has to be organized so that scholars and researchers can find just what they want in this enormous treasure trove.

Most of the researchers are ordinary citizens, but what they are looking for is not so ordinary. Treasure hunters are looking for the coordinates of sunken ships. Legal beagles are studying Indian water rights. Medical types are working on epidemiological studies about the health of Civil War soldiers. Although most of the storage area is filled with papers and pictures, someone is studying a half-eaten hamburger that is in the vaults to determine if it was filled with arsenic, and could have contributed to the demise of the original diner.

Controversy is nothing new to the 3,000 employees who seem to know exactly where everything is located. The recent movie about John F. Kennedy has prompted renewed activity related to the Warren Commission reports, which are all housed here. There were even some reports that the former president's brain was a part of the archives holdings; it is not.

But the Constitution of the United States is there, so is the original copy of the Bill of Rights, practically every foreign treaty, Hitler's diaries, Eva Braun's pictures, Nixon's resignation letter, the Watergate tapes and even the original manuscript of the Oregon Constitution.

One of the researchers retrieved this handwritten masterpiece for me to see. The document was formulated at a convention in Salem, and signed by M.P. Deady, President, September 18, 1857 (the same year great-grandfather started his Portland store).

To complement the excitement of actually seeing this historic piece, the same gentlemen brought out a report of a Lt. Neil M. Howison, U.S. Navy, who, in 1846, "examined the coast, harbors, rivers, soil, production, climate and population" of the Territory of Oregon.

His handwritten diary stated that the "whole population of Oregon, exclusive of thoroughbred Indians, whom I have always understood to omit, may be set down at nine thousand souls, of whom two thousand are not natives of the United States or descendants of American Indians. The people of Oregon had lived without law or politics until the early part of 1845; and it is strong evidence of their good sense and good disposition that it had not previously been found necessary to establish some restraints of law in a community of several thousand people."

The archives can, and do, correct many historical inaccuracies. In a book about her time as Franklin Roosevelt's secretary, Grace Tully wrote about her boss' December, 1941, message to Congress after the Pearl Harbor attack. She indicated that FDR had dictated the famous "date which will live in infamy" line. He did not. An archivist showed me the original manuscript which read "will live in world history." FDR, in his own writing, had crossed out the last two words and had inserted "infamy."

One wonders what significant documents historians will review from the 1992 national election cycle. So far I would say the "pickens" will be pretty slim.

FRIDAY SURPRISE

Dull knives never carve out that well-honed retail niche

*E*ver hear of a store called Condomania? Probably not, but chances are you will in the future. Yes, it sells just what the name implies, and it is doing a tremendous business in the East. The owner has plans to market his concept in major cities nationwide.

In Los Angeles, the Vagabond Vintage Luggage Company is doing a booming trade in a different field: luggage. No, not in the regular type that we see in the stores, but in quality used luggage. Pieces like old trunks and rounded-corner, real leather, double-handled Hartmann cases that haven't been a part of their regular line for several decades. (I can personally vouch for the latter model; I purchased two of them thirty-five years ago, and they are still in use after several dozen trips around the globe and relentless airline abuse during literally hundreds of cross-continental journeys.)

A small shop called Earth Scents in the Greenwich Village area of Manhattan has hit upon another bonanza: copying popular fragrances, such as perfumes, colognes, and the like. These folk stock most all of the ingredients necessary to duplicate the favorites that customers (1) can no longer find at the counters, or (2) do not want to pay the inflated prices asked by top-name resources.

These three different businesses are just a sampling of what is called "niche marketing," a concept that has caught fire recently, providing almost unlimited opportunity for those who have a certain spirit of adventure, combined with a unique or unusual idea.

Of course, niche marketing is really not anything new. The annals of successful entrepreneurs are filled with stories of past marketing giants who have had the vision and intestinal fortitude to do something just a little bit differently than the rest of the crowd. In a number of cases, the results were sensational.

Stanley Marcus took a sleepy specialty store in Dallas, Texas, from just another place to buy clothes to an operation whose name symbolized style and quality of the highest order. Neiman-Marcus, under his direction, became the ultimate for the up-scale customer. The main store itself was really nothing special to behold, but the superior training of the staff and the taste level of the merchandise made a niche for those who liked to throw their coats over the back of the chair with the label showing.

Marvin Traub made a special niche for Bloomingdale's in a different manner. Faced with immense competition in the world's toughest market (Manhattan), Traub practiced show-biz in its highest form to pack his store with customers who came to look, but stayed to buy. He did it with fabulous model rooms and glitzy cosmetic demonstrations and by sending his buyers all over the world to purchase goods for a China, an Italy, or even an Oregon products promotion.

But the late Sam Walton was the star of the lot. He, more than anyone else, saw that many department stores were getting old and tired and couldn't continue the niche of being everything to everybody as they had for decades. "Mr. Sam" capitalized on what most everyone knew, but didn't always put to work: deep stocks, local managers who could make decisions, a close relationship with employees and suppliers, and, most important, the customer is always right, even when he (or she) is wrong. And what a niche he carved for himself: more than 2,000 Wal-Mart stores with sales estimated at more than $55 billion this year.

Some of the giants of the retailing world had taken an overdose of sleeping pills or were lying on the shrink's couch trying to decide just what they were supposed to be. Sears and Montgomery Ward exemplified what happens when management does not understand what niche made them successful in the first place. Locally, remember when J. K. Gill was the city's leading book and office products store?

Wal-Mart is finding a lot of company in the special niche that has made it so successful. In Oregon, we are seeing a healthy birth rate in operations like ShopKo, Costco, HomeBase and PACE. They join Kmart and Silo and Target and a number of others in offering, in various ways, wide selections, larger size packages, dealing mainly in cash rather than credit cards, and sometimes membership operations. All have one major selling tool: lower prices. The discount niche is in danger of being over-crowded; it doesn't take a merchandising genius to forecast that not all

of them are going to survive.

The innovators of the nineties are asking: what are consumer priorities? How do I take advantage of new demographics (like two-job families)? What are the really satisfying aspects of current lifestyles? Toss these around a bit, and some exciting new niches may be a lot closer than we think.

FRIDAY SURPRISE

In the presence of a king? Awe, shucks, it was great

*M*eeting with a head of state, be it a king or a president, is an awesome and memorable experience, no matter what the title, the country or the setting.

I felt that I was standing in the presence of history when I walked into the memorabilia-filled office of President Habib Bourguiba of Tunisia several years ago. It was obvious that the gentleman was aging (he was deposed shortly thereafter). It was also apparent that he was a highly emotional individual.

He reminisced about his time with the American officials in Tunis just after World War II and about his association with Pierre Mendes-France, the ex-premier of France who had died shortly before our meeting. He walked among his trophies, pausing with obvious pride to explain the significance of his momentos.

He surely had not lost his political touch entirely. After the history lesson, he made a plea for assistance against Libya, hoping for rapid delivery of military equipment that had been purchased. He wanted to live long enough to personally review a parade in which these weapons of war would be displayed.

It appeared he did not want us (there were several American officials present) to leave his quarters. As various additional incidents were recalled,

he would first cry, then lash out at those whom he felt had betrayed him and his country. The lasting memory: a man whose time had come and gone but who was unwilling to face reality.

A visit with King Faisal of Saudi Arabia was a very different experience. In this case, I was alone. The schedule for the audience was not formalized until the day of the meeting; it took place in his palace in Riyadh. My mission at the time was to talk with Faisal about Middle-Eastern concerns; in preparation, I spent hours trying to cram into my head as many facts and figures as I could possibly digest.

I needn't have bothered. I didn't get a word in edgewise.

Upon arriving in the waiting room, I was astounded to see hundreds of Saudis wandering around the premises. In questioning this, I was told that there were periods set aside when the king would meet with any of his subjects who might have a problem, thereby keeping in touch with the mood of his people. Although he certainly did not have to think about elections, he carried on as if he were running hard.

Finally the appointed moment came, and I found myself in an enormous throne room, the size of a football field, or so it seemed. At one end, seated upon a throne chair befitting a head of state, was the king. Next to him was a small and much less pretentious chair, obviously for his visitor. I could feel large drops of nervous perspiration…it didn't help that the outdoor temperature was about 110, with a humidity to match.

Faisal was an impressive figure, with a serious, hawkish stare that never changed. Never a smile. He told me (through an interpreter) in no uncertain words how he felt about the official position of our country with regard to Middle-Eastern affairs (remember this was pre-Gulf War). His piercing eyes never left me; I was so taken by the strength of this man's personality that I had a difficult time at the end trying to recall what he had said.

How different was my visit with another leader of that area, King Hussein of Jordan. This experience took place in the library of his residence in the outskirts of Amman, the capital. Hussein was easy to meet and converse with, a comfortable person to be around.

It was apparent that he was in close touch with the mood not only in his troubled country, but in our nation as well. He was up-to-date on the political tides in Washington, D.C., as reported by our newspapers and magazines, which he studied daily. He had a firm grasp on the personalities that counted in our Congress and in the current administration.

Some of our own politicians could learn from this astute gentleman. He (and his staff) practice some of the subtle tricks of the trade. Every year since that meeting, I have received a holiday card from him, many showing off his attractive family.

During those several hours, the king, who was casually dressed in a sweater and slacks, never once raised his voice, never once uttered a harsh word. His was the demeanor and presence of a

statesman (although he is very short in stature), schooled throughout his life in the political and military turmoil of the Middle East. He has often been described as a true survivor. He surely is just that when one thinks of the problems of personal safety and position that he has faced nearly every day of his life.

Here were three important figures. Three who faced (one still does) vastly different problems in their countries. Each had that unmistakable charisma that sets a leader apart from his peers. They did not need titles to be special.

FRIDAY SURPRISE

Lose people's trust, lose the whole ballgame

*T*he highest national unemployment figures in eight years. The class of '92 having unprecedented trouble putting that hard-earned diploma to work. One major business after another declaring bankruptcy. The debt clock continuing to click, with the average family in the United States shouldering nearly $53,000 worth of an IOU approaching $4 trillion...yes, trillion dollars.

I submit there is no great secret why we are in trouble. It's not the fault of average U.S. consumers, who would like to buy more goods and services if they could save enough to keep the household bank account in healthy order. It's also not the fault of average U.S. workers, most of whom want to put in a good day's work and be fairly compensated for it.

Could it be that the fault lies in management? Managers who have gotten fat, lazy, more concerned with their own creature comforts than in their primary job: steering the wheels of U.S. industry in the soundest possible manner so that as many folks as possible can make a respectable living for themselves and those they support.

We are inundated these days with stories about the problems of the airline industry. Falling profits. Weaker outfits talking merger or Chapter 11. Thousands of employees being laid off, both in aircraft manufacturing and in the service end of the business. Hundreds and hundreds of mid-management jobs being eliminated. For heaven's sake, what were all those managers doing? Maybe, like their bosses, they were worrying about their own golden parachutes (or corner offices) rather than being concerned about the goose that was laying the golden eggs who made their jobs possible: the customer.

For twenty-four hours last week the newscasts were warning all who would listen that some major weather disturbances, including the possibility of tornado-force winds, would sweep through the mid-section of the nation, obviously causing some operational problems for the airlines. I was one who listened to the news, was foolish enough to travel through Chicago anyway, and fell victim (along with tens of thousands of others) to a superb example of lack of planning and supervision.

I am a strong supporter of United Airlines. In my opinion, United (and most other carriers) have able personnel manning their day-to-day operations... especially in Portland. But at O'Hare Airport in Chicago there was mass confusion of the highest order. Of course, nothing can be done about the wily ways of the weather witches. But something could and should have been done to prepare for this emergency.

Instead, on one of the busiest holidays of the year, with planes scattered and delayed over most of the eastern part of the nation, the relatively new, multi-million dollar United terminal in Chicago was a scene of bewildered passengers trying to cope. There was an almost complete absence of management personnel on the job trying to help those like the exhausted grandmother who had waited eight hours trying to find a plane to visit her family in Oregon.

Could it be that Stephen Wolf (United's CEO) and his management team were too busy figuring out the extent of their perks to worry about action on the firing line?

It doesn't have to be that way. It is no mystery why the Heathman Hotel in Portland is successful...have you ever been there when manager Mary Arnstad wasn't on the job? Ditto with Braley and Graham in the ultra-competitive car business. Buzz Braley, father Warren Braley and grandfather George Braley were (and are) always on the selling floor taking care of customers.

It's not just in business that the spectacle of weak leadership is obvious. The same goes for government, where we are witness every day to the appalling reality that while almost every member of Congress knows exactly what must be done to bring back fiscal sanity to our nation, they continue to be more interested in getting themselves re-elected (with the help of a staff of 37,000) than in redoing a spending-and-taxation system that is woefully unsuited to the economic health of the United States in the nineties.

Some of the military brass don't escape this comfortable cocoon of self-indulgence that has permeated our leadership ranks. The recent shocking examples of sexual harassment in the

U.S. Navy seem unlikely to have gone unnoticed for years by on-the-job commanders. Could it be that some of them were more concerned about not rocking their ships for fear of what might happen to their own promotional opportunities?

The CEO of Sears, an outfit caught in some pricing hanky-panky in their automobile service divisions, says, "Just trust us!" Trust in management is earned the hard way...mainly by ensuring that the public's welfare is priority No. 1.

FRIDAY SURPRISE

Eat, drink in old Portland? Speak easy, it's nostalgia

*A*fter a very political week, isn't it time for another subject? How about nostalgia? It's big everywhere in cars, in clothes, in food, in furnishings, in music. Sometimes the colors in the memories are turned up a shade or two, but it's still fun to look back a bit.

What was Portland like in the good old days? The days probably weren't always all that good, but our fair city has been a pretty great place to live, work and play for decades.

Where did people eat? Mainly at home in those days, as eating out was not always as popular as it is today. Before it was legal to serve alcoholic drinks, there was not a very wide choice of places. The Bohemian Restaurant was a winner. Portlanders flocked to Henry Thiele's to get huge German pancakes and to Yaw's Top Notch for the best hamburgers around. And when drive-ins became popular, the Speck and the Tik Tok were mobbed with oldsters and youngsters alike.

Late in the afternoon the biggest treat was waiting for the Good Humor wagon, complete with clanging bell. Price for an ice cream bar? A nickel. (Aren't today's gourmet bars two bucks?) Sometimes there was even a "good for a free bar" offer on the stick.

Milkshakes at Jolly Joan. Fresh turkey sandwiches at Huber's (they are still good). Popcorn from Paul's Wagon in the South Park Blocks by the old Lincoln High School. Gourmet food items at Sealy-Dresser, where Jack Luihn presided over the finest food specialty shop in town.

You weren't really "in" if your shoes didn't come from Armishaw's. Charles F. Berg was the place to buy hosiery ("Who's your hosier?"). Harold Kelley's appliance store in the Hollywood district was just about as busy as the boss, who was involved in nearly every worthwhile activity in town. M. & H.H. (to wags "Ma and her Herb") Sichel was one of the area's classy men's stores.

The tea room at Lipman's was a popular spot for lunch, and Roberts Brothers was the place to find a tremendous selection of piece goods. School supplies had to come from J.K. Gill, and what real Portlander didn't carry a Shed-Rain umbrella.

I guess it is only natural that I would remember some of the highlights of the "Friday Surprise" store (M&F). Joe, the doorman on Sixth Street, was a local institution. He would not only park your car, but would remember the kind of car and your name. Audrey Joy tied fancy flies for the fishermen in the sixth-floor sporting goods department. In the downstairs store, Isaac Hasson dispensed local fresh vegetables. Grace Lytle, the refined and informed lady who sat in the information booth under the clock, seemed to know everything not only about the store, but about the city as well.

And who were some of the unforgettable characters in town? Silver-tongued Edgar Smith gave great speeches. Frank Branch Riley was the area's unofficial ambassador. (There were always financial troubles paying for his trips. "Do you expect an ambassador to stay in the local YMCA?") Frank Sardam, an insurance salesman, was the most popular guy during the holiday season: he played Santa Claus on a local radio station (KWJJ).

Edris Morrison was the "everywhere" photog; Dr. Joseph Bilderback brought hundreds of young Portlanders into the world; and Dr. Ruth Barnett, a lady whose name was not mentioned in some circles, was the proprietor of the town's best-known abortion clinic.

For entertainment, dancing to the tunes of the big bands at Jantzen Beach was a special event. George Amato brought headliners to his supper club, stars such as Sophie Tucker and composer Harry Carroll and singer-wife Polly Baker. The Clover Club was another popular retreat, where members often ditched their refreshments under the table.

The Rose City got its news from a variety of papers, including the *Oregonian*, the *Oregon Journal* and the *News-Telegram*. Ep Hoyt at the big "O" and Phil Jackson at the "OJ" were prominent wheeler-dealers in town. Billy Stepp was a popular sportswriter of the time, and Gwladys Bowen (who just recently passed away) chronicled the social life of the city.

Visitors to town would arrive on the classy "City of Portland" streamliner. Swan Island was Portland's airport, and one of the treats of a visit there was dining in the excellent coffee shop on the grounds. The Portland Hotel was the architectural jewel of the city, but the Benson and Multnomah were equally popular.

What will a columnist on July 17, 2042, say about out city? Who, besides Mayor Bud Clark, will be listed as some of the city's real characters of our time?

Heed fresh tip for success, then milk it for all it's worth

A winning combination of family, fun, and great milk has made Alpenrose Dairy a premier Portland area institution for decades. At the site of the old Elco Dairy on Southwest Shattuck Road, the Cadonau family has built an unequalled reputation in the industry.

Today Carl Cadonau, Sr., presides over an outfit that has seen five generations of the same family adhere to a winning formula: make the parents happy with a good product, and do the same for the kids with an emphasis on show biz and a strong sports orientation.

During the summer, at Christmas and certain other special dates, the famed Storybook Lane is open for junior to pet and examine a stable full of patient and willing animals. On the spacious outdoor field, softball tournaments and other competition is encouraged by the civic-minded proprietors.

About 3,000 miles across the country in Norwalk, Connecticut, another family business with the same healthy motivations that has made Alpenrose so successful has refined a similar combination to an extent never before seen in this country. As a matter of fact, Stew Leonard is featured in Ripley's *Believe It or Not.*

Right in the middle of this quiet New England community, Stew Leonard has nurtured his reputation as the "proprietor of the world's largest dairy store." This is an understatement. Under one roof, in a showing of enormous stocks, compelling bargains and animated figures that talk and sing to wide-eyed youngsters and their elders, Leonard is doing more than $100 million per year in a store whose mission is "to create happy customers." This he does in spades.

Stew Leonard was a second generation milkman with a home delivery route until 1968, when a state highway construction project forced him to relocate his dairy plant. With the help of a half-million dollar loan from a bank and the Small Business Administration, he started this unique store around a glass-enclosed dairy plant. The rest is history. Today Leonard sells more than 10 million quarts of milk each year.

It takes many more animals than humans to run this enormous part of the business; only four men operate the completely automated dairy plant. And practically every container is sold the same day. If there is any left over at closing time, it is given away to some charity or worthwhile cause.

Nothing in Stew Leonard's store is kept over for the next day's sale. His son, Stew Leonard, Jr. (one of four children who are involved in the business), tells about some corn that was tried out by his own family. It seemed just a bit tough. In checking at the store, he found that fresh-picked corn did not arrive until 10 A.M., and the previous day's stock was being sold until that time. No more. Customers can't find any sweet corn until the farm fresh truck arrives each day.

One of the secrets of the success of this New England landmark is that the store carries only 800 items in stock, as compared to the average supermarket that stocks between 20,000 and 40,000 items. The 100,000 weekly customers find the best in every category, many with Stew Leonard's reputable name firmly implanted. For example, Leonard's sports drink, similar to Gatorade, is sold for just one-half the price of the better-known competitor.

A new store in neighboring Danbury, Connecticut, has just opened with more than 600 employees. It is expected to do $60 million in volume the first year, and, yes, a Leonard family member is there in charge. All of the family, from Dad down, are seen every day walking around the maze of merchandise (the store is not laid out like a normal supermarket) greeting customers and calling every one of the employees by name. Stew Leonard, Jr., carries a walkie-talkie, and is constantly suggesting something to his eager-beaver co-workers. "The talking cow's mouth needs repainting." "The corn should be turned around with the tassels facing the back." "The floor in the dairy room needs washing." (It looked spotless to me.) All of this surely pays off.

Each year the store sells 1 million pints of cream, 1 million cartons of yogurt, 100 tons of cottage cheese, 1,040 tons of ground beef and 2.9 million quarts of orange juice. To keep all of the customers happy, twenty-two bagging stations are staffed by store personnel at all times.

The show biz part? Customers can actually watch fifty bakers making the minute-fresh bread and rolls and other goodies. Milk cartons march by a show window to dramatize the freshness of the product. The kids can see a miniature zoo, à la Alpenrose, in the front parking lot. Suspended on a stage above the store's huge produce section is the "Farm Fresh Five," a state-of-the-art audio-animatronic robot show that performs original songs about milk, and, incidentally, about shopping at Stew Leonard's.

Fun, yes. But attention is paid to the smallest detail. Leonard knew I was coming for a visit, and the huge outside electronic board read "Welcome, Bryan (the *New York Times* restaurant critic) and Gerry." At lunch, an hour later, I commented on the board and the welcoming message. "Good heavens, is that message still up?" Minutes later it read three cantaloupes for $3.

(Update: Stew Leonard, Sr. was found guilty of tax evasion, and sent to jail.)

Oregon's reputation sparks NY callers, internal challenge

*T*wo weeks ago Joan Hamburg, the hostess of New York's most popular call-in morning radio show, asked me to be her guest...to talk about what's new in Big Apple stores and eateries. Joan and her husband were Oregon visitors at the end of the summer, and I put together a comprehensive state tour for them. She related her very positive experiences at the start of the show, and from then on, the hour became "What's doing in Oregon?" rather than "What's happening in Manhattan?"

All dozen call-in lines were continually lit up. The callers wanted to find out what to do and see here, if it really rained 365 days a year, if the streets were safe, how expensive were hotels and restaurants, could the kids find enough to do, and on and on.

Wine from Oregon? The couple at the next table at a trendy New York restaurant that same night questioned the waiter as if he were suggesting a drink that had just arrived from outer space! I listened closely for the taste test. The gentleman was full of praise as he performed the perfunctory ritual; his companion commented it was the best wine she had tasted in a long time. But where, again, did it come from?

We are often reminded that our state and its wonders and products remain something of an unknown to the rest of the nation. A fair number of our coun-

trymen don't know how to pronounce our name correctly, nor do they know exactly where Oregon sits on the map...oh yes, someplace out West near California.

Yet residents of Oregon are usually proud to wear their citizenship on their sleeves. The sense of uniqueness among us is also a sense of pride for both in-staters and expatriates.

The Oregon "mystique" survives.

Crook County in Central Oregon is now the last election bellwether in the nation, having the remarkable record of selecting the winner of the national popular vote in every presidential election since 1882. The explanation by one of the locals is that Oregonians tend to vote for the person they think is best for the job.

Labels don't mean that much here; we are a state that has elected a number of independent types such as Wayne Morse, Richard Neuberger and Tom McCall.

Despite the characterization that we live in a somewhat isolated, soggy and remote part of the nation, we are surely making our mark.

We rank second in per capita attendance at symphony, orchestra, classical music and dance performances, right behind the residents of the nation's capital.

Oregonians make good use of their library facilities. The Salem city library is one of the busiest, per capita, of any in the nation. Nearly one million items were checked out last year.

Numerous surveys, including one by the State University of New York, depict Portland as one of the most livable cities in the nation. Several years ago, Portland was rated the No. 1 best-managed city in the country.

Oregon City could be called the most civilized of all. It was the first incorporated city west of the Mississippi, as well as the original capital of the Oregon Territory. Elaborate plans are in the works here to commemorate the end of the Oregon Trail.

Lumber and wood products top our export list, with agricultural production crops and industrial and commercial machinery (including computer equipment) not too far behind.

In the area of foodstuffs, we are making a big impression. We have become a major contributor to the food supply of the region, the nation and the world. The value of Oregon agricultural products topped the $2.7 billion mark last year, with sales of $1 million or more gained by more than 170 different commodities.

Along the Oregon Coast, some of the best seafood in the world is abundant. Oregon salmon is a delicacy, and the region produces world-class cheese and dairy products. Orchards dot the full length of the western side of the state and produce some of the finest pears, peaches, apples and nuts in the nation.

Oregon's products don't take a back seat to those grown anywhere. The open spaces of the eastern side of our state produce the country's most prized wheat and a good share of the potato products consumed by our rapidly expanding fast-food society.

Several years ago, Bloomingdale's featured Oregon wines and foods in a number of stores. The event was viewed by more than 14 million customers; reorders for many of the more than 200 items shown continue to be placed with local outlets. Neiman-Marcus, the Texas-based home of high fashion, did a similar promotion; it reported sales approaching a half-million dollars.

Our ambassadors have organized successful trade missions into some of the potentially richest markets of the world. Oregon products can now be found throughout Europe, Indonesia, Thailand, Malaysia, Hong Kong and Russia. Japan, at more than $1.5 billion in purchases, is our No. 1 trade partner, Canada is second and South Korea, third.

But it is in our well-earned reputation as one of the great places in America to visit that we face our biggest challenge...and opportunity. How serious are we about keeping the environment of Oregon clean and inviting? (Last weekend, SOLV volunteers picked up more than 27,000 pounds of litter along our coast.) Are we going to allow the nation's finest park system to deteriorate because of lack of financial support?

Will we be willing to maintain Portland as a uniquely workable and livable community, without the pollution and transportation and crime problems of our neighbors?

![FRIDAY SURPRISE]

Yes, Virginia, there is an Oregon with gifts galore

*Y*es, Virginia, there are other things going on besides the election. Sometimes that is hard to believe, what with debates and demonstrations and polls and politicians seemingly dominating the news.

The past few days have underscored what we really already know: that there is a lot happening in our state that is positive. It is just that some folks like to dwell on the negative, looking for something or somebody to tear down. Well, let's build 'er up today.

First, there was a board meeting of the Oregon Coast Aquarium in Newport. To say that the locals in this bustling coastal community are all smiles is putting it mildly. They have had the biggest summer in history, with motel rooms hardly empty long enough to change the sheets, and restaurants, gas stations and kite shops racking up their busiest season ever.

The jellyfish and puffins have put on such an exciting show that in under five months attendance at this state-of-the-art facility has passed the 570,000 mark, a figure higher than was projected for the entire first year. Busloads of students from all over the state now know that it takes more than $10,000 annually to keep just one sea otter (there are three there) happy at the breakfast table, and Aquarium directors learned from head honcho Phyllis Bell the happy news that their "baby" will operate nicely in the black in the first year of life. Plans for phase two, perhaps including a dramatic shark tank, already are under way.

The scene shifts to the sparkling new Oregon Museum of Science and Industry at the site of the former Portland General Electric power station on the east bank of the Willamette River. Thousands of Oregonians got their first view this week of the magnificent building that puts any similar facility in the West to shame. Such an attraction does not just happen.

Before any more time goes by, let's record right here that if it hadn't been for former Portland General Electric chief Bob Short, all of this might not have taken place. He had the vision and led his board in generously giving the site for this most worthwhile venture.

When you combine a great location right on the river (there soon will be a submarine for kids to explore), with the design talents of Bob Frasca, the enthusiasm of OMSI boss and dreamer Marilyn Eichinger and the financial arm-twisting of experts such as Harry Merlo, Claris Poppert and Harry Demorest, you have a winner.

Down the valley, the spotlight was on Willamette University, where President Jerry Hudson has transformed a rather quiet and sleepy campus into one of the most attractive academic settings in the nation. Keeping the architectural integrity of the institution intact, Hudson has provided a twenty-four-hour library, a greatly expanded law school, a re-energized graduate school of management and, just last week, raised his knife and fork to open an eye-popping new student commons building. Named after Grace Goudy, a longtime patron of the university, this new eating emporium provides dining pleasures previously unknown on this or any other college campus. How about lunch by the river, with your choice of entrees from a half-dozen different food stations?

Up the Columbia River Gorge at the Menucha retreat center, there was Claxton Welch, a former Dallas Cowboy, University of Oregon and David Douglas High School football great. He led a crew of hand-picked high school juniors and seniors through a condensed course in our free enterprise system, with hands-on information from those who make the system work, such as Nan Alexander, an editorial writer for the *Oregonian,* and Linda Lohr, an attorney with the Oregon Department of Labor and Industry.

When the subject of discrimination in the marketplace came up, the young men and women proved that they were indeed aware of what was going on in the outside world. This yearly event, sponsored by the downtown Portland Rotary Club, insures that dozens of young people are going to be well-prepared to provide informed leadership in the twenty-first century.

On the bustling Marylhurst College campus, President Nancy Wilgenbusch was all smiles as she greeted returning alums at the last dinner before this historic Oregon academic treasure begins its hundredth year. Present for the dinner, where a large scholarship endowment grant from Nike's Penny and Phil Knight was announced, were members of previous classes (when it was a women's college) from as far back as sixty-four years ago. They couldn't believe their eyes at the transformation that has taken place in the past half century and propelled Marylhurst into one of the fastest growing institutions in the state.

The needy coffers of the local Multiple Sclerosis Society were bulging after the midweek dinner that honored Roger Breezley, guiding force at U.S. Bancorp.

Not one who enjoys sitting still while others talk about him, Breezley took the good-natured jabbing of friends and associates, such as Neil Goldschmidt, Bob Ridgley, Ed Jensen and Jerry Drummond, in the right spirit.

He emphasized that it was a long, long way from Bonetrail, North Dakota, to the corner suite at Portland's "Big Pink" and proved again that talent and commitment know no geographic bounds.

FRIDAY SURPRISE

Bob Straub tallest tree; have to go a fir piece to beat him

*W*hat many others would have considered a handicap to use as an excuse preventing them from achieving any kind of prominence, actually propelled a former Oregon governor into top public leadership in his adopted state.

Bob Straub, seventy-two, now a retired gentleman tree farmer and businessman, grew up with a common affliction: he stuttered. Although his friends and family didn't pay much attention to this problem, Straub found that it strongly affected his career plans. He really wanted to be a lawyer.

Born into a family of comfortable means, educated at Dartmouth, young Straub discarded the trappings of material comfort and concentrated on what he loved the most: the outdoors. As a teenager, he worked in a logging camp, later becoming a manager of a hotel at Mt. Moosilauke, New Hampshire. At a mountaintop camp nearby, he met a counselor whom he later married and who was to have a profound influence on his life. Pat Straub, whom her husband says has been the strong one in the family, packed up the couple's gear and settled in Springfield, Oregon, in 1947, when her husband went to work for Weyerhauser.

One of Oregon's most colorful politicians soon caught Straub's attention. He was Dick Neuberger, a very bright, liberal activist who was as much at home with the pen as he was at the podium. He asked young Straub to help him in his race against Guy Cordon for the U.S. Senate, in turn promising support for his admirer's interest in running for local office.

The combination worked. Straub became the very first Democrat to win a seat on the Lane County Board of Commissioners since 1892, shattering the widely-held belief that no one from that party could possibly be elected to such a visible position. And all of this occurred as the young politician struggled with his speech impediment when he appeared on public platforms.

In 1954, Straub was elected to the Oregon Senate in a race against one of his area's leading citizens, lumberman Ed Cone. (Cone later served, with distinction, as Mayor of Eugene.)

My first meeting with Bob Straub took place in the early 1960s, when he served as head of the Oregon Democratic Party. At the time, I was the chairman of the Oregon Economic Development Commission and had been asked to make a presentation at one of the party meetings in Lane County. I was enormously impressed during the evening's activities that the party chairman did not let his stuttering affect his very efficient running of the meeting, and also that he treated a Republican visitor with such class and dignity.

Straub's days in the midst of party politics were building ones, as the Democrats became a major force in the state legislature. Not one to mask his strong feelings about issues that he believed in, Bob Straub ruffled the feathers of several of the party's faithful, including Vern Cook and the "first lady" of the Democratic congressional delegation, Edith Green. But to his credit, Straub does not now (nor has he ever) engaged in any vicious personal attacks so common in today's political scene.

Who was this gentleman's political hero and one of his closest friends? None other than someone whom he ran against for the state's highest position. They were both bigger than life in stature, both shared an unending love of the outdoors and both loved to laugh. Here the similarity ends. Tom McCall was a gregarious people person who loved to entertain anyone who would listen. Bob Straub is a laid-back, private person who is uncomfortable with small talk.

One of Straub's favorite stories involves Dorothy Lawson McCall, Tom's mother, a lady well-known to political insiders as one who loved to use the telephone to vent her spleen about anyone who dared say a bad word about her politician son. After one of the McCall-Straub debates, she placed one of her infamous calls to let her son's opponent know that she was "shocked" by the comments about her beloved Tom. Straub related her strong rebuke to McCall. His response: "Just be glad she hung up when she did!"

Pat and Bob Straub raised six children (one was killed in a tragic auto accident) who still today gather 'round the family table at their farm in the outskirts of Salem.

Every free moment for Straub is spent playing with his trusty police dog, Shadrack, on this sixty-five-acre, timber-covered hideaway. Having been successful in building a comfortable financial foundation from real estate ventures, Straub keeps himself busy with a number of business activities. He enjoys playing the stock market, loves to be around his sixteen grandchildren, and camps out in Mexico with Pat when they want to "get away from it all."

But being out in the woods is still his true love. He has tree farms in Douglas County, Willamina and Fall Creek and an 8,000 acre ranch in Wheeler County.

Fond memories of public life? Yes, he has plenty of them and some strong views about current events. He credits Glenn Jackson as the one who showed the strongest support when he really needed it. He feels the Reagan-Bush years have been unnecessarily tough on lower income families. After fourteen years out of active political life, he would still love to be governor again. A profile in courage? You bet.

Today, Bob Straub hasn't a sign of a speech impediment. He tackled that problem with the same intensity that he did the Willamette Greenway and the housing needs of lower income Marion County residents.

He has been a winner in every one of these challenges.

Frankly speaking, he made Portland 'my kind of town'

*I*n his world there was no grey...everything was black or white. Those who knew him personally saw a tough and exacting exterior, with a soft, generous and fair side that wasn't obvious in a casual encounter. For those who knew him only by name, he was a commanding and controversial presence who was involved in just about everything that went on in the city and state that he loved.

During his early years, he developed a love for horses, spending many an afternoon riding his pony through the fields and woods of suburban Portland, in the days when what is now Washington Square was a rural paradise. He spent countless hours in the stables feeding and grooming the horses that pulled his family's store delivery wagons. And later, he put together a string of prize thoroughbreds and harness horses that was to bring many a blue ribbon to the maroon and red tack rooms where he loved to exchange stories with the likes of T. B. Wilcox and A. P. Fleming and Tevis Paine, who were major personalities at the Pacific International Livestock Exposition Horse Show.

Away from home, his horses competed with the finest animals from stables owned by Lurline Matson Roth (of shipping fame) and Carnation Farms (the milk people). During intermissions, he entertained at major shows in Oakland, San Francisco, Denver and Seattle dressed in a Charlie Chaplin outfit, almost looking more like the comedian than the actor did himself. When a tragic fire in Oakland and a disastrous train wreck in the Midwest killed the major portion of his stable within one year's time, he was crestfallen.

Not only in the arenas of the horse world did he show his lively spirit and sense of humor. These developed at an early age, about the time he doused his brown bag homemade sandwiches with castor oil to fend off interlopers who insisted on stealing his school lunches.

He loved to be around fun people. In the entertainment world the comedy teams of Amos 'n' Andy (radio) and Olsen and Johnson (stage and motion pictures) were his favorites. He became close personal friends with these gentlemen, and entertained them (and they him) on the boat he used for relaxation.

Athletics were always a major interest, especially when they involved young people. He played a major role in the careers of many outstanding Oregon athletes like Tommy Moyer (boxing), John Kitzmiller and Bobby Grayson (football) and Nancy Merki (swimming). He was President of the Oregon Amateur Athletic Union and an officer of the national organization as well.

It was not only in the sports arena

that he had a soft spot in his heart for youngsters. He was the one responsible for changing the selection of Portland's Rose Festival queen from the ranks of society matrons to a contest of popular seniors from our city's high schools. In addition, he worked side-by-side with folks like Anne Keil Robinson (locally) and Basil O'Connor (nationally) heading March of Dimes campaigns to eradicate the scourge of polio from our nation's youth. He gave the property that now houses Lewis and Clark College to that institution for a tiny fraction of its value. In 1930, he was named one of Portland's earliest and youngest First Citizens.

In his day, getting things done in the community was a lot easier than in today's world. Along with movers and shakers like Paul B. McKee (Pacific Power and Light), Dave Simpson (Norris, Beggs and Simpson), Ep Hoyt (the *Oregonian*), E.B. MacNaughton (First National Bank) and Ed Sammons (U.S. National Bank), he was a constructive voice in building the solid foundations of his community. But all was not sweetness and light. There were strong arguments about public versus private power, and the need for a city center hotel (the Portland Hilton). He was so pleased when the Union Oil Company bought the final $250,000 of Hilton bonds that he threw Dave Simpson's traditional straw hat out of the window of his 12th floor downtown office!

Although educated as a lawyer, and a retailer by profession, his real love was in the field of engineering. During construction phases in his business, he would drive local contractors like Andy Anderson and L. H. Hoffman crazy by showing up nearly every night to supervise the workmen. There was no room for compromise in his quest for quality.

Stories about his antics and activities and appearances in the department store that he headed are legendary. He would spend his Sundays inspecting the restrooms to insure that there were no cracked toilet seats or drippy faucets. He could be seen daily walking the aisles of his establishment picking up papers from the floor and making sure that no customer was waiting to be helped. On Christmas Eve, he would stand at the door and personally wish each of the thousands of Meier & Frank employees a happy holiday. Heaven help the new salesperson who did not know the short, heavy-browed man who seemed to be just about everywhere. The fuse was short and the temper, mercurial. Neatness and perfection were not just a pretense, they were mandatory. The lady (Judi Hofer) who now heads the business recounts with awe, even today, her early experiences as a stock girl, when she first met the boss who was then inspecting the back scenes areas where she was assigned.

I guess I should remember better than most anyone else the one-of-a-kind man that he was. His name was Aaron M. "Bud" Frank, my Dad.

FRIDAY SURPRISE

Musings on what lies ahead for the new year

Surely one of Oregon's least likely candidates for Governor was a gentleman who served in that office from 1939 to 1943. Charles A. Sprague was a starchy intellectual who had few social graces and little time for the usual political backslapping.

Sprague was the editor and publisher of the *Oregon Statesman,* Salem's most influential newspaper of that era. I recall the first time I visited with him in his office. He didn't lift his eyes from his typewriter, didn't ask me to sit down, carried on what little conversation there was in very few words, and dismissed me as if I were a local insurance salesman. It seemed to make little difference to him that I was representing his largest advertiser-to-be!

But there was no question that Sprague had lots going for him in the smarts department. His column, which appeared each morning on page one of his paper, was must reading for anyone who wanted to know what was "really" going on in our state, the nation and, indeed, around the world. "It Seems To Me" was the outlet for this man's vast knowledge and common sense commentary on contemporary American life.

I certainly would never place myself in the same league with this august statesman, but I would like to borrow his phrase. It does seem to me that as a new year approaches, there are some very significant things going on that will be shaping and influencing our lives in a very profound manner.

Are we witnessing the beginning of the decline of Japan as one of the world's wonder industrial nations? Several years ago we were watching with awe as our Japanese friends bought freely in the American real estate market. That spigot has been turned down. Many major Japanese industrial firms are showing some of the same bottom-line pains as some of ours, and financial scandals are becoming more commonplace. American competitors are learning that we have the savvy to be competitive in fields that Japan previously dominated, like automobiles and electronics.

It seems to me that we better keep our eyes on China as one of the dominant forces in the coming years. With the huge population of that country, and the work ethic that is a part of their culture, their potential seems almost unlimited. Just as we have seen the changing of the guard from World War II leadership to the baby boomer generation in our last election, imagine what will happen when the elder statesmen who are now in power in China call it quits.

Western Europe presents another important staging area for change. With economic cooperation now almost assured, the European bloc will be a very formidable competitor. But will the re-appearance of hate and unrest in

Germany slow that nation's influence? Will the persistent labor and political turmoil in Italy be a cause for concern? Will the British and French really be able to work together? Whose voice will emerge as the strong one...will it be John Major's?

Coming back home, it seems to me that the rather casual and unstructured atmosphere that we have known in the work place is a thing of the past. The easy give-and-take that had its pluses in the informality of life in our offices and stores and factories has led to many well-publicized minuses, as some folk took advantage of situations. Whether this change will affect the productivity of the American worker remains to be seen. But one thing is certain: intolerance and harassment will no longer be tolerated. Anywhere.

And a new day is dawning in the halls of Congress. Many will say that it is just about time. The American public is telling their representatives and senators that they should live by the same rules as the rest of us. Seniority, although still a vital part of our political system, is being assaulted by the wave of new faces in the nation's capital.

It seems to me that the mighty bureaucracy that we have put up with for years may be scheduled for some major surgery. Take, for example, the Agriculture Department. Fifty years ago there were more than 6 million farms in our country, and that department had 98,000 individuals taking care of their needs. A half century later there are one-third that many farms (just 2 million) and we have nearly 130,000 employees shuffling the papers. The message from the voters is crystal clear: too much is being spent on administration. Everywhere.

In the private sector, it seems to me that the same message is on the air waves, although some antennas are not picking it up as quickly as they might. No longer will it be business as usual in the health care field; we simply can't afford the soaring costs. No longer will stockholders sit still for the obscene executive salaries and bonuses that have become almost commonplace. No longer will American customers be content with sloppy and disinterested service.

The day of being everything to everybody is over. The giant niche-marketers (like Toys 'R' Us and HomeBase) will be even more of a challenge to the little guy. Next time you are in the East, visit a Bed, Bath and Beyond store. It's awesome, as the kids say.

This all sounds pretty serious. Let's end on a lighter and sweeter note. Don't let anyone tell you that we have become a nation of calorie watchers. Rich, gooey, fabulous desserts are very much "in" everywhere. It seems to me that is about the best economic news we could have at this time of year (given the implication for new and expanded clothes, more health club memberships, etc.) And if Charlie Sprague were alive today, he might even write a column about it!

FRIDAY SURPRISE

No matter who we are, U.S. still best place to be

*A*s is usual at the start of every year, we are awash in oceans of figures about our personal and our country's economic situations. We are told by various sources in the printed media and on television how very good or how very bad things are. Politicians, depending on their current status, chip in with comments that could, politely, be interpreted as being in their own best interests. There is no shortage of finger pointing. Most of us are at best somewhat confused by all these conflicting indicators, and at least somewhat turned off by the whole scene.

The highly regarded *U.S. News & World Report* tells us that consumers were better off four years ago than they are now. They report that rising unemployment and a weak job market have not been kind to family incomes. In addition, they mention the problems of an increasing debt load, which has had its effect on consumer spending.

Then the just-as-professional *Kiplinger Washington Letter* arrives with the statement that inflation-adjusted pay has not DECLINED, only SLOWED in the seventies and eighties. They say that pay did not fall in many areas and that self-employeds, supervisory personnel, government workers, teachers and some of those employed in agriculture showed robust salary gains over the past fifteen years.

In addition, the conference board said its consumer confidence index jumped to 78.3 in December from 65.6 in November.

So what are we to believe? As in so many situations, the truth lies somewhere in between. It depends on our own personal perspective. Do we personally have a job, and is it better than the last one? How have we personally been treated with regard to promotions, pay scales and bonuses? What is our own job security? If we are retired, how does our income (and taxes, buying power, health benefits) measure up against previous years? If there is blame in any area, if our new situation is not so hot, the politicians get most of the wrath.

How about corporate America? *U.S. News* tells us that weak profits and a continuing debt position left over from the highly-leveraged 1980s have prevented American companies from investing in necessary new plant equipment and the research and development that is necessary to stimulate our productivity and growth.

Kiplinger has a much sunnier outlook. He claims that the American economy is doing very well, points out that we are the world's biggest producer of goods and services, and that we lead on a per-capita basis in output per person among major world powers. Further, we are told that we are first in overall productivity in every major sector. Productivity GROWTH slowed a bit, but is now on a fast track, with our average factory worker 20 percent more productive than his (or her) counterpart in Japan.

Some folks like to blame our tax structure for all economic problems, but contemplate for a moment that there was only one country among the Organization for Economic Cooperation and Development's twenty-four members (Turkey) that has a lighter tax load than the United States.

All of this was played out "ad nauseam" in our recent election. President Bush was the optimist (he has since been proven correct in some areas); Governor Clinton the nay-sayer (but he is now cautiously more positive); and Ross Perot chimed in with "we are not making anything anymore." Most of us considered the sources, making our evaluations (and directing blame) on the basis of how it affected our own business, our own income, our own future.

On the social agenda, certainly education and health care are at the top of anyone's list. *Business Week* provides figures showing that America's schools are turning out more graduates than ever before, but that the cost of higher education is up at a time when real wages for less educated workers are sinking. They also quote huge rising medical costs, like a 5.1 percent annual increase (1960-1990) in hospital costs, and a 7.4 percent annual cost increase during the same period in nursing home care. It's easy to blame greedy doctors and inefficient homes and hospitals.

Kiplinger tells us that America's top universities are the world's best, that our basic research is topflight. But in public elementary and secondary schools, despite high per-pupil expenditures, our schools aren't doing the kind of job they should in preparing youngsters for today's skilled jobs. He blames the parents who don't ask enough of their kids. Others are quick to point out that our schools suffer from bloated administrative costs.

Then there are the serious social problems that face our nation, like AIDS, child neglect and abuse, racial unrest, an out-of-control drug situation and crimes increasing at an alarming rate in nearly every sector.

Consider this: most recent figures show that the increase in the percent of children living below the poverty line in our country is 17 percent. In Canada it is 9.6 percent. In Britain it is 10.7 percent.

In 1990, handgun homicides in our country totalled 10,567; in Canada, 68; in Britain, 22.

Numbers of prisoners (per 100,000 people), same period: United States, 426; Britain, 98.

Blame is spread well here also: a too-lenient judicial system, not enough support for police agencies, lack of family control (divorces, two working parents, etc.).

Sure, it is easy to criticize and complain and blame others. And again it all depends on where each of us is personally coming from. But serious problems and challenges are nothing new to our country. We have thrived on them. The only difference today is that with modern communications, we are much more aware of what is going on around us.

But would you honestly want to trade places with citizens of any other nation on Earth?

Mickey's boss does well, but public smells a rat

*M*ost everyone has a vision of a "dream job," the ultimate if one could so choose. For me, that job would be the head honcho at Walt Disney. Why? Because it has always seemed that outfit brought more fun and pleasure to more people than any other.

All I know about the current Disney C.E.O., Michael Eisner, is what I hear and read about. He seems to be having a great time. And well he should.

From the time he joined Mickey and his friends (1984), Eisner has produced a stunning performance. On the purely financial side, he has racked up a compounded total return to shareholders of an amazing 35.4 percent per year (up to 1992), a level of performance that placed Disney at the 94th percentile of the 300 companies with the highest value of outstanding shares.

Just over a year ago, Eisner decided to sell 5.4 million shares (from stock options), giving him an aggregate pretax gain of $197.5 million. When combined with his salary and annual bonus, Mr. Eisner made more legally in any single year than any other executive ever. Of course, he will have to pay some taxes on his gain to the feds, something like $61 million, and another $21 million or so to the California coffers.

The Disney directors no doubt felt that his performance was worth these astronomical returns. Eisner also proba-

bly feels that he was worth it. I have no idea of his motivations as far as the company is concerned, whether they are purely financial, or if he is having such a great time overseeing the far-flung empire of amusement parks, movies, TV shows and Disney merchandise that money is secondary. For one thing, I would imagine that he has not been too happy with the way Mickey and his friends have polished their French accents...the theme park outside Paris has not been a winner so far.

But the spectacle of perks and salary in this range is so obscene and so out of sync with the present-day mood of America that it serves as a wake-up call for some serious soul searching for the leadership of our nation, both on the political and business side.

Stockholders are telling their companies to pay fair salaries, bonuses and stock options...and stop all the other gimmicks. Do something about the expanding list of perks: club memberships, automobiles, extra life insurance, golden parachutes, extravagant expense accounts, company planes.

They are also saying that boards better pay more attention to what is going on. We have seen the beginnings of this with upheaval at General Motors and IBM and American Express. The troops are saying that non-CEOs should be added to compensation committees. Forget about the consultants who are getting fees from the company. Rewarding directors with stock is being suggested as a desirable form of payment for those overseeing businesses.

Government agencies have gotten into the act. The Securities Exchange Commission has recently issued new rules for the disclosure of executive pay in proxy statements They require that compensation committees explain the reasoning behind executive pay decisions. Figures comparing the company's five-year shareholder return to that of a broad-based index and an industry or peer group index must be published. And finally, proxy statements must include a series of compensation tables for the top five execs of the outfit.

This is just the tip of the iceberg, a reaction to things that are bothering Main Street. Americans want reform, and they want it right now.

In politics, most everyone agrees that elections cost too much. Overall spending limits must be put in place. The advantages that incumbents have in elections must be eliminated. The perks of Congress have to be changed, just as well as the perks for a private company's corner offices.

Something has to be done to trim the fat off political institutions as well as private ones. If we see downsizing at Sears and Boeing, then how about the same on Capitol Hill? Is it necessary to have so many committees that most every member of the majority can become a chairperson of some sub-committee? And why in the world do you need 37,000 aides and assorted hangers-on to run the place?

Those who are looking farther down the road understand the importance of doing something dramatic with our educational system. Right here in Oregon we are facing decisions that will have a profound effect on the social health of our state. The fallout from Measure 5 is beginning to be felt in the limbs and branches of our education tree of life. But we must keep up the research and development dollars that help spread manufacturing ideas to the multitude of small companies that provide so many jobs. The feds can sure help in this process: shift the bucks from research that works on killing people to projects that will improve our quality of life.

We no longer live and work in a vacuum. Overseas markets provide one of the exciting hopes for expansion of American business. But what a mess we are in. We have twenty-eight agencies that presently deal with exports; the little guy finds it almost impossible to work through this maze. Besides his emphasis on redefining our health and welfare systems, President Bill could make a real contribution here. How about making Coca-Cola prexy, Roberto Goizueta, the "export czar"? He has done a pretty good job with his own product!

Oh yes, Mr. Eisner could help, too. How? By acting like one of a great nation's leaders and being ready, willing and able to share his talents and resources to help others around the world, while helping to make life easier for families right here at home.

FRIDAY SURPRISE

And now for the real story behind political squabbles

*W*hen someone was praising a local politician during a conversation at a public meeting not long ago, the officeholder's wife responded, "Don't be impressed; I wash his socks!" There is always the tendency to look at public figures as special individuals who do not have the personal frailties and needs and social problems that the rest of us have. Nothing could be farther from the truth.

History has shown that the personalities and relationships between those who occupy positions of leadership often is a significant factor not only in the manner in which their office is conducted, but also in the kind of legislation that is passed during their terms of office.

Oregon has had its share of strong personalities in political seats both in Washington, D.C., and Salem. The chemistry between some of them provides a fascinating backdrop for the history of our time.

I have had the opportunity to know a number of them in various capacities, ranging from sitting in her classroom (Maurine Neuberger) to serving as his Chief of Staff (Mark Hatfield) to competing against him in horse shows (Wayne Morse).

How did these folk, and a number of others whose names are well-known in current Oregon folklore, get along? Well, my friends, what you heard and

read about was not always the real story!

One of the most fascinating associations was that of two very intelligent and determined gentlemen, who were associated not only in the classroom, but also in the mighty halls of the United States Senate: Wayne Morse and Richard Neuberger.

For a short time Neuberger studied under Morse at the University of Oregon law school. One can only imagine how impressed any young person would be with the agile and brilliant mind of a professor like Morse. And obviously Morse recognized the unusual literary talent of his student. Neuberger even wrote a favorable article about Morse for the *American Mercury* magazine. But as the years went on, and both of them entered the political arena, tensions grew to the point that vitriolic letters were exchanged, culminating in a very rocky professional relationship.

I asked Maurine Neuberger (Dick's wife, and later a senator in her own right) what happened to destroy this mutual admiration society. She thought that a flattering profile of Neuberger, as one of the nation's up and coming new senators, that appeared in the *New York Times* was not looked upon kindly by his senior associate. It was all downhill from there.

During that same period, in the House of Representatives, there were also some ladies and gentlemen with very well-honed egos and very definitive agendas.

Edith Green will go down in Oregon history as one of the best-informed legislators on educational policy to have been in Congress. This she came by naturally, as she also was a school teacher. But her knowledge and leadership in the area did not sit well with Morse, who also rightfully claimed expertise. There was a continuing battle between the two to claim credit for various legislative initiatives.

Wendell Wyatt, a lawyer and former FBI agent from Astoria, and a Republican, had varying experiences with Democrats who served with him in Congress. Before Wyatt was elected to the House, he was nominated by President Eisenhower to serve as a Tax Court judge. Morse, unhappy because of Wyatt's support of former Governor Douglas McKay in a previous U.S. Senate battle, found him "personally objectionable;" therefore, he was not confirmed. There was no love lost between the two.

On the other hand, Wyatt and Green (a Democrat) developed an increasingly close friendship during their terms in the House. Wyatt claims this was because Green became more conservative in her views, but it is frequently true that members of different political parties get along better than those who share the same label. After serving in the House for twenty years, Green retired at the same time that Wyatt did. (He was there ten years.) Now a federal building named after both of them stands in downtown Portland.

Robert Duncan, a Democrat, served as Speaker of the House in Salem during some of the period when Mark Hatfield was governor. They worked well together. Later, Duncan ran against Hatfield (for his first senate term in 1966) and lost in a very close election. (Our involvement in Vietnam was the big issue.) Duncan went on to serve in the House in Washington from the Portland area (1975-1981), and he and Hatfield became close friends, working co-operatively on a number of legislative initiatives.

Recent events have cast a spotlight on the relationship between our present two United States Senators, Bob Packwood and Mark O. Hatfield, both Republicans. Once again it started as a professor-student relationship at Willamette University, where Hatfield taught political science. Both of these gentlemen are students of politics and articulate spokesmen. But there the similarity ends. Hatfield is basically interested in how political power can be used; Packwood has always been more fascinated with the process itself.

The association of Hatfield and Tom McCall (former Republican governor) was another intriguing (and edgy) one. These two were miles apart: McCall, an outgoing, off-the-cuff newsman's delight; Hatfield, a studied and private person. Private and public sparks flew. But both saw enormous progress during their governorships: McCall in the environment and Hatfield in economic development.

The real strength in any family or community is in the diversity of its members. The same is surely true in politics.

FRIDAY SURPRISE

Andy Rooney keeps dinner lively with non-stop talk

*D*o you have any idea who might have said this, commenting on chefs: "I don't like food that is too carefully arranged; it makes me think that he's spending too much time arranging and not enough time cooking. If I wanted a picture, I'd buy a painting!"

Or this, on pets: "If dogs could talk, it would take a lot of the fun out of owning one!"

Some hints. He is seventy-four years old, writes a syndicated newspaper column, is the author or co-author of a number of books and does a weekly television commentary that is seen by over 35 million viewers. Oh yes, he also has a very decided view on practically everything. There is just one person that fits this description...Andy Rooney.

I heard that someone recently described my segment on KPTV-12's weekly *Northwest Reports* news magazine as a wrap-up commentary à la *60 Minutes* (but for sure, I'm no Andy Rooney). I never imagined that soon I would have the opportunity to spend an evening with the gentleman who does this piece. Well, it happened last week over dinner in a New York restaurant. And, my friends, this American institution is just as colorful in person as he is on the screen.

The other guests at the informal affair were Andy's wife of over fifty years, Marguerite, who insists on calling her partner "Andrew"; Emily, one of their twin daughters (they have four children), who is under consideration for executive producer of Peter Jennings' *World News Tonight*; and Bryan Miller, the *New York Times* restaurant critic, a friend of Rooney's son, Brian, who himself is an ABC television personality.

Rooney started the evening by bringing out a copy of the new book *Hot Potatoes,* a recipe collection of well-known potato lovers, put together by Enid Nemy, who also writes a Sunday column for the *New York Times.* Contributors to the unusual volume include Ann Landers, Robin Leach, Joan Rivers, Barbara Walters and, of course, Andy Rooney. His contribution: potato ice cream. "Place the cooked potatoes in a blender with cream and a dash of paprika for color, and blend well...only after dinner should you throw out the potato peels...don't ask why." Rooney read the entire recipe aloud to the group, muttering that he was afraid some readers might take the whole thing seriously!

On other subjects, it was he who was more serious. One of the biggest concerns he has is in the quantity of mail he receives. Over 1,000 letters a week come to him at CBS, and stacks more arrive at his homes (an apartment in New York, a residence near Albany, New York, and another in Connecticut). He can't possibly answer all of them and he feels that he is being rude to his admirers.

Rooney finds that some of those who write are just as opinionated as he is. Take the letter he received from the daughter of famous Army General George Patton (whom Rooney wrote about during his World War II stint with the newspaper *Stars and Stripes*). Rooney was not complimentary about the legendary war hero. "My father would not have liked you, either," the family member steamed.

The dinner conversation covered a wide variety of topics.

Rooney makes furniture in his free hours to relax and to be productive. He could not understand why I didn't know about some obscure tool store in lower Manhattan.

Food seems to be a big thing in his life. He had strong views about any number of Manhattan restaurants and food stores. He thought (and I agree) that the trianon chocolate cake from Mme. Colette's upper east side bakery is superb. This was about the only time I felt I was on equal ground!

He thought that Jacques Barzun, a former professor at Columbia University and author of the *Modern Researcher*, was the fourth smartest person alive. He wouldn't tell us who the first three were.

When very down-to-earth wife Margie could get a word in edgewise, she turned out to be just as strong in her views as "the old man." She wanted to know the latest news of her college chum, Portlander Helena Biddle Dick.

It was inevitable that the dinner talk would finally turn to politics. It turns out that Rooney is an unabashed admirer of our new president and particularly positive about his communications skills. As a TV pro himself,

Rooney was fascinated to see Mr. Clinton skillfully departing from his script during his speech to Congress several weeks ago. He was equally complimentary about the fellow who ran the glass script monitors and was able to follow Clinton's many off-the-cuff remarks without a hitch.

Then someone mentioned Rush Limbaugh. Boy, did we get an earful! "He only appeals to the uneducated..." and much more. When I casually mentioned that I knew a number of rather well-schooled individuals who found some wisdom in a few of Limbaugh's opinions, Rooney wanted to know who they were, what college they went to, if they graduated, and what kinds of jobs they held.

At the end of the three-hour dinner, Rooney piled us all into his white Jeep for an hour's tour through the bowels of Manhattan, mainly for the benefit of his Boston-based daughter. It turned out to be vintage New York, even to a Greenwich Village scene with unclad New York University students scaling a huge, street-corner artifact, much to the delight of their fellow classmates and to the disgust of some of New York's finest, who stood by covering the eyes of female observers!

Whether it was on youthful bare-bottoms, or aged white wines, Rooney had the pithy comments one might expect. Life around his house would certainly never be dull!

G.I. relives World War II from KP to Lucky Strike

Someday I am going to ask a person who knows about those things why it is you can remember well what happened years ago, but it is sometimes impossible to recall where you had lunch yesterday!

This came to mind vividly the other evening when friends were telling stories from their days in uniform. Some of the experiences as a GI in World War II feel as if they occurred last week; maybe it is because we were all so impressionable in our teens.

I had enlisted in the Army when I entered Stanford University, but it was some time later that I was called to active duty (as a buck private) at Fort Lewis, Washington. There were a number of Oregonians who had received greetings from Uncle Sam at the same time...most were students at various schools throughout the West. It was somewhat reassuring to see an old friend, Graham Barbey of Astoria, at Fort Lewis when we arrived. He was on the induction staff there, having been summoned to duty some time before.

A memorable event happened early. As a matter of fact, the second day of Army life.

The sergeant in charge of our group of very raw recruits gathered his charges together on the second floor of the barracks to show exactly how an army bed should be made. For some reason unknown to me (I assume it was by chance), he chose my upper bunk in the middle of the room for his demonstration. As he tore the blankets off my resting place, all manner of comic books (and some not so comic) flew out over the floor.

"Whose blankety-blank (and some other expletives I had not learned in English 101) bunk is this?" "Mine, sir." "Don't call me sir, I'm a sergeant." "Yes, sir. I mean, sorry sergeant." "Nothing, I mean nothing, is to be put under your mattress. Understand that?" "Yes, sir, I mean sergeant." "Do you see that pile of rocks (he pointed to the yard outside the window)? Report there in one hour."

Much to the delight of my buddies, who were gleefully enjoying this early indoctrination into matters of military discipline, I was assigned to spend the rest of the day moving the rocks from one location to another, then back to their original resting place. I thought to myself if I could find the so-and-so who had been assigned my bunk in the previous training class, I would have had a few to things to say to him. Oh well, off to a good start!

In what seemed like an eternity of physical exams (ex-military personnel reading this will know the type) and KP (kitchen police) duty and shining buttons and shoes, we were finally told that basic training would be real close by...at Fort Bragg, North Carolina. We were piled into a troop train that was to be our home for the five-day journey. Of course, the travel route was not announced, but we were excited to learn that the first stop (for just two hours) was to be at Union Station in our hometown, Portland, Oregon.

Everyone rushed to the phones to call parents, girl friends, buddies, etc. Fellow trainee Clint Eastman, Jr., from Lake Oswego, called his father, who was so pleased to hear from his son that he ran the entire way from his office at Sixth and Morrison (yes, at the Friday Surprise store) all the way to the railroad station. Mr. Eastman was not a small person (he must have weighed 225-plus pounds). He was a wet wreck when he arrived at train-side, but he sure was a welcome sight not only for his son, but for all the rest of us. He had brought some good things to eat!

The sands and the humidity of Fort Bragg (and nearby scenic Fayetteville, North Carolina) provided too many opportunities to dig fox holes and run obstacle courses. Then there was more schooling, this time in uniform, in engineering at Loyola University in Los Angeles. Next stop, supposedly to get in shape by learning how to transport 75mm pack howitzers (we were in a field artillery battalion) up and down hills, was at Hunter Liggett Military Reservation in northern California.

Back to the East Coast again, this time to prepare to go overseas with the Eighty-ninth Infantry Division. Most everyone was looking forward to this. How many more training sergeants did we need to listen to?

The journey overseas, on the converted troopship *S.S. Uruguay,* was originally destined to end in England. In the middle of the Atlantic two things happened: (1) we were diverted to Le Havre, France, and (2) we were told there were a number of subs in the area and to be ready for any eventuality. I kept chocolate bars in my pocket.

Unloading in mid-winter in the middle of the night on the coast of France was a unique experience. We were loaded into open trucks, like cattle, for a journey to the "cigarette camps" (mine was called Lucky Strike) for staging. Camps? Tents in the middle of nowhere. First instructions were to be careful when going to the latrines... there were snipers nearby.

Friend Charlie Crookham of Portland (he of recent State Attorney General fame) sauntered over from his infantry section to see how I was doing. Neither of us will ever forget the evening. The artillery commanding general, who shall remain nameless, didn't mind a shot or two to shield himself from the intense cold. Privates Crookham and Frank found themselves almost carrying the star-shouldered oldtimer outside his tent so he could relieve himself. Generals had to do that, too!

The race across Luxembourg and Germany with General George Patton's Third Army was the journey of a lifetime...once. It sure made an indelible impression; I can still almost recall every place we set up camp.

And there was no time for comic books to be stuffed into the well-used, olive drab sleeping bags!

Times may be a-changin'; but names often retained

*W*hat would it be like if we could be magically transplanted back to the 1880s in Portland and surrounding communities? Would we see any familiar names? The answer is a resounding "yes." And would we recognize any local institutions that are still important parts of our lives? Again, the answer is a very definite "yes".

As a matter of fact, we probably would be reading this very same newspaper, for the *Oregonian* was founded in 1850. Each edition was five cents, a price that held for nearly one hundred years.

If you lived down the valley in the Salem area, you would be reading he *Oregon Statesman,* the state's second-oldest newspaper, which began publishing on March 28, 1851, in Oregon City in opposition to the Whig newspaper (the one we now hold in our hands). The *Oregon Statesman* moved to Salem in 1853 when the territorial capital relocated there. A well-known name of the period was founder Asahel Bush II, who was active and influential in Democratic causes.

Bush sold the *Statesman* in 1863, and went on to a career in banking and other businesses. He established the well-known Salem bank, Ladd & Bush Bankers, in 1869 (now Ladd & Bush branch office of the United States National Bank of Oregon), which was the center of commerce in those days.

During the decade of the 1880s, the *Capital Journal* was started in Salem with the twin purposes of promoting the Republican party and making money. Will H. Parry was the founder (1888). He soon sold the paper; since then it has had a long succession of owners and editors.

The predecessors of a number of other well-known newspapers of today were "must" reading in that period. Original names on the mastheads were different. The *Albany Democrat-Herald* put out its first edition in 1859 (the year our state was born); the *Corvallis Gazette-Times* began life three years later; and the *McMinnville News-Register* first saw the light of day in 1866. The next year, one of the West's best papers, the *Register Guard,* started serving Eugene, and the *Roseburg News-Review* was born at the same time. *The Daily Astorian* dates back to 1872.

If we wanted some legal work done in those days, we might well have gone to the predecessors of the current Portland firm, Miller, Nash, Wiener, Hager & Carlsen. Of course, those were not the names on the door at that time: the firm was founded in 1873 by Henry H. Northrup and William B. Gilbert. They set up practice in the Dekum Building.

Later on, Northrup served as a Multnomah County judge, and Gilbert was a member of the U.S. Ninth Circuit

Court of Appeals for thirty-nine years.

If a member of our family was thinking of going on to college (not so common in those days), some of today's most prestigious institutions were in the forefront in the educational world. Our pioneer institution is Willamette University in Salem, where the first students were admitted in 1842. A seat of higher learning with a sterling reputation for nearly 150 years, Pacific University of Forest Grove has roots going back to 1849. St. Mary's Academy was founded in 1859; Lewis and Clark College in 1867; Oregon State University in 1868; and the Oregon Episcopal School in 1869.

What would we have paid at Willamette? Tuition for the College of Liberal Arts was $13 a term, and board (in "comfortable rooms" in town) set the student back $2 to $3 a month! The library had all of 2,500 volumes, and there was to be no profanity and no tobacco on campus. Students were to attend chapel services every day.

Lewis and Clark College was founded in 1867 as Albany Collegiate Institute by Presbyterians who were anxious to find a place to educate their children in the New England tradition. The first graduating class (four women) received their diplomas in 1873.

If sickness struck, we could have gone to St. Vincent's Hospital, dedicated on July 19, 1875, the Feast of St. Vincent de Paul, as Oregon's first permanent hospital. The pioneer founders had less than $5,000 in their pockets when they started construction. Good Samaritan Hospital dates back to the same year.

The farmers of the eighties would recognize the name R.M. Wade Company, an agricultural supply business that was founded by Robert M. Wade in Salem in 1865.

When our trusty mode of transportation (the horse) needed some equipment, we would go to the Cronin Company (now in the floor coverings business); they would have provided the necessary harness and saddles. This predecessor of Electrical Distributing (now a Cronin fourth-generation operation) was started in 1878.

By the latter part of the nineteenth century, the Holman Funeral Service was well-known in Portland. The business was first established in 1854 as A.P. DeLin & Company (at 151 First Avenue). Later it passed to Edward Holman, DeLin's son-in-law, who changed the name.

Hungry Portlanders of the 1880s could find the same great turkey at Huber's Restaurant (founded in 1879 as the Bureau Saloon). If a customer bought his beer for five cents, the food was free. In 1888, bartender Frank R. Huber bought out founder W.L. Lightner.

Shoppers in mid-century had their choice of three, well-stocked department stores: Lipman Wolfe (1851); Olds & King (1851); and Meier & Frank (1857). Only the latter still survives, now a part of the May Company.

In 1885, M&F moved into a new two-story building on Taylor between First and Second streets. Founder Aaron Meier died one year later; his partner, Sigmund Frank, then became the principal officer of the business. He had no office; his headquarters were in front of (and in back of) the counters.

A very significant event took place one year later, on April 29, 1887. It was Friday Surprise sale Number 1. After an absence of many years, Friday Surprise is re-born. Today is number 4,255!

FRIDAY SURPRISE

Holocaust memorial brings back more memories of World War II

Several recent events brought renewed focus to a period of my life that in one way had been almost forgotten, but in another way was still very vivid, indeed.

The first was the unexpected, but certainly very welcome, outpouring of calls and letters from dozens of former GIs who wanted to share their World War II stories after my column of several weeks ago recounted some of my more memorable days in an Army uniform during that period.

Then the recent opening of the United States Holocaust Memorial Museum in Washington, D.C., was more than just a passing news story. Once again, the unforgettable mental pictures of seeing firsthand what this new museum is all about flashed through my mind.

So, for the past week, I have searched my memory and my files, in an effort to come up with a few more details of that once-in-a-lifetime military experience.

One of my Portland army friends, interested in finding out more about the convoy that took us from Boston to Le Havre, France, in mid-winter of 1944-45, thought that it would be fascinating to get a copy of any documents in the Pentagon files that related to our troop movements. Although some of the technical language was not very illuminating, there was a rather interesting report

sent by the Convoy Commodore (Capt. O.L. Wolfard, USN) to the Commander of the Tenth Fleet Convoy and Routing Office in Washington, D.C.

The ship that our Division (the Eighty-ninth Infantry) was assigned to for the North Atlantic passage was the *S.S. Uruguay,* a converted passenger liner. It turns out that we were one of the thirty-six ships that sailed in this convoy, a fact that we had no way of knowing at the time.

What we did know was that the weather was pretty awful. The report from the Commodore indicates that it was so rough that one of the ships (*USAT Lakehurst*), with 350 troops aboard, had a cargo of locomotives break loose. The report indicates that the ship was ordered to leave the convoy because it was impossible to secure the equipment safely.

It was also necessary to change the course of the convoy to permit several other ships to secure their cargo. This accounts for some of the changes in direction we only heard about through the grapevine; the other was the change from the original landing target (England) to the French port. German submarines in the area also caused tactical re-routing.

The rough weather resulted in the almost universal seasickness of the troops, stacked five deep in no-ventilation bunk areas. It was a scene that had to be witnessed firsthand to be properly described.

Three and a half months after landing in France, our Division came to a halt just short of the Czechoslovakian border in Saxony. At the Moselle River, we opened a route for the Eleventh Armored Division to slash enemy remnants still west of the Rhine River. In just fifty-seven days of action, Major General Thomas D. Finley's Eighty-ninth Division troops advanced 350 miles and captured 43,512 prisoners.

There were several dates that will not soon be forgotten. One was March 26, 1945, when at three points along the West Bank of the Rhine, our Division pushed off in assault boats at Wellmich, at Oberwesel and at St. Goar. I was in the latter crossing. At the time, frankly, I didn't know where we were or what we were doing. Later I learned that the mission was to secure and hold a bridgehead at any cost.

Another memorable date was April 6, 1945. A village (Eisenach, Germany) that had been converted into a German strongpoint when the Fourth Armored Division bypassed it to take Gotha, was given the worst artillery blasting by our outfit of any town since the Rhine crossing. It was a town where Martin Luther was supposed to have thrown the inkpot at the devil.

We learned later that this drubbing was deliberately administered when surrender negotiations were broken off in mid-conversation upon direct orders from Adolph Hitler. About 35 percent of the town was demolished; the Vorburg Castle, where Martin Luther translated the Bible, was splattered by shrapnel and bullets. The Germans had used it as an observation post.

But the most memorable incident of all took place that same month when our division liberated a large concentration camp at Ohrdruf, where several hours previous to the arrival of the American forces, SS guards had shot all the prisoners who were too weak to move.

About thirty German officer candidates were herded into a closed corner of a large classroom. Most of them spoke good English as well as several other languages. There were American uniforms hanging on the walls, obviously to be used for spy purposes as they tried to infiltrate our ranks.

A search disclosed nearly 3,000 bodies burned and buried in pits north of the camp. A group of German citizens, by order of Army authorities, were made to witness these horrors: including the whipping block, the gallows, and the crematorium.

I will never forget the sight of half-dead prisoners staggering around the Ohrdruf compound. Or the sight of hundreds of bodies, stacked like railroad ties, lying in the ditches. Or the pervasive smell of lime...and death.

It is almost too much to believe that there are still some people who think that all of this did not happen. Hopefully, the horror story of the extermination of 6 million Jews and 5 million non-Jews that is now so graphically portrayed in our nation's capital will cause future generations to pause and remember.

Politics, parades, paving; the news doesn't change

*I*t is Sunday and time to put a few thoughts together. The end of a busy week for many; for others, there is delight in looking forward to a day of relaxation or perhaps some time with the family or in much-needed work in the garden.

It is also the opportunity to spend a few moments digesting the news from the Sunday paper.

A front page story describes an important speech that a very prominent Republican made in Washington, D.C. In it he says that, "Tonight we are reading nobody out of the party. We want all of them in the ranks, and they have the opportunity to establish their claim to Republicanism by that which they shall do in both houses of Congress by helping to enact the legislation which is now before them."

The article goes on to report that the audience stood up and cheered as the speaker declared that his party was not rigid in its demands. It is so broad and liberal that it permits differences of opinion.

Partisanship was mentioned. "It is not that the Democrats are not patriotic or good citizens, but it is that the expression of 'Democratic Party' does not mean a compact, cohesive party of men who can make progress in this country."

Then there was a piece about the new building boom in Vancouver, Washington. Mention was made of a hospital that was being built, about a new theater, a new church, and various city government projects, including a new sewer and improved streets between the city and the military reservation.

A fascinating story about the advisability of making hard-surface improvements on Corbett and other streets in South Portland cornered a good deal of space. A gentleman who represented several area citizens thought that the present improvements on Corbett were ample and that no paving was required. He released a statement to the press lamenting the fact that some citizens had the effrontery to misrepresent the number of persons interested in the improvements.

In racing news from Los Angeles, the headlines told of some sensational new records in stock car competition. Two of the best in the business reeled off mile after mile under the 40-second mark, and completed the ten in 6:35.6.

From Bend, we learned the important business news of the establishment of another bank, and that the great financial prosperity that is following up the Deschutes Valley promises to double the deposit holdings of the local banks before the summer has ended.

There is special excitement coming from the quiet coastal community of Gearhart in Clatsop County. There are definite plans for the opening of a new hotel in this resort community. It will be quite a structure. There will be a seawall; along the top of the wall a twenty-foot-wide park will be built. Publicity releases say that it will become as well known as the famed Boardwalk in Atlantic City, New Jersey. Additional features will include golf links, tennis courts, and rowboats on the Neacoxie and Necanicum rivers.

From the hallowed halls of Congress come reports of a Northwest senator who speaks so much that his peers have become super-critical. The story indicates that when he rises to speak, most of the other senators leave the chamber, and he addresses eighty or more empty chairs.

Of course, Rose Festival time is rapidly approaching. Festival officials have declared that, "The event will be the most wonderful week of amusement and pleasure ever arranged west of the Rocky Mountains." The motor car pageant will include 1,000 decorated automobiles, with some of the cars featuring as many as 5,000 rose blooms.

One of Portland's most prominent citizens indicates that the equestrian parade will be the greatest mounted procession ever presented in the City of Roses.

It was the advertisements in the paper that really caught my attention. What bargains! As a former retailer, I was impressed to see kids' headwear at 25 cents; woolen yardage at $1 a yard; women's stockings at 25 cents a pair; a mattress for $8.95; Hart, Schaffner & Marx trousers selling for $5; a twenty-two-karat gold tooth for as little as $3, and a full set of teeth for $5.

Sounds like a full day of news, eh? Well, my friends, the paper was the Sunday *Oregonian* of April 10, 1910, but many of the news stories could have appeared last Sunday.

The rousing speech in the nation's capital was given by President William Howard Taft before the League of Republican Clubs in the District of Columbia.

Vancouver's building boom included a hospital to be built for $125,000 by the Sisters of Charity of Providence.

The cars involved in the Los Angeles race carried the names of Simplex and Fiat.

At the time of the opening of the new bank in Bend, deposits in the pioneer institution in the city, the First National Bank, had reached the astounding record figure of $200,000.

The big development in Gearhart, which old timers will certainly remember, had a total price tag of $75,000.

And the verbose senator was Senator W.B. Heyburn of Idaho, whose remarks were included in every issue of the Congressional Record for that entire session.

None other than Ambrose Cronin was president of the hunt club that was to put on the great Rose Festival parade; his heirs are still active in Portland civic circles.

The caps for the youngsters, the yardage and the stockings were available from Roberts Brothers (not too long gone from the local retailing scene); the bargain trousers were advertised by Sam'l Rosenblatt & Company at the corner of Third and Morrison streets; the mattress from Wm. Gadsby & Sons; and Dr. Wythe's Dentists, Inc., at 148 Fifth Avenue, could provide the classy teeth.

There is some validity to the oft-repeated statement that the more things change, the more they stay the same.

Fallout from Clinton's haircut may have him pulling it out

*T*here is a big difference between campaigning for an office and performing the duties required upon winning that position. In private business, certainly the same thing is true. Articulating an idea for a new venture, then implementing that plan and running an operation take very different efforts and very different talents.

Some people get their adrenalin going being a part of the tough battles for office. Others enjoy governing. We have a very good example of this with our two present United States senators from Oregon. Before his recent problems, Bob Packwood was very much at home in the rough give-and-take of partisan campaigning. He was good at it: he speaks convincingly, he loves to raise money, and he is tough as nails.

On the other hand, Mark Hatfield does not really enjoy many of the necessary activities on the campaign trail...the unending meetings, the fundraising, the accompanying backslapping. But he does know how to get satisfaction from governing and he has had plenty of experience in the game. It has been his lifetime career.

It was obvious in the last presidential campaign that Bill Clinton really enjoyed the day-to-day demands he faced on the campaign trail. He relished diving into the crowds to shake just two more outstretched hands. He got satisfaction out of criticizing the Reagan-

Bush years. He was at his best when articulating new programs that he wanted to put in place if elected.

On the other hand, George Bush acted as if it was beneath him to have to go out and sell himself once again to the voters. He thought that his previous performance in office was enough to make us vote for him again. Many feel that Bill Clinton did not really win the last contest; George Bush lost it.

Mr. Clinton was no stranger to either the campaign trail or to a major political office. He had been through a number of gubernatorial campaigns, all but one of which was successful. He had served as a rather innovative, and generally quite successful, state chief executive.

Given this background, I find it difficult to understand how our young president, obviously a very intelligent gentleman, has allowed himself to get into such political quicksand.

If it had been just one or two problem episodes, it would be understandable. But there have been quite a number of events for the relatively brief stint in the Oval Office. No definite plan in the Bosnia conflict. All manner of trial balloons for how national health care is going to be funded. Weekly pronouncements and backtracking on a realistic spending and tax program. Uncertainty in implementing his campaign ideas concerning gays in the military.

Then there is the personal side of it

all. Hillary and Bill Clinton have been in the public spotlight long enough to know that perception is a major factor in this business. Not that some of the things that they are being criticized for are all that important, but they do stick in the public's mind. They are much easier to understand and relate to than balancing trillion dollar budgets and implementing complicated health delivery systems.

A $200 haircut in Air Force One on the tarmac at the busy Los Angeles airport? Moving a relative in to organize the White House travel office? Hillary Clinton personally managing stocks in some outfits in the health care business? Come on. It doesn't take a super-sensitive nose to smell the lurking problems in all of these cases.

The underlying difficulty, of course, is the lack of mature judgment by some people surrounding the first couple, and maybe even a bit of the same as far as they both are personally concerned. It is very disappointing, because a lot of folks (myself included) had, and continue to have, high hopes that this pair would provide a much needed breath of innovative air to the musty halls of the White House and Congress. But it's only fair to remember he hasn't even finished half of his first year in office.

It's no secret that the great majority of Americans are middle-of-the-roaders. As such, they are ready to follow nearly anyone who articulates most of their values. They want, as someone has aptly suggested, an individual who acts as the nation's cheerleader. Ronald Reagan, as sleepy as he sometimes seemed, was just that kind of person, someone whom they felt comfortable with. The beltway gang knew that; this is why Reagan was so successful in getting so many of his programs through Congress.

So here comes Bill Clinton with his own agenda, surely a bit left-of-center, but not enough to cause him any trouble at the polls. What does he do about choosing a crew to help him? First he delays any number of important decisions, leaving a good number of the agencies and departments without much leadership. Then he picks some individuals who can't help but be lightning rods to many of those whose support he could use in Congress. Not just Jesse Helms, whose antagonism he could expect, but other less emotional decision makers.

Clinton has compounded his problems by surrounding himself with a sizable number of Washington, D.C., novices. Not a bad idea on the surface, but you need some crafty and experienced warriors around, too.

The results could be predicted. The president is now being accused of lack of focus. Translated, this means he is losing middle America.

We will all be the losers if he doesn't start doing a bit of arm stretching to bring some folks into the fold who have a little bit more grey hair than our leader had clipped the other day at LAX.

FRIDAY SURPRISE

Three pioneers in their fields carved their own Oregon Trail

*T*here is a very good chance that your life, or that of someone in your family, has been touched by the generosity of three pioneer Oregonians whom you probably did not know.

These individuals, all former Portland residents, were a diverse group. The first had only an eighth-grade education but was one of the most successful businessmen of his time. Another put $6,000, which his father gave him to go to college, into a radio repair business that led to the establishment of a world-class electronics firm. And the third was the son of a successful timber baron who began his career sweeping out a pulp and paper mill in Salem without telling his bosses that his father was a major shareholder and director of the company.

But they also had several important characteristics in common: they all were extremely hard workers; they all had a well-defined vision for their businesses and their careers; and they all cared about the people they were associated with and the region that made them eminently successful.

They were Fred Meyer, Jack Murdock and Truman Collins. The foundations that today bear their names, the Meyer Memorial Trust, the M.J. Murdock Charitable Trust and the Collins Foundation, have disbursed hundreds of millions of dollars to good causes throughout the Pacific Northwest.

Fred Meyer was born in 1886 in Brooklyn, New York, the son of a small grocery operator and the nephew of seven uncles, all of whom were in the food business. His first investment in Portland was near the Union Station, where he opened a store and began peddling coffee door-to-door.

Pioneering in a commodity that eighty-four years later was to become one of the "hottest" around, Meyer's operation grew to the point that he had to hire six more salesmen. He then sold his routes and established the Java Coffee Company at First and Washington streets in the old Washington Street Market.

Ever the entrepreneur, Meyer was soon managing the whole market for a 50 percent split of the profits. Evidently the outfit's chairman of the board didn't relish the financial success of this young upstart, and he relieved Meyer of his duties. It was a bad decision. As soon as Meyer left, the market went back into the red.

Next it was an "all package" grocery store at Fifth and Yamhill, where Meyer learned that customers wanted conveniently-sized units instead of buying bulk amounts of sugar and coffee and flour.

One of his off-shoot businesses at the time was called "Mybros" (meaning

Meyer Brothers), so named because of his association with brother Harry. The two of them also negotiated for the franchise of Piggy Wiggly (grocery) stores, but a family disagreement ensued. They went their separate ways.

The rest is history. Today, Fred Meyer stores operate in most every major community in the Pacific Northwest, doing $2.85 billion in volume during the last fiscal year, and employing over 24,000 co-workers.

Fred Meyer was a tough, but benevolent, operator. He relentlessly toured his stores, knocking down tall pyramid displays with his cane because they were not "consumer friendly." He would have none of the trappings of a fancy office. For years, he sat in the middle of an open office next to all of his cohorts. He gave sizable amounts of money to outfits that believed (as he did) in reincarnation. In the end, he directed that his estate be used to establish a trust that in the first ten years of grantmaking provided $105,325,202 to worthy Northwest organizations.

Of the five trustees, two (Oran B. Robertson and Pauline Lawrence) were long-time Meyer employees; one (Gerry Pratt) is a former *Oregonian* columnist and for a time CEO of Fred Meyer Savings and Loan; the other two (Warne Nunn and Travis Cross) held prominent positions in Oregon state government and in major Oregon business and non-profit outfits.

Jack Murdock was a natural soft-sell salesman. His success in repairing Stromberg-Carlson radios in a small shop that he started in 1937 led to an association with an electronics genius, Howard Vollum. This partnership, with the valuable advice of lawyer Jim Castles, led to the establishment of the Tecrad Company in 1948, and then to Tektronix, a leading manufacturer of cathode-ray oscilloscopes. Today, Tek is one of the world's largest electronic instrumentation companies, with annual sales of over $1.3 billion.

Murdock, a life-long bachelor, was not well known in his community. Eventually he moved to Vancouver, Washington, not just for tax purposes but also so that he could live the private life he enjoyed. He was killed in a tragic seaplane accident on the Columbia River in 1971; his body was never found. The Murdock Trust, started in 1975 with assets of approximately $90 million, has awarded 1,818 grants totaling over $174 million. Trustees include Castles, FEMCOR founder Walter Dyke, and Lyn Swanson, founder of a Beaverton high tech firm.

The Collins Foundation, a family operation controlled by Truman Collins' widow, Maribeth Collins; her sister-in-law, Grace Collins Goudy; her daughter Cherida Smith; her niece Lee Collins; and Ralph Bolliger, has given over $51 million to worthwhile local outfits, with Willamette University (Collins' alma mater) a major recipient.

Truman Collins was an exceptionally modest man. One would never suspect, upon meeting him, that he was the heir to one of the proudest names in the nation's timber industry. He was a lieutenant commander in the U.S. Navy in World War II, and served for six years as President of Willamette University's board of trustees.

Today these three foundations, with a strong commitment by their trustees, provide nucleus funds to a host of programs in education, the arts and the humanities for kids and the underprivileged and for health-related causes. Their benefactors would be very pleased.

FRIDAY SURPRISE

Taking a stand guides Hatfield's long service

*O*n the 26th day of this month, Mark Odom Hatfield, Oregon's senior senator, will have the distinction of serving in the august body of the United States Senate for the longest time of any Oregonian in history. The previous record, 9,725 days, was held by the late Senator Charles L. McNary of Salem.

It has been quite a career for this educator, politician and statesman: member of the Oregon House of Representatives, member of the Oregon State Senate, secretary of state, two-term governor, and now in the middle of his fifth term in the "most exclusive club in the world."

I have been an observer and participant in a major portion of his career, as a campaign worker, eight-year volunteer head of the state's economic development program when he was governor, as a dollar-a-year man in Washington for six years, and (until May of 1992) as his chief of staff. This diverse and exciting political trail has been unusually productive, always exciting, unfailingly educational and sometimes rather bumpy.

What kind of a person is this very private, highly intelligent, sometimes controversial man?

First and foremost, he is a superb politician. His early interest in government came mainly from a strong mother, Dovie Hatfield, a self-sufficient and highly motivated lady who earned her stripes as a school teacher in rural Oregon. A keen sense of timing, so important in the political world, seemed to come naturally to this young man, although it was certainly finely honed by time as a political science professor at his alma mater, Willamette University in Salem.

Mark Hatfield's parents (his father was a railroad blacksmith) provided their only child with a fine education, but with no economic base upon which to embark on a public career. Where there have been problems in his political life, many can be directly traced to his lack of personal financial resources. He has been far more skilled in handling multi-billion dollar federal budgets than in trying to balance his own personal checkbook.

Hatfield's strong belief in the sanctity of human life accounts for many of the positions he has taken on issues that have divided his electorate. Although a majority of Oregonians are considered to be pro-choice, the senator has been re-elected each time by rather comfortable margins despite his anti-abortion stance. In his first race for the United States Senate, his then-unpopular anti-Vietnam War views were a major problem in the contest against former Congressman Robert Duncan.

But Mark Hatfield, unlike so many public figures of our time, has never personalized his policy disagreements.

Although on opposite sides in the abortion question and on military aid to Israel, he and junior Senator Bob Packwood have had a good working relationship. Duncan, now retired, remains a close personal friend of Hatfield. The Senator even has kind words to say about one-time opponent Wayne Morse.

This same non-partisan stance is true in the body of the United States Senate. Although Hatfield (the second-ranking Republican) has been on the losing side of many important votes over the years, he enjoys respect from Democrats and Republicans alike. His liberal positions have not kept him from enjoying campaign support from party conservatives like Barry Goldwater and Bob Dole.

One of the toughest early decisions this ambitious young politician faced was whether to enter the 1958 Oregon governor's race. The favorite of the Republican party at that time was long-time State Treasurer Sig Unander. Hatfield knew he would incur strong resentment from party regulars if he filed against their man. He was right.

The decision to enter the battle was made at an off-the-record meeting at the home of Warne Nunn, then a Hatfield staffer in Salem. Present, besides Hatfield and the host, were long-time friend and advisor, Travis Cross, political consultant Ralph Emmons, Salem businessman Lee Ohmart, and several other close friends. The decision to go was not an easy one; it was Hatfield's keen sense of timing that was the determining factor.

Another major chapter in the career of this very durable politician took place at the 1968 Republican National Convention in Miami, where he was under top consideration as a possible vice-presidential candidate with Richard Nixon.

Hatfield was to give one of the seconding speeches for Nixon's nomination. The party higher-ups, however, were very nervous about this because of the senator's strong opposition to the administration's Vietnam policies. I was the liaison assigned to work with then top Nixon aide John Mitchell on the contents of Hatfield's remarks. To say the least, it was a real no-give and no-take battle between two very strong personalities. The senator didn't soften his stand, and Spiro Agnew was named the vice-presidential candidate. How different history could have been!

There is nothing "off-the-cuff" about Mark Hatfield. He is a voracious reader, a student of the lives of all former presidents, particularly Abraham Lincoln and Herbert Hoover, and a keen observer of international politics. Every one of his speeches, every meeting he has with constituents in his office or in the field, is carefully prepared. He is a perfectionist when it comes to facts. He enjoys policy decisions, but abhors nagging personnel matters.

Where does he go from here? Hatfield will be seventy-four years old when his present senate term ends in 1996. It is no secret that his wife, Antoinette, her husband's strongest political influencer, would like to see him close the books on this chapter of his life.

No matter what that decision may be, there can be no question that Mark Hatfield will go down in the history books that he so much loves as one of the most colorful and significant players in twentieth century Oregon life.

FRIDAY SURPRISE

Portland's past peopled with fabulous characters

*T*here are some folks who are truly unforgettable...and Portland has had its share of such characters. Stories about them never seem to fade; as a matter of fact, a number of these ladies and gentlemen take on an almost "bigger than life" reputation after they have left us!

Few, if any, clergymen were better known and better loved in the Rose City than the late Right Reverend Benjamin D. Dagwell, Bishop of Oregon from 1936 to 1958. Full of fun, this very human man of the cloth was a favorite at any gathering. At the same time, he had a serious side that was an inspiration to all who knew him or who had the privilege of listening to him speak.

Bishop Dagwell, a life-long bachelor, made his home at Portland's sedate Arlington Club, in the days when that establishment was a men-only domain. He held court in his quarters on the top floor, receiving friends and parishioners who sometimes wanted spiritual advice, and other times just wanted a good laugh.

I remember calling on this distinguished fellow with a friend, who happened to be a member of the Trinity Episcopal Church congregation. The attendant at the club had been told to announce any of the Bishop's guests. On this occasion, to have a bit of fun, we used the names of two other members of this church with whom the Bishop was well acquainted (no names, please, as the individuals in question are still very much around).

We knew what the response would be when the Bishop thought he would have to entertain the two un-named gentlemen. "Sorry, I'm tied up," came the reply to the embarrassed telephone operator, knowing full well what was going on. The two of us went upstairs to Dagwell's room anyway. Of course, as we suspected, he was anything but busy. He thoroughly enjoyed regaling us with stories of how he liked to pick and choose those who came calling unannounced.

When it was time for any youngster in Portland to learn to swim in the early part of this century, there was just one person whom the mothers and fathers of the era trusted. Her name was Millie Schloth, a buxom, leathered woman whose trademark was an unglamorous black bathing suit and a whistle that could be heard for miles around.

Millie would parade up and down the side of any pool she was visiting, nagging at her charges until they were too exhausted to admit that they were really scared of the water. Some of her pupils went on to take advanced training from the famous Multnomah Club swimming coach, Jack Cody, who sent a number of his more able girls to represent the United States at the 1948 Olympic Games in London.

Speaking of teaching, few Ainsworth Grammar School graduates will ever forget Miss Kate Protzman, the no-nonsense eighth grade teacher in the 1930s whose sole mission in life, it seemed, was to make sure that the young girls and boys in her class knew the fine points of English spelling, punctuation, grammar and the like. If this very stern lady ever smiled, no one could quite remember; however, all will never forget the fact that few, if any, of her students ever failed college English entrance examinations.

Shriners and retailers in the Rose City still talk about R.R. "Rube" Adams, one of the last of the real "feel" merchants of our time. He could look at a piece of merchandise and instantly know the value and the saleability of the product. This man was also an advertising genius. Adams would sit at his desk atop the Friday Surprise store cutting out ad proofs, redesigning page after page to please his practiced eye.

But there was much more to him than just making cash registers jingle. He was as much at home leading an in-store amateur chorus in rollicking songs at co-worker parties as he was at the forefront of the Shriner's All-Star football games, where he probably raised more money for crippled children than any other person in the city's history.

Adams liked nothing better than putting on dramatic fashion shows at the start of each selling season. He would personally direct the models and the lavish entertainment (like a recreated, in-store ice rink) that drew thousands of spectators to his performances. And there was a romantic side to all of this. After a lengthy illness took his first wife, Goldie, Rube Adams married Lina Louise von Schmidt, the top fashion model of mid-century Portland.

Truly a giant of the time was our most unforgettable politician of this century, Tom Lawson McCall. No one played center stage more effectively than this completely public man, whose huge stature and accompanying charm made most Portlanders feel that he belonged right in their living room (he also was a TV commentator) rather than in the governor's chair. Whether it was trying to quiet down his outspoken mother, or marching shoulder-to-shoulder with Democratic opponent Bob Straub on environmental issues, or announcing to the nation, "Come visit Oregon, but for heaven's sake don't stay," McCall was a walking news conference.

Not an Oregon native, but a transplant, feisty Ira Keller quickly left his indelible handprint on the foundations of Portland's Urban Renewal program. Small in stature but big in vision, this industrialist-cum-civic booster was as tenacious an activist as this city has ever seen. We can thank him, also, for seeing (ahead of most of his contemporaries) the importance of a first-class science and technology graduate center in the metropolitan area.

Of course, there were untold others, including Rose Naftlin, who made big cakes famous at her Rose's rendezvous; this newspaper's boss man for many years, E. Palmer (Ep) Hoyt, who went on to become one of the nation's top publishers in Denver, Colorado; and Margaret Malarkey Cartwright Cabell, who reigned for decades as our city's most elegant "grande dame."

The jolly yule elf got a ho ho for wearing a 'mirthday suit'

*I*t isn't even Thanksgiving, but we are already being rather subtly influenced to begin our Christmas shopping. The 19 million people who are employed one way or another in the nation's retail industry are giving us hints on satisfying those holiday lists, and the stores that they represent have all the colored lights and fancy packages set in strategic places to get us in the proper buying mood.

I had not really thought too much about the approaching holidays until a friend asked the other day if I knew where he could get a Santa Claus suit to use for an upcoming party. No problem. I have one that has been carefully packed away for a number of years, since two rather devastating episodes ended my impersonation of the jolly big fellow.

The first disaster took place some years ago at the family department store. At that time, Portland's most attractive and personable young ladies manned the twenty elevators that served the store. As a rather young fellow co-worker, I was excited to be invited to their Christmas breakfast. Just one catch in the invitation: I was to be the entertainment!

What better, I thought, than to appear as the spirit of Christmas himself. But what to do once I was in the proper outfit? Well, I spent days coming up with feeble rhymes that included some colorful interludes in the lives of the ladies who came into contact with thousands of shoppers every day.

In the middle of my presentation my audience erupted into sustained laughter. The stories were not really that funny, it seemed to me. But then...

My Santa Claus outfit included a pillow stuffed in my pants, held together with a safety pin attached to the top portion of my trousers. All of a sudden in the midst of the uproar, I felt a distinct draft in my lower extremities. You guessed it. The safety pin had broken, the pillow had become dislodged, my Santa pants were sitting on the floor. There I was, in my underwear, the boss' son, half naked in front of all those thoroughly amused co-workers. It took several weeks before I was once again able to ride the store's elevators.

The final blow that put the outfit into mothballs was when one of my friend's young sons, age five, did not have the reaction I expected when I awakened him on Christmas Eve fully disguised (it seemed to me) with the proper whiskers and ho-ho-hos. The youngster couldn't have been less excited, and announced to all who were watching the scene that, "Santa Claus sure looks and sounds like Uncle Gerry."

Many things have changed since that time. If you look back a generation or so, you will remember that it was a period when major department stores told us what to wear, how to decorate our homes, what to use for what little leisure time there was. The stores knew their customers; before there were credit cards, many of them simply allowed the customer to sign on their charge accounts. The successful retailers built their reputations on informed service by salespeople who had been there forever. Then, too, the shopper never had to worry about returns; many of the stores would even take back items that they never sold. (I can remember when I worked in the drug and cosmetics department we even gave an unhappy customer credit for the false teeth she returned!)

The retail environment has changed drastically. The emphasis now is on targeted marketing: special stores and sections for the ladies with mature figures or for gentlemen who want to select from the largest possible assortment of athletic shoes.

This has meant that traditional department stores have seen their share of the market drop in several significant and highly profitable areas, like apparel. Along with that, after-tax margins have dropped, and return on net operating assets has decreased by more than half, from 7.7 percent to about 3 percent.

But this is no time to be concerned with such dull figures. It is time to explore the crowded counters and tables of our favorite stores to see what will be prominent on the Christmas wish lists and what we may find under our own trees. To get a proper perspective, I spent last weekend in and out of more Portland area stores and malls than I want to count. I pass along to you my findings:

The kids are going to find dinosaurs coming out of every package under the tree. There are dinosaur figures,

dinosaur tee shirts, dinosaur games. For the folks a bit older, but who still like to play games, the mystery angle will be the biggest hit for Christmas, 1993.

There are mystery jigsaw puzzles, like "The Ghost of Winthrop" or "The Last Chill and Testament" or "Burning Evidence." And if you want to entertain your guests properly, you could ask Santa to bring you some murder-à-la-carte games for your spooky parties. These games, like one entitled "Wall Street Scandal," have their share of the necessary ingredients: blackmail, sex, larceny, deceit and murder. The trappings include cassette tapes that reveal details of the murder, a blueprint of the murder scene, even guest invitations and envelopes.

For those who prefer a bit less stressful recreation, the book stores are filled with stacks of popular titles like Margaret Thatcher's fascinating *Downing Street Years,* and Rush Limbaugh's *See I Told You So.* The sports enthusiast will want Shaquille O'Neal's *Shaq Attaq* and the fitness buff will surely need Joyce Vedral's *Bottoms Up!*

Mother and Dad will want bread-makers and pasta or espresso machines. There is renewed interest in all manner of home furnishings, especially luxury bedding. The price resistance so evident in apparel is absent in merchandise for the home.

But there will be one very significant difference in the Christmas morning scene at many homes. It used to be that Dad was kept busy putting together kids' gifts. This year the kids will be showing their parents how to use all the great electronic gimmicks of the nineties.

Now, more than ever, Oregon needs ingenuity

*O*regonians have been known to be independent folks, not always doing things by the book or operating in the same manner as individuals in other parts of the country.

We have elected a number of politicians with a truly independent streak, although only one Oregon governor (Julius Meier in 1930) won a general election with this label.

With the increasing numbers of Oregonians who are opting out of public life these days (Bob Smith, Mike Kopetski, Ted Kulongoski among them), many are wondering if we will continue to see special people present themselves for public service. Are those with a unique flare, the likes of a Tom McCall or a Wayne Morse or a Dorothy McCulloch Lee going to be willing to face an electorate that seems intent on focusing on the negatives?

One only has to look around our state to see where an unusual touch has made a vast difference. The Oregon Coast is a prime example. How fortunate that Governor Os West put 90 percent of our beaches in public hands years ago.

Then there are the wild and scenic rivers that provide so much enjoyment for boaters and fishermen. (Or should that be fisher-people?) Far-sighted individuals have set aside a multitude of parks throughout Oregon for the permanent enjoyment of residents and visitors alike; few states can equal our inventory. The bottle bill started here. Remember how devoted the late John Piacentini (Plaid Pantries) was to this cause? To make sure that vital parts of our Oregon heritage are not forgotten, special people like Doris Bounds of Hermiston have used their resources to save unusual pieces of our history. Her fabulous Native American collection will soon be available for all to enjoy at the Oregon High Desert Museum.

Oregon air waves have played host to some unforgettable individuals. Surely one of them, a very independent lady, was Peter Mudie, who pioneered a daytime radio talk show for Fred Grubmeyer, more commonly known today as Fred Meyer. Her squeaky voice and rapid patter gave listeners the latest consumer news and was a popular feature of mid-century Portland.

Oregonians are quite independent in their religious practices, too, it seems. Recent surveys by the Ray C. Bliss Institute and the University of Akron revealed that our state has the highest percentage (17 percent) of non-believers in the nation. The average nationwide is just 8.2 percent. Those who analyze figures like these speculate that non-believers may be attracted to the smaller and more rural "frontier" communities.

Where many cities discard their older neighborhoods, Portlanders have taken a special delight in bringing a number of them back to life. The talent and resources of Sam and Bill Naito have made Old Town sing again. Enterprising operators along S.E. Hawthorne Boulevard have made their area one of the most popular eating and shopping districts in the city.

And look what has happened to Northwest Portland! Nob Hill, since the 1880s one of Portland's most colorful communities, has emerged as a prime residential area. As a matter of fact, this neighborhood has more dwellers per block than any other district in the city. The old is remembered by the street names–pioneers like Burnside, Couch, Davis, Everett, Flanders, Glisan, Hoyt and so on. Then there are the great area houses of the early century: among them the Charles Adams (2363 N.W. Flanders, 1904); Bates-Seller (2381 N.W. Flanders, 1908); and Frank Dooly (2670 N.W. Lovejoy, 1901). The new is represented by talented entrepreneurs who have brought some of the city's most popular eating establishments to the district: Besaw's Cafe (2301 N.W. Savier); Foothill Broiler (33 N.W. 33rd Place); Papa Hayden (701 N.W. 23rd); and Zefiro (500 N.W. 21st). In addition, there are first-rate take-outs like the Elephant Deli (13 N.W. 23rd Place) and Marsee's Bakery (1323 N.W. 23rd).

It would be hard to find two more unique merchandising outlets than Michael Powell's huge bookstore at 1005 West Burnside or the unbelievable "gizmos and stuff" at Hippo Hardware at 1040 East Burnside. The folks behind the counters at these two popular establishments are just as independent as those who are making the purchases!

Talking about uniqueness, how about the late Leo Adler of Baker City? He started, of all things, a magazine distribution business in this relatively small community, feeding it with innovative ideas so successfully that when he died a few weeks ago, at the age of ninety-eight, he left a $20 million estate for worthy outfits in his hometown.

When it comes to good causes, we have many who are actively looking for innovative projects. Lee Weinstein, Susan Schreiber, Jackie Gango, Ann Carter, Christina Blackwell, Marty Forsman and others have opened Our Children's Store at 510 S.W. Broadway in Portland. The idea for the project is a very simple one: involve interested children's charities in selling marketable products in one store with all the proceeds going directly back to the charities. The innovators have been joined by First Interstate Bank, KINK Radio and our favorite morning newspaper as sponsors. The Schlesinger family provided space for the store, and Richard Rife donated over $50,000 worth of antiques to help display the merchandise.

The sponsors realized that they could not rely just on volunteer help, so in stepped Mt. St. Joseph's residence, who agreed to a loaned executive program to provide necessary management systems. How great that those who are most concerned with taking care of seniors have joined forces to help the juniors of our community. Hats off to Mt. St. Joseph's Mary Jaeger and Bill Swanson.

If there ever was a time in our state's exemplary history when the independent and the innovative fabric of our society must continue to operate, it surely is now. And a lot of Oregonians have shown us how it can be done.

FRIDAY SURPRISE

Strategies for taking U.S. to the top of the mountain

*L*ast weekend we were treated to headlines that the economy was doing better than expected, people were said to be more optimistic about the future, and the unemployment rate was going down. But before we go out and celebrate, it might be well to digest a few facts and figures.

The experts say that if you really want to put your audience to sleep, bore them with a lot of numbers. But, I'd like to remind them that the rosy outlook heralded by the administration and others can be rather deceiving, at best.

Let's take a look at the budget deficit situation. Remember that our deficit has grown from $994 billion at the start of the Reagan era to $4.4 TRILLION at the time our new president took up residence at 1600 Pennsylvania Avenue. It is predicted that we will add about $255 billion (4.1 percent of our gross domestic product) to this figure this year.

It is important to understand just what the components of the federal budget are: social security (20.5 percent); defense, without the pension factor (17.8 percent); net interest on the national debt (13.1 percent); Medicare and Medicaid (16.2 percent); with the rest made up of a variety of other programs.

The deficit can be difficult to understand. Just whom are we indebted to? Well, governments, like the State of Oregon and City of Portland, own about 18 percent of federal debt securities; for-

eign investors, another 17 percent; the Federal Reserve System, 10 percent; individuals about 9 percent; with commercial banks, private pensions, insurance companies, corporations, and mutual funds holding the remainder.

Just for the record, don't forget that we have been promised balanced budgets/deficit reduction, with great flourishes, at least four times during the past decade.

Several things are worth remembering. The first is that the main problems are entitlements, like Medicare and Medicaid. The second is that debt equals 52 percent of our entire economy. And third, the announcement that certain new programs will be paid for by savings from reduction plans should be taken with a large grain of salt. (The $22 billion that the Senate expects to use for the new crime bill has already been earmarked for two other causes!)

To keep the entitlement problem in the proper perspective, it is well to note that in 1964, with total federal spending at $119 billion, entitlements made up 24 percent of the total. Thirty years later, with federal spending reaching $1,497 billion, entitlements consume 49 percent. In other words, spending on benefit programs has been expanding at the unhealthy rate of 12 percent a year.

What's going on in the rest of the world in budget activity? Japan and Sweden make for some meaningful comparisons.

Japan is the only major power that is presently operating with a government budget surplus. The yen is the strongest currency in the world today, and the unemployment rate in that country is just a little over 2 percent, compared to our 6.4 percent. (Who won World War II?)

Another significant fact is the cost of capital in that country. In October, when the Bank of Japan dropped the discount rate to 1.75 percent, it set a record for the lowest rate ever posted by a central bank in any major country.

On the other hand, in Sweden, where the government is paying its citizens who were unemployed or sick or just wanted to stay home to take care of the kids 100 percent of a Swede's working income, the country's industrial production has plunged 15 percent since 1989, and the jobless rate is 12 percent and rising.

It is easy to lose sight of the human factor when all these bewildering figures are thrown around.

Remember for a minute how many folks have been given pink slips recently: in aerospace, 86,000; in computers, another 86,000; in retailing, 62,000; in food processing and consumer goods, 23,000; in transportation, 12,000; and on we could go. The number of U.S. autoworkers has gone down from nearly 1 million in 1985 to 750,000 today; steel employment has plummeted from 772,000 to 421,000.

I mention all of this to bolster my contention that competition and productivity are two vital areas where we are not doing as well as we should.

Did you know that per-worker output in our country is currently about $20,000 a year less than it would have been if we had maintained the productivity trends in place a generation ago?

If we had continued as we were, the savings rate would have been higher, and so would investment rates. There could also well have been a meaningful decline in our deficit.

How do we go about reaffirming our nation's long-standing leadership in the marketplace? Not easily.

One of the first moves has to be right at the top. Maybe "greed" isn't too strong a word. The earnings of chief executive officers in our major corporations have increased from 33 times the mean income of U.S. workers two decades ago to 157 times the average today. In Japan, the boss man earns no more than 25 times that of his typical worker.

Next we have to push more private-sector competition in a variety of fields where government is inefficient.

Then, cut down the size of government, beginning right on Capitol Hill where 37,000 aides and functionaries set a very poor example for the rest of a nation that must downsize.

Cut down on entitlements or we shall never get out of our monetary maze. One easy place to economize: the latest figures show that 25 percent of all federal entitlements went to households with annual incomes of more than $50,000. Just to get the juices running, consider the fact that our nation's unfunded liabilities—benefits promised to the workers of today in excess of funds available to pay them—total 14 trillion dollars, two and a half times today's already vast national debt.

Finally, we must go on a national diet. We have to stop the unhealthy habit of consuming more than we have actually earned, especially the platters of government largesse for which we have developed a very unhealthy appetite.

What a difference a day makes – a century ago

*W*ell, the latest list of honor is out, and there are a number of familiar names: Chapman School, Marylhurst College, Muir & McDonald, Reedwood Friends Church, Sacred Heart High School in Gervais and Tom Busch Home Furnishings. They have all been around our fair state for at least 100 years.

They join a group of firms founded in the early 1890s, such as Finley's Sunset Hills Mortuary and Cemetery, Gimre's Shoes, Jake's Restaurant, Nielson's Jewelers and the Schwabe, Williamson and Wyatt law firm.

The *Oregonian* leads the list, starting publication in 1850; New York Life Insurance and the predecessors to the *Statesman-Journal* in Salem date to 1851; Holman Funeral Service was founded in 1854; Blitz-Weinhard in 1856; and the parent company of the Friday Surprise (Meier & Frank) in 1857.

What was life like in Portland when Marylhurst College and the others were new? I can't tell you from firsthand experience, although some days that feels possible. But faithful readers plus old letters and stories paint a colorful picture of what it was like in the oft-mentioned "good old days." Do you really think they ever DID exist?

Can you imagine living without information highways, telephone answering machines, jammed freeways, Lorena Bobbitt, unisex earrings and Rush Limbaugh?

A hundred years ago, Portland was THE place for fun and games, not just for the lucky residents, but for folks from all over the state who came to the Rose City to see the bright lights and beautiful ladies, eat great food and take in outstanding entertainment.

The Union and North Bank train stations were busy places (Union Station is still around, of course). For overnight guests, hacks from fancy hotels such as the original Imperial (now the Vintage Plaza), the Oregon and the Benson lined up in front of the stations. Some visitors from The Dalles and Astoria arrived by steamboats that tied up at wharves along the riverfront.

There were several legitimate theaters: the Baker at Broadway and Morrison and the Heilig at 11th and Morrison, where the classiest of the traveling shows played to capacity crowds. Premier seats sold for about $2, in those days the average daily wage for most men. Of course, if you wanted to sit in the back of the house, a 50 cent piece would be adequate.

If you could afford it, the Orpheum at Broadway and Taylor was No. 1 in vaudeville, including great magicians, comedians, animal trainers and gorgeous chorus girls. Admission ranged from 15 to 75 cents.

The Empress at Broadway and Yamhill and the Pantages at Broadway and Alder were for the really big spenders with really important dates. Top price: 25 cents.

A different type of entertainment was available at Oaks Park, on the river, accessible by jumping on a trolley at First and Alder. Admission price was a dime, and that let you to take in a free vaudeville show in the open-air theater.

For motion picture entertainment, all roads led to the Columbia, the Peoples, the Arcade, or the Star (still standing at 9 N.W. Sixth). A shiny nickel would get you in the door.

A.P. Ankeny's New Market Theater opened in 1872 at 50 S.W. Second Ave. The building, restored outside to its old glory, remains. But the vegetable stalls on the first floor and the theater on the second are no more. In the 1890s, there were two places for those with more sophisticated tastes: the Marquam Grand Opera House and Cordray's.

Popular local entertainment included Portland socialites in a program to benefit the Portland Women's Union. They were the forerunner of the popular Junior League follies of the 1920s and 1930s.

Old programs tell of an elaborate Multnomah Athletic Club production of *Babes in the Woods* at the ornate Marquam Grand. The orchestra was under the direction of W. H. Boyer, and male club members took all parts (including women's roles). Some of the names ring a familiar bell, with family members still in Portland: R.T. Platt, C.F. Swigert, Ivan Humason, James H. Murphy, J.D. Malarkey, D.J. Zan and George C. Stout.

Rose Coursoen Reed formed the popular Ladies Chorus in the 1890s; it later became the Treble Clef Club. During the same period, the Portland Symphony Society was formed, and the Portland Art Museum was started with a gift of Greek and Roman casts from Senator Henry W. Corbett.

Dance halls were very much in vogue. The swankiest was Mrs. Foreman's at 19th and Washington Street. Classy cotillions were organized by Portland society, with silver trinkets, bangles, powder boxes and jewels given as favors. The first of the Cinderella parties, held in 1895 at Parson's Hall, had guests arriving in Louis XIV costumes.

The horse and buggy era took a new turn on November 7, 1899, when Henry Wemme, a tent and awning maker, bought a Locomobile from Stanley Bros. of Massachusetts for $600. He made history when it arrived, the first automobile in Oregon. Wemme also bought the first Reo in Portland, the first Oldsmobile, the first Thomas Flyer, the first Pierce Arrow and the first airplane. What a guy!

In 1903, Otto Wilson (his family still lives in Salem) brought the first auto to the Capital City, an Oldsmobile, and pioneered the way for cross-country automobile travel: 61 days.

Speeding soon became a problem, and the Portland City Council did something drastic about it. In 1906, it set up speed limits of 8 miles per hour within city limits and 15 miles per hour outside.

Portland established the first one-way street in Oregon in 1912: Council Crest Drive. The same year, the first gasoline station with a pump was built at the curb at Sixth and Oak streets.

"Good roads still are our greatest need. No development can come without them." Sound familiar? History does repeat itself. These words came from Governor Os West addressing the 1915 Legislature. And, that same year, the first jitney bus was started here. The fare? Five cents.

FRIDAY SURPRISE

Olympic Star Dan Jansen sets pace for all to follow

*L*ast week we were treated to leadership at its very highest level. When Dan Jansen won the speedskating Olympic gold medal, it was the rare individual who didn't have moist eyes. Here was a fellow who, in 1988, while performing as a tribute to his sister who had recently died of leukemia, fell twice. Four years later he did not skate up to snuff, and earlier in this year's games during his specialty, the 500-meter race, he again had an annoying problem.

But not to worry. This obviously sincere, friendly, homespun, talented gentleman showed what it takes to make a comeback at the highest level, thrilling the thousands of spectators in the arena and millions more at home. As he mouthed the words of our national anthem, and scooped up baby daughter Jane in a whirl around the ice, one could not help but think that here was a great athlete, yes, but more than that, a courageous guy from Greenfield, Wisconsin, who had his priorities in order: family, friends, his country, his chosen field of expertise.

What a leadership example for all, young and old. Leadership does not necessarily mean being at the head of a business organization or holding a political office.

One thing comes through loud and clear: the leader must set an example, must not let temporary setbacks deter from finishing the job, must have vision about where he or she wants to go. Boy, does Dan Jansen qualify…in spades.

We are now seeing significant changes in the name plates on the doors of corner suites in some of the City of Roses' largest outfits. A number of familiar names are handing over the keys to the executive washroom to newer and younger players. Most of the replacements have sizable challenges; their ability to inspire associates will be a determining factor in how well the organization performs under a new command.

A forty-seven-year-old power executive from Jackson, Michigan, takes over the reins at PacifiCorp from longtime, in-house executive Al Gleason. Not since Bruce Willison came to town some years ago to take over the driver's seat at First Interstate Bank has anyone arrived with as positive an initial reaction. Willison and his equally personable and talented wife, Gretchen, immediately made their mark in just about every charitable and business oriented game in town. When he left to assume major responsibilities at the home office in Los Angeles, the entire community felt the loss.

Now Frederick Buckman assumes the top job at PacifiCorp, one of our area's major businesses. His credentials are outstanding; those who have rubbed shoulders with him since his arrival say that his friendly and outgoing personality is contagious. His priorities will be in re-emphasizing the importance of the basic business of the firm: power. He is doing all the right things: learning more about his company, meeting his associates in small and large gatherings, finding out about our community structure so he can begin to exert his influence. Lucky for our United Way. This charity needs all the strong hands possible. Buckman is a big supporter.

At U.S. Bancorp, the scenario is a bit different. Roger Breezley, a no-nonsense banker and civic enthusiast, wants to take life a bit easier. In his place, Bancorp's directors (I am one) chose a man who has already spent a lifetime in the outfit. Gerry Cameron is a born-and-bred product of the company, having spent thirty-eight years in a journey to the desk where the buck stops. Cameron's advantage will be not only his knowledge of the bank, but the highly desirable quality that the troops know him well, and respect him highly.

Cameron's big job will be to get Bancorp's expense structure in shape, which is a real challenge in today's climate. Making the bottom line look good, and, at the same time, keeping up the morale of the troops is an awesome job. His leadership talents will be put to the toughest kind of test.

High profile Nike is also witnessing a changing of the guard. Richard Donahue, second man to founder Phil Knight, is trading his running shoes for some more frequent use of his house slippers. In his place comes a talented marketer, Thomas Clarke.

With competitors taking straight aim at Nike's position in the athletic shoe business, Clarke will have his hands full maintaining the Nike mystique so carefully crafted by local ad agency Wieden and Kennedy. As a former retailer, I am

in awe of Nike's success in their specialty, but at the same time I'm puzzled at how poorly they have done in creating a really first-class athletic clothing line. The new man's job will surely be to sharpen up the pants and jackets and sweats, before the competitors eat them alive in this arena.

Changing of the guard at U.S. West Oregon headquarters results from the untimely illness of Marsha Congdon, an executive who literally climbed the pole to success. Her demanding job, in an industry where new players on the information highway are going at breakneck speeds, will be taken by popular back-scenes executive Charles Lenard.

One of Lenard's priorities will be to bring the customer back to the driver's seat in the complex telecommunications business. With all the advanced technology, the industry has forgotten that the person at the end of the line pays the bill. Customers are baffled by the competitive claims and bewildering substitution of buck-passing for service. Lenard has his work cut out.

Ron Tempe will become number one at Standard Insurance when a legendary figure steps aside this summer. Ben Whiteley, one of the nicer of the nice guys, leaves Tempe with the daunting challenge of encouraging a new generation to become career agents in an industry that doesn't project much glamour. With success in operating at lower levels at Standard, and a track record with local charities, Tempe has a formidable start at the leadership hurdles.

Whether it is running a utility, a bank, an athletic gear house, a telephone company or an insurance outfit, the basics are the same. Dan Jansen exhibited them in a dramatic fashion. It remains to be seen if our local leaders take heed.

FRIDAY SURPRISE

Around-the-world jaunt begins in exotic Bangkok

*H*ow about joining me on a twenty-three day odyssey around-the-world? Transportation is by any number of means: jet aircraft, historic train, motor boat, rickshaw, ferry, taxi, motor coach, automobile and ocean liner.

Seventeen hours across the Pacific is not as numbing as it sounds. As a matter of fact, the three major American carriers from the West Coast (United, Delta, Northwest) are so competitive that they do just about everything to make the long journey as comfortable as possible.

A refueling stop in Taiwan breaks up the long haul to Bangkok, Thailand, the exotic southeast Asian city that sits on the banks of the busy Chao Phraya River. There are three words that best describe this intensely pulsating city: people, pollution and patience. One especially needs the latter.

Eight million-plus mainly happy souls inhabit a city that combines magnificent attractions (like the Temple of the Emerald Buddha), huge office towers, a bevy of world-class hotels, unique shopping stalls that offer magnificent silks and unique handicrafts, and fast food outlets that vary from American chains to corner carts. Hundreds of restaurants offer exotic cuisines from Japan, Taiwan, Mainland China, Hong Kong, India, and Malaysia. But it is the native Thai dishes that are so special.

Seven hundred years of indepen-dence has not allowed this capital of the Thai kingdom to accommodate, efficiently, the throngs of motorcycles, bicycles, meter taxis, buses, tuk-tuks (three-wheeled open air taxis), trucks and pedestrians. Gridlock is the way of life. A favorite story of locals involves a private car owner who spots a friend walking down the street. "Want a lift?" the thoughtful driver shouts. "No thanks, buddy, I'm in a hurry!" comes the immediate reply.

Trips across town that should take twenty minutes can become four-hour nightmares. The accompanying exhaust of idling vehicles accounts for the extremely high level of air pollution.

Bangkok lives by water transport. A journey on the klongs, the colorful waterways, provides an immediate insight into the lives of ordinary Bangkok families. What was once a picturesque scene of rural and lush tropical vegetation is now a mish-mash of stilted shanties, tourist-grabbing markets, offices and apartment structures, nestled between rice paddies and banana trees. It is not unusual to see members of klong families bathing, washing clothes, scrubbing eating utensils, dumping garbage and urinating in the same pollution-filled water.

The most memorable part of a visit to this intriguing land is the contagious friendliness and graciousness of the people. To lose one's temper is considered by Thais to be the ultimate in bad manners. Smiles are the order of the day. Their attitude is summed up in their words "mai pen rai." Translated: no problem, never mind, tomorrow will do.

On to Singapore. There are plenty of ways to get there from Bangkok, but none as nostalgic as the Eastern & Oriental Express train, conceived and operated by the same outfit that revived the Simplon-Orient-Express in Europe several years ago. The journey of 1,207 miles down the Gulf of Thailand and through Malaysia to the tip of the peninsula is the culmination of a dream come true for James Sherwood, chairman of Orient-Express hotels.

Sherwood had been on the lookout for suitable rolling stock for a new luxury train for some time. His opportunity came when he discovered thirty-one unused, Japanese-built sleeping and restaurant cars from the Silver Star and Silver Fern trains that ran between Auckland and Wellington, New Zealand.

This ambitious entrepreneur bought the rolling stock for just $3 million, but it took ten times that much to convert the carriages into a twenty-two-car train capable of carrying 130 passengers on the forty-two-hour trip. Forty crew handle the operation, which includes white-linen tablecloth service in the two dining cars.

The setting is tailor-made for the background of that great movie *Murder on the Orient Express*. There is live piano music in the bar car, aging matrons showing off their best 1890s jewelry to mysterious looking business types, and modern couples splurging on a memorable honeymoon experience.

In addition to the once-a-week trip each way between Singapore and Bangkok, there are overnight excursions from Singapore to the spice-trading port of Malacca in Malaysia, as well as from Bangkok over the infamous bridge on the river Kwai to Wang Po and on to Ayutthaya, the ancient capital of Thailand.

What a contrast it is between the crowded and disorganized city of Bangkok and the orderly life of tiny Singapore. Here the authorities control the traffic congestion by charging a daily fee to all vehicles entering the inner city.

Besides being one of the largest and busiest ports in the world, Singapore is noted, along with Hong Kong, as a non-stop shopper's paradise as well as a premier hotel destination. Dozens of huge shopping malls teem with throngs of visitors, who soon find few remaining bargains in this legendary merchant town.

Visitors are quickly warned about the rules of life here. The cost of being caught with a firearm or drugs is death; if it is just a knife or a sharp object, seven years and a dozen lashes. The result: an almost crime-free community. Could we learn a lesson?

If there is just one special place to see, it is the completely restored Raffles Hotel, the grand old lady of the East. The hotel dates back to 1887; it was just one year later when Rudyard Kipling dined here on his own round-the-world journey. It was too early for him to try a Singapore Sling, the fabled house drink that was created by a Chinese bartender in 1915. The whole place reeks of romance.

Next stop: India. Then on through the Indian Ocean, the Arabian Sea, the Red Sea, and the Middle East. Stay packed.

FRIDAY SURPRISE

From amazing India to the ancient kingdom of Sheba

*L*ast week's "Friday Surprise" traced the first leg of a round-the-world adventure, starting in Thailand and proceeding on to Singapore. This week takes in the underbelly of Asia; the final portion of the twenty-three-day experience–through the Suez Canal, the Middle East and Europe–comes next week.

Overwhelming is perhaps the most accurate word to describe India. A country that claims over one-fifth of the world's population, a nation that is unequaled in its variety of races, religions, languages, food, clothing and contributions to the arts, literature and medicine, India is indeed a very special experience.

After eight visits to this legendary land, it would be natural to assume that the odors and the colors and the poverty and the suffering would not seem quite so overwhelming. But the opposite is true. India last week was just as fascinating as it was during my first visit over a quarter of a century ago.

Watching the snake charmers, bartering with the nimble merchants, and walking among badly handicapped street youngsters whose mothers used them as come-ons for begging brought back vivid memories of unique times here.

Surely one of the saddest cities in the world, Calcutta's litany of problems seems unending: overcrowding, power cuts, protests, traffic jams, unemployment. But now there are worries over a new problem...or maybe an old one that no one has paid much attention to. Noise pollution. This grand city of imperial India is slowly, inexorably, turning hard of hearing. The city's average sound level is over 75 decibels, about the level most industrial factory workers are subjected to at their workplaces. Such intense sounds could only happen in this country!

I have been in Calcutta four times over the years. Spending time in this teeming bazaar with Mother Teresa somehow renewed faith in our fellow human beings. Here is an aging, frail saint of our time administering to the homeless, to abandoned children, to lepers. Even though her undertakings seem impossible, there is always a platter of love being offered to all with whom she comes in contact.

Then there was a visit with Mrs. Indira Gandhi when she was Prime Minister. How is it possible for any one person to govern a nation so torn by diversity? She was one tough lady; it was obvious that political responsibilities weighed heavily on her shoulders. My time with her was in the company of Senator Mark Hatfield, who was visiting India some years ago on a government assignment. I well remember the early morning session, with the silk-clad Indian leader obviously suffering from severe stomach cramps. Who wouldn't, with such enormous problems to deal with day after day.

Bombay last week was still a colorful mecca, the industrial and business hub of India, its second-largest city, and one of the world's great ports.

In a society of planned marriages, the city's leading English language newspaper publishes a section entitled "Lifemate" where eligible men and women in their search for a bride or groom list colorful descriptions before someone else does it for them. Last week, one asked for responses to a plea for a "beautiful educated homely Bengali Brahmin girl within (sic) twenty-four for a Naval officer posted on land." One can only presume that his mailbox was filled the next day!

A week at sea was quite a change from the heart-wrenching scenes of the sub-continent. There was nothing but blue sky and calm waters in the Arabian Sea as we sped toward the Gulf of Aden.

As wondrous as the ancient sights of India, the wonders of modern navigation seemed almost as incomprehensible. Here we were, in the middle of a massive body of water, navigating by satellite. The legendary ship's wheel was no more (although I did see a small one that looked as if it belonged on an automobile). But there were telephones, FAX machines, television sets with four channels, VCRs, yogurt machines–all the trappings of modern life.

Ships need fuel just like automobiles, so a stop was necessary at one of the most remote Middle Eastern nations: South Yemen. If you get out your world atlas, you will note that this tiny outpost occupies a prime location for shipping en route to the Red Sea and on to the Suez Canal; thus, its importance over the years during war times.

Aden was once part of the ancient kingdom of Sheba. Later, the seventy-five-square-mile city-state was controlled by the British. They were driven from the area in 1967; shortly thereafter, South Yemen was formed with Aden as its capital. Neighboring North Yemen, with a larger population, has had a sometimes rocky relationship with its sister Muslim state.

Government, business and personal travels over the years have taken me to over 130 countries and territories on all seven continents, but I can honestly say that I have seen few as poor and desolate as South Yemen. It surely would not be on any list of recommended stops for vacation travel.

Despite recent oil discoveries, and a strategic location, the country is the poorest in the Middle East with the highest infant mortality rate and the lowest literacy rate in the region. Because of Yemen's sympathy with the Iraqis in the Gulf War, Saudi Arabia expelled one million Yemeni guest workers; this has cost the country over $1 billion in annual remittances.

Everywhere on this diverse and ever-changing planet one learns something new about how people adjust to their unique surroundings. In Yemen, it is qat. These are leaves, chewed by the natives, that produce a pleasant, euphoric effect that provides an instant happy feeling and a sense of intellectual power before depression sets in. In this unbelievably remote land, one can understand the need. Over their daily qat sessions, the Yemenis will smile and tell you that they never give up hope for something better. Amen to that.

FRIDAY SURPRISE

Mouth-watering memories of old Portland eateries

*I*f you were going out to dinner in Portland on May 19, 1894, chances are you would have ordered oysters for the special occasion. In those days, Portland had a number of colorful restaurants and because of the popularity of this seafood treat, most all of them featured this delicacy on their menus.

You might have tried Cram & Groski, at 1711 Third Street, where they served oysters and ice cream all day and all night. The nearby Broiler, at 127 Fourth Street, also served oysters (and steaks) day and night. So did Rasmussen's Cafe, at 268 Alder Street, where proprietor A. Rasmussen held court. The Knickerbocker, at 108 Fourth Street, operated by the Haehlen Brothers, also billed itself as an oyster and coffee house.

After dinner, a big night out one hundred years ago would have included a visit to Cordray's New Theatre. Covering a quarter block at Third and Yamhill, this showhouse was billed as the "favorite amusement resort of Portland, Oregon." The proprietors and managers were John F. Cordray and O.A. Wass, and they made sure that everyone who came to their establishment behaved properly!

The seats for the opera, comedy and drama performances fetched thirty cents, forty cents and fifty cents, while the fancy box seats, only for the really big spenders, were sixty cents. It was duly noted that children occupying seats must pay full price; mothers and fathers were reminded that the seat is what they were charged for, not the size of the child!

There were more explicit rules. Profane or boisterous language was not tolerated. Intoxicated or improper characters were not admitted to the auditorium. Customers were warned that anyone who did not comply with the rules of the house should not be surprised if they were invited by a house police officer to vacate immediately.

I think that I can even remember the house telephone number: 694. And, happily, there were no answering machines or recorded voice mail choices. US West: take note.

A sparkling evening performance might have included the Montaliens (Swedish specialists), Frank Gardner (comedian), Baker and Brown (merely listed for selections), and George Harrison (German impersonations) in a program directed by one Silas Robinson.

Just as sourdough French bread has been a trademark of San Francisco for decades, so have oysters played a significant role in the gastronomic history of our city. In 1907, Louis Wachsmuth carted boxes of live crabs, live lobsters from the East, shrimp and all kinds of fish and oysters into the City Oyster Company at 252 Ankeny, right next to the present location of his Dan & Louis' Oyster Bar. Louis and his partner, L. Roland Mills, started a business that would become a long-running favorite for seafood-loving Oregonians.

Some years later, in 1930, a young newspaper travel editor, the late Edward Miller, joined the staff of the *Oregonian*. His contemporaries told Miller about oyster expert Louis Wachsmuth. As Miller was an oyster enthusiast, he and the Oyster Bar owner became fast friends.

Miller took a trip to the Yaquina Bay oyster farm and later wrote a column for his paper describing the operation. Wachsmuth told Miller, who was later to become the Managing Editor of the *Oregonian,* that the best way to eat oysters was, of course, to consume them alive!

Portlanders have had love affairs with many old-time restaurants. There was the wonderful green apple pie at Roberts Restaurant. At the McCoy Coffee Shop, individual two-cup coffee pots were plugged in right at the table. Special occasions called for dinner at Kelly's Restaurant on Broadway. Waiters wheeled around a soup tureen to make sure there were no empty bowls; their dessert cart was the talk of the town. The Coffee Cup on lower Broadway had a huge namesake outside complete with rising steam. Stories abound about the magnificent display of goodies at the inside buffet for those with massive appetites.

If you took the train from Astoria to Portland, the parlor car steward, Sherman Dennis, served a tasty gourmet dinner, complemented by white tablecloths and sparkling silver.

Some of the better known eating houses of mid-century Portland have now disappeared from the scene. Bill's

Gold Coin, West Burnside at 20th Place, had great Chinese food and a very colorful clientele. Bogaard's, also on West Burnside, was one of the few true Indonesian restaurants in the United States in those days. Now, of course, Indonesian fare is popular everywhere. The Golden Knight, in the Multnomah Hotel, was a gourmet paradise. A real dinner in this famous room would last up to three hours.

The city's best-known personalities would meet at the twenty-four-hour Hoyt Hotel restaurant for great steak dinners. Impresario Harvey Dick was usually on hand to recount tall tales of his past in the beautiful, gaslit saloon.

Also very popular in mid-century Portland were the Hazelwood establishments. These elegant houses, one on S.W. Washington Street and the other on the east side, are still remembered by history-prone citizens of the City of Roses. The dining rooms were complete with palms, an orchestra and a busboys' quartet.

Eleanor Tunno of Portland tells stories of her father, who started as a busboy, rising up the ladder to become candymaker and later a soda jerk at what was officially known as the Hazelwood Cream Store.

A century ago, you could also have had some fine oysters at the predecessor of Jake's Famous Crawfish Restaurant, an outfit that is now celebrating 102 years of feeding hungry Portlanders. These are expanding times for Jake's, with their much-anticipated new Grill at the Governor Hotel scheduled to open next month. Specials will maintain Jake's famous seafood traditions, with a number of meaty additions. Our great-grandparents would feel right at home!

FRIDAY SURPRISE

Oregonian adds his voice to London conversation

*I*t was a propitious time last Friday in London to gather together a group of Cambridge University classmates from all over the world. That morning's *Times of London* reported on the front page that Cambridge University, for the third straight year, was named Britain's best university, beating out its ancient rival Oxford (Bill Clinton, take note) and the dozens of other institutions of higher learning in this country.

Assembled around the table at the rather musty Oxford and Cambridge Club on Pall Mall in central London were old friends, most of whom had distinguished themselves since graduation as captains of industry throughout the British empire, as leading physicians in the nation's public health program, as educators and lawyers, and some, as members of the British parliament. As the only American from our college (Trinity Hall) at that period, there were no other voices from the United States to answer the bevy of questions that ranged from the state of American television shows to what was happening to the media in our country to an evaluation of the present occupants of the White House.

In London, the American influence is still obvious everywhere. There are plenty of Wendy's and The Gap and American movies. Clothing styles reflect our tastes, and menus feature a number of typically American dishes.

But the strong British institutions haven't changed very much. There was majestic Buckingham Palace, where the changing of the guard still takes place. The London theater is very much alive and kicking, with a fair number of familiar musicals, but also features some great local and French comedies. We particularly enjoyed one titled *Don't Dress for Dinner*, considered to be one of the most skillful examples of the type of light fare popularized in France as Boulevard Comedy. Many London theaters are small and intimate, giving the audience a feeling of being a part of the action on stage.

The famous Claridge's Hotel used, for almost one hundred years, as a pied-à-terre by some of the world's most illustrious names, still reigns as the city's premier lodging facility. Harrods, a store renowned for immense stocks and quality merchandise, was as exciting a shopping destination as ever. The store's unique food halls were filled with an unbelievable assortment of every kind of cheese, meat, bread, candy and fresh produce imaginable. The only addition to the store was a noticeable number of security personnel, perhaps necessary because of recent bomb threats connected with the troubles in Northern Ireland.

As one might well expect, politics was subject number one at the dinner.

A major election takes place in early June to determine British representation in the new European parliament. Candidates from the three major parties (Labor, Conservative, Liberal Democrat) have differing views on where European unity should be headed. The general consensus was that a type of federal system, not unlike our own, rather than a strong central European parliament, would win out.

At home, Prime Minister John Major, who has seen his popularity slide even though the country's economic health is improving, remains a lackluster leader. Whether his Conservative party can win the next election remains very much in doubt.

On the Labor side, the death of popular politician John Smith was a real shocker. The leading contender now for party leadership is Tony Blair, a man noted for his youth, vigor and modernity. There is talk that a popular member of parliament, Margaret Beckett, might be the ideal number two on such a ticket. The last female leader, Margaret Thatcher, remains much more popular in our country than she does in her native land.

As one of our dinner partners was a native of South Africa, it was only natural that current events in that country occupied some of the evening's conversation. This gentleman, Duchesne Grice, a prominent lawyer and bank board member from Durban, who has been a Portland visitor, called the recent election a "miracle." He pointed out that it was unique, indeed, for a sitting government to give up power, and that is exactly what has happened in his country. President Nelson Mandela faces a tremendous challenge, especially in the education and job sectors, in a country where large population increases make employment difficult for the nation's young people.

After the euphoria of the recent election wears off, Grice predicted that his country would see more cases of sporadic violence, similar to what has been going on in Northern Ireland. Although those responsible for recent outbursts are a part of a relatively small group, there is still a reservoir of fear and prejudice among a certain element in that nation.

The Oregon Health Plan was well known by the members of the medical community who attended the dinner. Hearing them talk was not much different than listening to conversation in our own country about the ever-increasing costs of providing decent health care for the majority of the population. Although government-paid health care is available to all citizens in England, there is still the overriding question of how much can be spent for individual treatments, and who receives priority care.

It was pointed out that the Oregon tourism industry might take note that in Britain the number of tourists visiting gardens has risen by nearly 80 percent in the past seventeen years, as amateur horticulturalists seek inspiration from professional displays. Over 17 million folks visited gardens in Britain last year; their popularity is increasing at twice the rate of museums, wildlife parks and historic properties.

Despite differences (elevators are lifts, wash cloths are face flannels, sweaters are jerseys, desserts are sweets and the English phrase for keeping one's spirits up has a very different meaning for us), the Brits remain our most loyal and trusted friends in today's complex world of geopolitics.

FRIDAY SURPRISE

Green fields of N. Ireland seen through bulletproof windows

*W*hy in the world are you going to Northern Ireland? This was the usual question recently when I mentioned that I had a trip planned to that part of the world. "Don't you know that they have some serious problems over there?"

Yes, I did realize that there was unrest in the region, but I wanted to have a chance to understand the problems firsthand. In addition, one of my Cambridge University classmates is now a key player in the judicial system of that country, and I looked forward to the opportunity of visiting with him and seeing a bit of his homeland.

When Lord Justice John MacDermott and his wife arrived at the Belfast airport to pick me up, I sensed immediately that all was not well. The jolly, outgoing Dickenesque figure (he is six feet, four inches tall with bushy white hair at the temples) was certainly preoccupied. He had reason to be.

Just before leaving his chambers that day, the justice and his associates had been the target of another terrorist attack. He related the all-too-familiar scene as if it was a matter of daily life in a country that outwardly seems so quiet and peaceful and satisfied.

Three suspected IRA members had heaved a bomb over the fifteen-foot high security fence into the Law Courts building area, where construction was underway for more security facilities.

Nine workmen and a passerby had been injured by what the locals call a "coffee jar" bomb: one loaded with explosives that detonates upon impact, wickedly throwing its content of nails over a wide area.

As if that was not enough to unnerve Lord MacDermott, that same evening a Royal Air Force Boeing-built Chinook helicopter crashed just across the water in Scotland, killing at least twenty-nine members of the armed forces and the Special Branch, the outfit that is charged with intelligence in anti-terrorist control. The worrisome part of the tragedy, besides the loss of life, was the amount of valuable insight these individuals had about the troublemakers throughout Northern Ireland and in the Republic of Ireland to the south. Officials in Belfast could not understand why so many of their most informed agents were aboard the same aircraft.

During my entire stay with the MacDermotts, there were security people with him at all times. Several agents guard his home day and night, bulletproof windows have been installed in his residence and at no time is he allowed to go out of his home unaccompanied by an armed guard. How do he and his wife cope with this unusual life? Well, he says, it has been the pattern for over twenty years and one just gets used to it.

Security is big, big business in

Northern Ireland. Most public buildings have installed special barriers or barbed wire fences. Airport checks are exceedingly thorough. Even in the smaller country villages, armed personnel periodically check cars going in and out of city centers, likely targets for terrorist activity.

Northern Ireland receives an annual subsidy of over $5 billion from the British taxpayer. Of this, about $2 billion is for security, including a sizable amount for terrorist damage. Every man, woman and child in England, Scotland and Wales is paying about $30 a year in extra tax just because of these problems.

To complicate the situation, there are also loyalist terrorists in the country. They have committed many more murders in the past three years than their better-known adversaries, the IRA.

No one seems able to be very optimistic about a satisfactory solution for the violence. It is really not a religious issue of Protestant versus Catholic, but more a clash of lifestyles that have exceedingly different historic roots. Many residents of Northern Ireland are unable to answer the question so often put to them by foreigners: where is your real allegiance? Are you Irish? Or are you a Brit?

The only thing that all agree upon is that a cessation of violence has to be permanent. There must be verification of the handing over of arms. Informed leaders say that there is little point in attempting to bring people into political dialogue if it is done on the basis of "we'll give it a try, and if it doesn't work, we'll go back to the bombs and the bullets."

On more pleasant subjects, life in Northern Ireland, especially in the magnificent green countryside, is exceptional, casual and relaxed. The Irish are great sports enthusiasts. They have many opportunities to participate in and watch athletic events. Food prices are reasonable, the economy is healthy, good housing is affordable.

One of the most unforgettable experiences during this visit was an overnight stay at Jamestown House, located several hours west of Belfast, near Ballinamallard, in rural County Fermanagh. Here Arthur and Helen Stuart preside over a one hundred-acre country haven that was built in 1760. In the midst of a lush lakeland, the place has to be heaven for the outdoor enthusiast. Pheasant, duck, snipe, woodcock, trout and salmon are all available nearby. So is golf and horseback riding. Their table can only be described as bountiful; best of all, the price is right, starting at thirty-five dollars per person per night, bed and breakfast. My advice: get packed. No blarney!

There is a contagious charm and sincerity about these Irish folks. One cannot imagine a people more alien from terrorism. But who is going to come up with the magic answer?

Citizens in the limelight held to different standard

*T*here is a temptation to regard some celebrities, sports stars, politicians, television and movie personalities and other prominent individuals as somehow larger than life. They live differently, they aren't subject to the day-to-day stresses that the rest of us face, they don't put their socks on one at a time like everyone else does. Oh, yeah?

Surely this kind of a scenario was exhibited in the extreme last weekend with the unbelievable, and tragic, end to the star-studded career of football great O.J. Simpson. "The Juice" had millions of television viewers glued to their sets as the chase over Los Angeles freeways ended with the hero handcuffed and taken to a nine-foot by seven-foot jail cell with only a toilet, sink and bunk for conveniences. Quite a difference from the multi-million dollar digs he had been used to.

The general reaction seemed to be one of sincere sympathy for the Simpson children, whose life will never be the same. But more than that there was a feeling of disbelief. How could this man who had captivated millions, first on the gridiron and then running through airports, commit such a heinous crime? Was he a victim of fame and adulation, or was he so human that something snapped and he became a killer in a personal struggle of a far different type than the football struggles he

had conquered before?

There are many who question the activities of the Los Angeles police department. Why had they dealt so softly with his previous domestic violence? How could they have allowed him to escape momentarily this time? Was it because of that celebrity awe factor?

But it is not just in violent episodes like this that we exhibit special feelings about folks in the limelight.

Recall the tremendous outpouring of respect for Jacqueline Onassis a few weeks ago. With the exception of a particularly nasty piece in one of the London papers, there was a genuine sense of respect for a lady who had, with great dignity, served as an example of unbelievable strength after the assassination of her husband. She had raised two children in the glare of public lights, and had done it very well.

No matter if she didn't speak, only smiled, when passersby on the streets of New York would greet her. She was a celebrity. But how could such a special person, with beauty, means and position, be taken away so suddenly? That just happens to people and families we know in our own lives. Mrs. Onassis was a celebrity, therefore supposedly somehow different.

The other evening, I was invited to a small dinner in Portland to hear former Federal Reserve Chairman Paul Volker discuss the current economic outlook. In the business world, this towering giant (in height as well as position) is considered very much a VIP. When he predicted, in a very upbeat fashion, that the current outlook was "too good to be true," there wasn't a challenge from the assembled banking luminaries. Most any one else would have been severely challenged, but not Volker. With his name in the papers for years as THE voice of fiscal fact, how could he possibly be wrong? In the world of high finance, he is indeed a celebrity.

When I was starting out in the retail business, it was my ambition to meet presidential counselor Bernard Baruch. You remember: he was the man who sat with our nation's leaders on a park bench in Central Park in New York, dispensing pearls of wisdom to the occupants of 1600 Pennsylvania Avenue. Through the courtesy of then-Governor Mark Hatfield I did indeed have the thrill of visiting with Baruch...not on a park bench, but in his apartment at the Waldorf Towers in Manhattan. I was scared to death. What in the world does one talk about with a man so filled with great knowledge?

It turned out that this distinguished statesman was easy to be with. There was no pretense. There were no outward signs of his tremendous mental capacity. But there was common sense in abundance, and this was his genius. There was an aura of fame around him. No matter how down-to-earth he seemed, he was someone very special: a celebrity in his own way.

Different people handle their celebrity status in different ways, as the Simpson tragedy illustrates so well. Media attention can be addictive. Peter Jennings, a man whose face is instantly recognizable to millions of television viewers, is secure enough to have time to greet most everyone personally. Katie Couric, one of the most talented and attractive personalities on the tube, is just as pleasant in person as she is on the box.

On the other hand, for whatever reason, Tom Brokaw comes across as arrogant and I-don't-have-time-for-you. The late Danny Kaye, in person, had to be one of the rudest individuals I have ever encountered. Ronald Reagan charmed everyone by being totally unimpressed with his status; his wife, Nancy, was just the opposite. Again, I guess we expect too much from some of the folks who are so much in the limelight.

In Oregon, happily, we have had a tradition of very approachable politicians. The great majority of them are comfortable to meet and generally pleasant to be around. Governor Barbara Roberts, despite the beating she has taken recently in polls, remains one of the state's most charming individuals in public life. Former Governor Bob Straub, now enjoying an active retirement life at his rural Salem home, is one of the most down-to-earth public officials this state has ever elected. Ditto for former Governor Vic Atiyeh. Celebrity status certainly hasn't gone to the heads of any of these leaders.

If there is anything to be learned from the pressures and intense scrutiny our prominent citizens are subjected to, it is that they are being held to a higher standard than the rest of us. Whether or not this is correct, it is a fact of life in modern-day America.

Perhaps before we are so quick to question and criticize, we might place ourselves in their positions. How well would we handle the heat in the kind of kitchen in which they work?

Serving Oregon a way of life for Otto Frohnmayer, family

*L*ast week, over lunch with the legendary Otto Frohnmayer, there were few signs of his years of service: he is eighty-eight years young, as trim and as sharp as ever and, just as significant, as involved and as concerned with the well-being of his state and nation as he has always been. Our lunchtime companions, all long-time professionals and golf buddies of Frohnmayer, look up to him as their shining example of how one can blend family, profession, and community together...and do it all effectively with style and grace.

Frohnmayer's family came to this country from Goppingen, Germany, in 1906; his father soon became a toolmaker for the old Portland Railway Light and Power Company.

The younger Frohnmayer started his career as a bellboy at Portland's Washington Hotel. Soon his talents were recognized: he was promoted to become the hotel's night clerk.

A college degree was the most important goal for this aspiring young man, and in the mid-1920s he enrolled at the University of Oregon in Eugene. To make ends meet, he first ran the elevator at the Eugene Hotel, later using his experience to become the night clerk. It was a full day for this hard-working student: working at the hotel from eleven in the evening until seven in the morning, then attending classes until noon. Rest and sleep were in short supply, but Frohnmayer's ability and devotion to his career were immediately obvious. He became a hotel auditor, then a day clerk, finally graduating from the university in 1929.

After a short stint with Pacific Gas & Electric Company in San Francisco, Frohnmayer came back to Eugene to pursue a law degree, which he received in 1933, graduating at the top of his class. His beginning salary as a law clerk that year was forty dollars a month.

The next several years were spent learning the ins and outs of the legal world, but more importantly commuting between Medford and McMinnville in a long-distance courtship with the lady who has been his loving partner for over fifty-eight years.

Marabel and Otto Frohnmayer raised four children; each one has become distinguished in his or her own chosen field.

Probably the best known of the clan is David, now the acting president of the University of Oregon, a former state attorney general, and one-time candidate for Oregon governor. He and his wife, Lynn, have had serious medical problems with their children. In typical Frohnmayer style, they have been an inspiration to all around them in their constant search for solutions to the problems that they, and other families around the world, have faced with fanconi anemia. David's father makes no bones about the fact that he hopes he lives long enough to see his son a member of the United States Senate.

Son John made headlines for several years when he served as Chairman of the National Endowment for the Arts in Washington, D.C. It was not a happy experience; the job, at best, is a controversial one with the administration and the Congress constantly taking potshots at the agency's leadership and operation. John is now doing a good deal of writing and speaking, besides keeping his musical talents in good order.

All of the Frohnmayer children inherited their musical ability from their mother. Son Philip is a professor of music at Loyola University in New Orleans, and daughter Mira Jean is a professor of music at Pacific Lutheran College in Tacoma, Washington.

Who was the elder Frohnmayer's role model? Not surprisingly, the late Glenn Jackson of Medford, probably the most influential Oregon citizen of this century. It was Jackson's unselfish approach to civic leadership that caught his townsman's eye; it was also the uncanny ability that Jackson had never to show any signs of anger, no matter how tense or difficult a situation might be.

Frohnmayer's own list of civic accomplishments has gained him the title of "Mr. Southern Oregon." One of his proudest accomplishments has been the progress of Medford's Rogue Valley Memorial Hospital. In 1937, along with his former employer, attorney Porter J. Neff, Frohnmayer helped convert a struggling private hospital into a nonprofit community facility. Over the years, he has chaired numerous drives to bring needed expansion money to the hospital. He still serves on the foundation's board of directors.

Not long ago, Otto and Marabel Frohnmayer gave six acres of prime property to the city of Medford for an expansion of the Donahue-Frohnmayer Park. Other community involvements have included serving as a director of the Oregon Community Foundation, the Medford School District, the Northwest Hospital Service and Oregon Health Sciences University and serving on the Oregon State Bar's Board of Governors.

Nearly every major political candidate of the past several decades has come to Medford to ask the blessings of this gentleman who has so much common sense and practical wisdom to offer. They are rarely disappointed. Republican or Democrat, liberal or conservative, if they have the right stuff, Otto Frohnmayer will support them.

Today he stands even taller than his imposing 6 feet, 1 1/2 inches.

Oregon's visionary leaders mark places in history book

*W*hen the history of the twentieth century in Oregon is written, who will appear on the cover as the man or woman of the century? Who has been the most significant individual, the one whose accomplishments have had the most positive effect on our state?

It is only natural, I suppose, to look first at the politicians. They certainly have been the most visible, and have been in positions to do things that have had a lasting influence.

If we go back to the early 1900s, we see the important work of the Direct Legislation League and the Progressive politician W. S. U'Ren. His role is all the more significant at the present time, when we have so many initiatives appearing on upcoming ballots.

U'Ren and his followers were the ones responsible for passing the initiative and referendum bills in 1902, the direct primary in 1904, a corrupt practices act in 1908, and the recall in 1910. The Oregon tradition of direct participation in the electoral process was thus put in place; we have provided a model for other states ever since.

These days, we take for granted the number of women who are serving in prominent positions in government; it hasn't always been that way, of course. Over the years, there have been some outstanding women in political office in our state. Nan Wood Honeyman, elected in 1936, was Oregon's first female representative in Congress. Edith S. Green from Portland, a former school teacher, served with distinction in the House of Representatives for twenty years (1955-1975). Our first woman mayor in Portland was Dorothy McCulloch Lee, who assumed office in 1949. She was credited with running a very ethical administration.

The third woman to serve in the United States Senate was Oregonian Maurine Neuberger. She was elected in 1960. Mrs. Neuberger, who is currently a resident of Portland, was part of a famous husband-and-wife political team. Husband Richard Neuberger was a highly visible Oregon Democrat, whose pen and voice were influential in the halls of Congress and in the nation's press.

We can thank the foresight of one of the early governors of our state, Oswald West, a Democrat, for insuring that our magnificent beaches are, for the main, permanently in public hands. West served in the state house from 1911-1915.

Another governor who certainly will go down as a major player in the history of our state is Tom McCall, a Republican, who was first elected in 1966 and re-elected in 1970. A journalist by profession, McCall had an uncanny ability to attract support for many of his proposals with his imposing stature and voice and his colorful phrasing.

McCall's environmental program will certainly have a lasting impact on the quality of life in Oregon.

One of McCall's off-hand remarks, "Come visit us, but for heaven's sake, don't stay," made national headlines. To this day, many folks from around the country remember this comment first when Oregon is mentioned as a place to live.

Probably the most durable Oregon politician of the century was McCall's gubernatorial predecessor, Mark Hatfield, who served as chief executive from 1959-1967. Prior to his election to the state's top office, Hatfield served as a state representative, state senator, and secretary of state. After leaving the governor's office, Hatfield was elected to the United States Senate, where he is currently serving his fifth term.

As governor, Mark Hatfield put strong emphasis on the diversification of the state's economy, long dependent on the timber industry. To this day, he remains probably the best informed individual in Oregon on our natural resource base. Hatfield will undoubtedly be remembered for his service on the Senate Appropriations Committee, where, as the ranking Republican (and one-time chairman) he has been able to bring hundreds of millions of dollars to the state for a variety of projects. The Oregon Health Sciences University has been one of the major recipients of his legislative efforts.

A true visionary, Neil Goldschmidt, former Portland mayor, Oregon governor and secretary of transportation in the Carter administration, should certainly be included among the century's outstanding public servants.

The only Oregonian to have a place on a national ticket as vice-presidential candidate (although unsuccessful) was Republican Charles L. McNary from Salem. McNary was originally appointed by Governor James Withycombe to serve out the term of Harry Lane, who died in office. McNary was elected in his own right in 1918 and re-elected four times (1924, 1930, 1936, 1942). He died in office in 1944. As a senior member of the United States Senate, McNary was highly regarded for his statesmanship.

If one was to name the most colorful Oregonian to serve in the United States Senate during this century, it certainly would be Wayne Morse, at one time dean of the law school at the University of Oregon. Morse was elected as a Republican in 1944 and re-elected in 1950. He registered as an Independent in 1952, and in 1955 became a Democrat. Morse was re-elected in 1956 and 1962.

Known for his keen intellect and a legendary knowledge of the parliamentary system, Morse was one of the finest debaters ever to serve in Washington, D.C. Although he did have considerable seniority, he was never able to assume a top leadership position, probably because of his rather prickly personality.

Conventional wisdom places the late Glenn L. Jackson of Medford as the most influential citizen of our time. Jackson, whose base was Pacific Power and Light Company, was also active as a newspaper publisher, rancher, and chairman of the State Highway Commission. He was intimately involved politically and personally in dozens of major Oregon projects. It was a rare individual who was able to say "no" to this unselfish dynamic gentleman.

There are dozens of other men and women who have made major contributions. Do you have a nomination for the cover of that thick book that will document this unbelievably productive era?

FRIDAY SURPRISE

Much today goes awry due to lack of discipline

A quality that has almost disappeared from prominence in so many aspects of life in the nineties in these United States is discipline. The most obvious breakdown in this precious commodity, which has been responsible for so much success in our nation's way of life, has been in the capital city.

For decades, the work of the House of Representatives and the Senate was highly structured. The chairs of the various committees were extremely powerful individuals, guiding legislation through their spheres of influence and control with strong hands. Newly elected members of their bodies were seen, but not heard; it was rare, indeed, when a junior representative or senator would rise to take exception to his chairman or a congressional leader.

Whether one judged them right or wrong, individuals like Lyndon Baines Johnson and Sam Rayburn were very much in control. If they wanted a bill passed, they darn well knew how it could be done. Depending on the political complexion of the White House, the president usually knew exactly where the necessary pressure points were located.

All of that is past history. The turmoil we saw last week in the life of the crime bill, and what we are continuing to witness with health care legislation, would never have happened thirty

years ago. Nor would there have been conflicting testimony by treasury department personnel on a matter such as Whitewater.

The key difference is that today nearly all members of Congress consider themselves experts on nearly every subject, and they are in no mood to buckle under to the exhortations of their so-called leaders.

Can you imagine congressional chiefs in mid-century turning over the manufacture of major legislation to a 500-member task force of self-anointed experts (as was done with health care)? Can you imagine the leadership of the Congress asking their members to read (and hopefully, by some miracle, to understand) a 1,300-page document on the subject? And now the presiding officer of the Senate, George Mitchell of Maine, has come up with his own plan: this one is 1,410 pages long!

The American public can only digest so much political fodder at one time. Each one of us has a myriad of other things to think about, to worry about, to do something about. We need to be fed in small doses by our elected leaders. We look to them to establish priorities. This is where discipline comes into play.

Think back for a moment to the dark days of World War II. President Franklin Roosevelt was able to galvanize the American public in support of the war effort, and the lend-lease arrangements with our allies, by the sheer power of his words. "There can be no appeasement with ruthlessness," he exhorted the nation in one of his fireside chats. He reminded his audience that if Britain fell, all of the Americas would soon be living at the point of a gun. He was successful, just as Winston Churchill was, because he knew how to influence the hearts and minds of his people, and because he had an understandable plan, sold with the necessary discipline.

It is not just in government that we see this valuable tool disappearing. With mothers and fathers both working, and kids subsequently left to their own devices, the family control that we used to know is becoming a rarity. It seems to matter little if homework is done, if the bedroom is left in disarray, if late night outs are the norm rather than the exception. And if the offspring is grounded for one reason or another, we see name calling, the threat of law suits, even murders, by unhappy youngsters.

Pity the teacher of the nineties. Not only does he or she have to put up with larger classes and edicts from layer upon layer of supervisors and boards, the matter of discipline in the classroom is almost laughable today. No longer can Susie or Johnny have her or his bottom whacked for some obvious infringement of common decency. In today's world, that would be cause for dismissal of a teacher.

The marketplace is no different. The manager of a restaurant establishes a dress code for the waiters and waitresses in his establishment. One of the young servers appears, flaunting the rules. "Where is your tie?" the manager asks. "In my pocket," comes the reply. And there is no action to correct the infraction. The employee is just asking for some overt action, so he can claim harassment.

Whether it is in government, where the rule of the majority is still our guiding principle, or in the home, where parental supervision has proven to be so vital, or in the world of business, where top operators run a tight-fisted operation, someone must be in charge. Is there any doubt why outfits like United Parcel or Federal Express are successful? Was there any question who was running the store when Fred Meyer was building his empire?

Last, but not least, the same rules apply in the sports world. Would the disgraceful strike situation we now see, with overpaid players and greedy owners, have been possible a half century ago?

A ten-letter word sorely needs to be brought back to the front burner to replace the four-letter words we hear too much today.

FRIDAY SURPRISE

Whale of a time a shoo-in in Warner Bros. proposal

*O*regonians could be in for a whale of a time! Yes, whale watching has been especially spectacular this year along the Oregon Coast, but there is more to come. Permanently. The star of the Warner Brothers hit movie *Free Willy* may be going to take up residence in our state.

Keiko, the killer whale who was the star of the popular saga, has been having a very bad time in Mexico. He has been confined to a much-too-small tank in a Mexico City marine park where the water temperature (80 degrees instead of his native Arctic Sea's 40 degrees) is too warm to suit his natural lifestyle. His teeth are being worn down by constant rubbing on hard surfaces and from chewing on his exhibit walls. In addition to all that, Keiko is suffering from a virus quite similar to herpes, and he is two tons underweight.

The folks who read the fan mail at Warner Bros. are almost as unhappy as their marine charge. They are tired of the bad publicity from environmentalists who look upon the conditions in the Mexican tank as being absolutely intolerable.

Finding a suitable home in California for the twenty-one-foot-long, 3.5-ton Keiko would be exceedingly difficult, because of all manner of state regulations. Time Warner, who have even been criticized in their own publications (*Life, Entertainment Weekly*) do not want the unhappy mammal to be a part of any show. They feel he has done his share of tricks, and they are willing to spend big bucks to end his present miserable living conditions.

One might think that returning the whale to the open seas would be the right answer. But marine biologists disagree on whether this would be in Keiko's best interests. Re-introduction of a species to its native haunts is best used for populations of endangered species, they say. Killer whales are presently not so classified.

Oregon steps into the picture in two ways. First, the sequel to *Free Willy* is presently being shot in Astoria, but not with live mammals. The marvels of technology have taken over to spare the kind of tank troubles Keiko has already endured.

Next, in their search for a happy retirement home for their ward, representatives of the entertainment company paid a visit to Oregon's charming coastal community of Newport and to the Oregon Coast Aquarium, the two-year-old destination attraction that has so far attracted nearly two million visitors.

What they saw at this modern facility made them smile with the hope that at last they had found an answer to their prayers. And if you thought they had grins on their faces, it was nothing compared to the excitement of the Director of the Aquarium, Phyllis Bell.

The embattled company executives were willing to invest $10 million to build a state-of-the-art tank to house their problem child; in addition, they talked about additional funds to allow for the upkeep of the popular gentleman. It is no small order to consider his culinary needs: Keiko eats 300 pounds of fish daily. To take care of the logistical needs of the new resident, aquarium officials estimated it would be necessary to hire three additional staff members. This was also covered by the Warner proposal.

Bell and her associates could hardly believe what they were hearing. Here was a multi-million dollar addition to their $25 million facility being placed right in their laps, without any of the usual wear and tear necessary to even consider such an expensive addition.

The potential for ongoing attendance was even more heaven-sent. The excitement of being able to see this unusual movie star was obviously something that would bring kids (and their parents and grandparents) back to the aquarium over and over again.

Several weeks ago, Phyllis Bell presented the offer to her board, most of whom appeared incredulous at the thought of such a windfall. They had a multitude of questions. What was the timing for construction? What would happen if Keiko passed out of the picture? Was there adequate space in the long-term plan for the aquarium to house a 2-million-gallon pool? What about state and federal regulations? Would this new feature be included in the overall admission charge to the aquarium?

The answers seemed only to intensify the excitement. Meetings were held almost immediately to make the final decision. No worry if twelve to fifteen-year-old Keiko was no longer around. (The average life span of a whale is thirty years.) The tank could be used for underwater viewing of another whale or even of killer sharks. There is a prime area adjacent to the present facility that would be perfect for the huge new tank (even desirable as far as delivering the daily grocery order).

State and federal officials see no insurmountable problems, but transporting Keiko to his new home will certainly be a major undertaking. No, visitors will not have to pay extra to observe this new tenant.

During a period when each telephone call to her office almost caused apoplexy, Bell received the good news. After extensive discussions with a Seattle-based funding coalition and the San Francisco environmental group Earth Island, the Oregon location was selected as the number one choice. Earth Island had acted on behalf of Warner Bros. in scouting possible sites for the animal's relocation and rehabilitation.

Although necessary documents have not yet been signed, design and engineering work is already well underway, and it is hoped that construction will begin in late September, 1994.

Don't you imagine that after hearing this news most Oregon kids (and the late Tom McCall) would want to rework that oft-repeated saying to something like this: "We're glad you are coming to visit, Keiko, but we're particularly happy that you are going to stay."

FRIDAY SURPRISE

Good or bad, foreign policy rests with the president

There are 435 members of the House of Representatives and 100 members of the U.S. Senate in Washington, D.C., who think that they should be President of the United States…and a goodly number of them think that they should also be secretary of state. We can add to that impressive list of candidates at least one former president, Jimmy Carter, who has become a considerably more distinguished statesman in retirement than he ever was while in residency at 1600 Pennsylvania Avenue.

Can you imagine former Secretary of State Henry Kissinger sitting back and allowing anybody, even a former president, to steal the headlines in a major foreign policy crisis? And can you picture the former master of international affairs, Richard Nixon, letting one of his predecessors serve as the point man in delicate overseas negotiations?

As we watch the fascinating story of Haiti, a poor and ravished country that hardly produces a blip on the world radar screen, unfold before the daily eyes and ears of hundreds of cameramen, foreign correspondents, network anchors and foreign policy gurus, we are reminded about the ever changing face of our United States Department of State.

Unlike our British friends across the pond whose foreign policies seldom get off course, our international affairs have had unsteady sailing. This is partially due to the rightfully changing priorities of different Democratic and Republican administrations, but it is also due in many instances to a lack of true leadership and discipline at the highest levels of our government.

Besides Kissinger, we have had strong secretaries of state in recent times, individuals like George Schultz and James Baker III. They have backed up presidents weak in foreign affairs (like Reagan) and others who found great fascination in the world geopolitical scene (like Bush).

Today, Bill Clinton, who came to the White House with scant interest or knowledge of the striped-pants world, has seemingly been unable to put together a cohesive foreign policy team. Warren Christopher, the current secretary of state, arrived with favorable credentials–distinguished service in the Carter administration, early support for our current president–but he has hardly turned out to be a charismatic spokesman for our causes. Anthony Lake, the current National Security Advisor, until recently was barely known to the American public.

So it was not too surprising to see President Clinton turn to Jimmy Carter for help in defusing crises in North Korea, Cuba and now Haiti. Carter has been anxious to play just such a role.

However, it looks as if the president got more than he bargained for, as Carter took things very much in his own hands, becoming almost a one-man State Department. He even personally lined up travel companions General Colin Powell and Senator Sam Nunn for his Haiti mission. It is not difficult to imagine the consternation and distress this has caused, not only at the White House, but also at Foggy Bottom (the State Department headquarters).

During my twenty-six years in Washington, D.C., I traveled to over 130 countries (mostly at my own expense) in a variety of assignments for Senator Mark Hatfield. This was an immensely interesting and educational experience, and gave me a good deal of insight into the kind of men and women who make up our foreign policy team. As in any organization, there are the strong ones and there are the weak ones, but generally speaking, we can be proud of the caliber of individuals who represent us in foreign and Washington, D.C., posts.

They are busy with immigration problems, economic assignments, political information gathering and a host of other duties, in addition to serving, at times, as reluctant chaperons to hordes of office holders who feel that overseas junkets are a vital part of their jobs.

In Oregon, we have had the distinction of having several natives serve in top State Department assignments. Portland businessman and political activist Alan (Punch) Green served the Bush administration as our Ambassador to Romania. Edward Perkins had a high profile job when he represented our country during troubled times in South Africa. William Hall (whose father-in-law, Jay Bowerman, was an Oregon governor) had an exceptionally productive career as U.S. Ambassador to

Ethiopia and later as Director-General of the Foreign Service, the branch that makes personnel assignments. Bill Lane, the second generation of the family who founded *Sunset Magazine*, had a turn as ambassador to Australia. Lane currently maintains his Oregon ties as a director of the Oregon Coast Aquarium.

Several foreign service personalities stand out in my memory. One is Carol Laise, our Ambassador in Nepal when I first met her. She carried out a long-distance courtship and later marriage to another distinguished state department careerist, Ambassador Ellsworth Bunker. Ms. Laise was particularly influential in getting our Peace Corps in Nepal organized (with a number of Oregon volunteers), turning it into one of the most successful in that worthy worldwide program.

There are, and always have been, any number of capable folks who want to play major roles in the conduct of our foreign affairs. The Senate and House Foreign Relations Committees, although lacking in strong leadership on the Senate side, have some very well informed members, like Richard Lugar of Indiana and Nancy Kassebaum of Kansas.

But the bottom line is very clear: we have only one individual who is ultimately responsible for the conduct of our foreign policy, the president. The buck stops in the Oval Office, no matter how passionately Jimmy Carter believes in the causes in which he has become involved. One would have thought he learned that when he, himself, sat behind that desk.

FRIDAY SURPRISE

Modern marketing means you always get to choose

*D*o you remember when you went into your favorite ice cream parlor, with the neighborhood's most popular youngsters behind the counter serving as the soda jerks, and asked what was the choice that day? Vanilla, chocolate and perhaps strawberry. Not today. The current menu now includes rainforest crunch, wavy gravy (ice cream?), white Russian, coconut almond fudge chip, chunky monkey and dozens of other flavors whose names have to come from the most hip of the dessert marketers.

But ice cream is no different than dozens of other commodities. We are living in an age of remarkable change in where we shop, how we shop and what we shop for. Never before have we had such a selection of merchandise to choose from, and never before have we been offered so many shopping facilities.

To be successful today, companies must be fast on the uptake. We are extremely fickle customers. The outfits that are going to be successful must spot the current trends, and then be in a position to do something about them. Take the sneaker business. Most of us can remember when the choice was Keds or Converse, and that was about it. Now there are running shoes and walking shoes and basketball shoes and jogging shoes and bicycling shoes and soft shoes for just about any other activity you can name. There are dozens of stores that

sell only these goods.

Is there a day that goes by when you don't receive some kind of a come-on from a communications company offering a new and different kind of service, or a special deal if you sign up right away? To be honest, I think they have just about reached the saturation point here; how do we know that the plan that we signed up for yesterday is better than the one being offered today? In my opinion, these companies are just about at the edge of losing their most valuable sales pitch: consumer confidence.

Also in the service area, what about the proliferation of credit card deals? There are hundreds of them, offering every imaginable kind of premium: special rates, air miles, hotel stays, merchandise discounts, you name it.

The buzz word in this wild and wooly world is niche marketing. This means that many of our desires and habits are being minutely scrutinized by the experts, so they can bombard us with the latest data on merchandise that appeals to our particular lifestyle. They know, for example, if we order electronic items from the maze of catalogues that appear almost daily in our mail boxes. If we do show an interest, say in computers, then we will get data on every conceivable new product there is in this rapidly changing field.

They know if we are the kind who respond to the magazine outfit prize games. Their marketing tactics intrigue me; some time ago I sent back some of their order forms. Now I receive two or three new "you are in the final winner category" mailings daily. Have you ever met anyone who has really won those prizes? A friend of mine is so addicted to this game that she has now run out of magazines to order. How about the one on "how to win contests"? Now that is real niche marketing!

We could go on and on. I was reading the other day that Sony provides more than 100 varieties of Walkmans, that Seiko has upwards of 3,000 different watches in their line, and that Philips has 800 different models of color televisions. There once was a day when you walked into the radio department of your local department store and saw RCA Victor, General Electric, Atwater Kent and not much more.

Then there are the superstores that dot our landscape. For a time these behemoths were a long drive from the central city, in areas where land was cheap and plentiful, and new housing tracts were being rapidly developed. No more. The superstores are coming to town, to downtown.

In city after city, huge Barnes and Noble bookstores, offering not just vast selections of reading material but also coffee, tea and milk, plus lectures and magazines and quiet reading areas, are making it tough for the small bookseller to compete. The big category busters like Toys 'R' Us (Toys); Bed, Bath and Beyond (home furnishings); CompUSA (computers and accessories); and Home Depot (everything for the home) are putting a severe strain on local hardware and gift and accessory outlets. Today, stores are not just in the merchandise business. They are also in the entertainment business.

The space in many of these stores is measured in acres. The shopping carts, to encourage us to pick up more goodies, are twice the size of the usual supermarket variety. The aisles, on the average, are fifteen feet wide. Forklift trucks rush back and forth reloading the never-ending shelves. The variety of merchandise reaches to the ceilings, with dozens of clothes hampers and hundreds of kitchen gadgets vying for customer attention.

We have regional malls and strip malls and neighborhood malls and factory outlet malls, so I guess it was inevitable that we would have the anti-mall! Of course the place where such a new concept would be born had to be southern California. It is known as The Lab, and the target audience is the dual-channel generation that is interested in clothes with a short lifespan (there are no Nordies or Gaps included). This is a place where the shopper can "plant sunflowers or buy broken tiles to decorate walls" with proceeds going to a charity for the homeless.

There is no scientific formula for keeping up-to-date with the newest and the trendiest. However, if you want to keep abreast of what is going on, and make the best use of your hard-earned bucks at the same time, there are a few relevant hints. Read everything you can; specialty newsletters and papers like *USA Today* (and of course, our favorite morning newspaper) tell you what is currently happening in the marketplace. Monitor what is happening in trend-setting cities like New York and Los Angeles. Watch what the celebrities are wearing and doing. Analyze new consumer priorities. Watch the emerging demographic groups.

Choices, choices, choices. I'll take just plain chocolate, thank you.

FRIDAY SURPRISE

Special group of 10 VIPs are major community asset

I want you to meet some Very Important People in our community. No, they are not politicians, or big business tycoons, or television stars or celebrated authors. Some of them may well be your neighbors, and chances are good that, in some way, one or more of them has touched your life or that of a member of your family or your circle of friends in a very positive way.

In a world with a serious lack of role models, these ladies and gentlemen are exactly that. They serve as examples for all of us, young or old, students or seniors, professional persons or housewives, hamburger flippers or horticulturists.

The first one is a gentleman who has done more than his share of volunteer work in the health field. He has been a member of the Board of Directors of Good Samaritan Foundation for a decade and was prominent in the campaign for that hospital's Heart Institute. He was a volunteer for the American Lung Association and an active member of the steering committee for the Robert S. Dow Neurological Science Institute.

In the business world, he was a part of the prestigious Young Presidents' Organization, and used his leadership talents in training youngsters through the Junior Achievement program. His name is Robert A. Sprouse.

The next VIP I'd like you to get to know works in a very quiet and unassuming manner. He greets incoming hospital patients and escorts them personally to their rooms. It was his idea to have a "belongings cart" to make sure that all patients' personal items are put in the right rooms. Besides countless hours comforting those who are not feeling well, Don Sherwood and his wife find time to be active in their church, scouting, Little League and school office activities. One word to describe him? Dependable.

Charlotte Schwartz's bio reads like the honor list of Oregon's non-profit organizations: Cystic Fibrosis Society, Guide Dogs for the Blind, Juvenile Court of Multnomah County, Jewish Family and Child Services, Marysville School. In all of these she has been an advisor, tutor or development worker. In addition, this gregarious lady was long the district manager for ten Kelly Services (temporary employment) offices in the Portland area. Her dream is to help create a Recreation Center for the Handicapped, a facility she helped organize in San Francisco years ago.

Although a Portland resident for just eleven years, Arlitria Proctor quickly became a key volunteer in a number of worthwhile organizations, such as the Urban League of Portland, the Albina Ministerial Alliance and the Energy Assistance headquarters. She has spent countless hours assisting needy families in the north and northeast sections of our city with the paperwork they need to apply for help, at the same time using her needlework skills to make hats and blankets for the young and old to keep them warm during the cold winter months.

I have a particularly soft place in my heart for the Portland Police Sunshine Division. It was one of the first organizations I became involved with after returning to Portland from army and university days. Portlanders with long memories will recall Jack Luihn (now deceased) of the famous gourmet shop, Sealy-Dresser. He was the sparkplug who got many of us started with this unique program that offers food, clothing and furnishings to the needy.

The Sunshine Division would not be what it is today without the expertise of Leland Stanford "Bud" Lewis. Bud was a sergeant in the patrol division and director of the safety education unit of the Portland Police for nine years, after a thirty-one-year career in the military. But there's more. Bud became involved with the Crime Stoppers program, Red Cross blood drives, and now gives private driving instruction to sixteen-year-olds. What a guy!

William "Pete" Knox has given a lifetime of service to the Boy Scouts as a District Commissioner, Scoutmaster, and Rotary Club Camp Enterpriser volunteer. If there ever was a role model for young people, it is Pete Knox! His Silver Beaver award says it all.

Besides an almost full time job in the real estate business, this lady finds time to work for the Camp Fire Girls and the League of Women Voters, the DePaul Center, Loaves and Fishes and Neighborhood House. And she doesn't just sit in committee meetings. Phyllis Buckingham personally visits the home-bound who have no relatives or friends in town to see if they might need some kind of support.

Someone once said that music makes the world go round, and Charles "Chuck" Bradford has been making melodious sounds practically all his life. He was a music and band director with the Portland public schools; since his retirement he has joined a group of musical devotees in organizing the Providence Stage Band, an outfit that re-creates the big band sounds of the thirties and forties. Bradford and his cohorts not only bring musical pleasure to countless civic organizations, he and his wife also bring hot meals to the needy through the dependable Meals on Wheels program.

A frustrated actor, yes, but Kenyon Bement has turned his stage interests into good deeds for a big audience: the Salvation Army, the Muscular Dystrophy Association, the Portland Rotary Foundation. His hobby is collecting hats, and practically every one of them signifies involvement in something positive for his community.

Our last VIP is none other than our 1994 Oregon Mother of the Year, Margie Keller. She is largely responsible for the Recovery of Hope Drug Rehabilitation program, a counseling and support system for individuals with drug and alcohol problems. Keller houses addicts in her home after their treatment, getting them to stay in touch with the program. But that's not all. This magnificent lady also began the annual free Thanksgiving dinner for the homeless and needy of our community.

The OASIS program recently honored these ten role models for their community work. Today we honor them for what they stand for…service to their fellow men and women. VIPs, to be sure.

Veteran institution at bank closes account on career

Someone who came to work in a temporary position (at $300 a month) forty-two years ago and just left that same job? Someone whose position was so special that there was no title or real job description? Someone who outlasted eight chief executive officers at his bank? Someone about whom no one has ever said an unkind word? Is there really a person like that?

Yes, there is. His name is Floyd Bennett, and just last week he retired after one of the most productive and unusual careers in Portland banking history. To say that he was an institution is putting it mildly: he touched the lives of countless Oregonians.

A native Portlander, this gregarious individual was plagued with health problems during his early years. Before the days when tuberculosis was conquered, he spent several years in TB hospitals. Sheer determination, a hallmark of his entire life, got him through some very tough years.

Bennett's first job was in the sports department of the *Oregon Journal.* There he perfected his writing and public relations skills; they were to come in very handy in his coming career.

In 1952 he went to work "for a few days" at the First National Bank, then an outfit that was small enough for everyone to know most all of their co-workers. It was obvious to the powers that be right from the start that their young

intern possessed special talents in the people-handling area.

He has made all of his bosses look good. First it was the legendary E.B. MacNaughton, who ran the bank and the *Oregonian* and Reed College (at different times) with an iron hand. Next it was Frank Belgrano, whose handwriting (totally illegible) was as famous as his lifestyle: he arrived from San Francisco with a chauffeur and a Chinese houseboy, almost unheard of in mid-century Portland.

Then it was homemade C.B. "Bill" Stephenson who moved into the corner suite. He was just the opposite from his predecessor: a low-key, no pretense boss who was loved by everyone.

When a group of Portland businessmen decided that our city needed a major downtown commercial hotel, C.B. Stephenson assigned Bennett to be the bird dog in helping to raise funds. Soon the big chiefs found that their young recruit could open almost any door in town. That hasn't changed over the past four-plus decades.

Bennett's next boss was Ralph Voss, a fine banker who still resides in the City of Roses. Bob Wallace, a strong and heavy-handed leader if there ever was one, was next; then figures expert Bill Wilke; succeeded by extremely popular Bruce Willison (now in Los Angeles at the bank headquarters); and followed by the genial and reserved Jim Curran.

Although each of these prominent Portland leaders had his own style, Bennett was at their side, doing all the things that either they did not have time to do or did not want to do in the first place.

Directors' meetings away from home base? Bennett would make all the necessary arrangements, see that the proper people were invited, order the food, execute the theme (like a western barbecue), and insure that the directors' spouses had special activities of their own.

A charity drive that the boss got himself involved with as chair? Bennett would take over, make the endless calls, twist the arms of local corporate types (many of whom, of course, had bank connections), and generally make his chief a hero.

Special guests coming to town under bank sponsorship? Bennett would be the fellow who took care of accommodations, special food requests, transportation, and all the details that many of the prima donnas thought they needed. He says that the recent Portland visit by Margaret Thatcher, which he organized, was probably the easiest and best (and last) of his career. She turned out to be a pleasure to work with, much less demanding than others who hadn't begun to achieve her prominence.

In between all of this, Bennett administered the donation program for the bank. Like so many highly visible institutions, First Interstate Bank is besieged with requests for monetary donations for every imaginable cause. It was up to this savvy operator to evaluate the many requests, then recommend a figure that was practically always accepted as the final say so. Even though he had to say "no" in many cases, no one ever accused this gentle-man of not listening to the needs of our community.

And he has had his own public involvement agenda. He was president of the Rose Festival, president of the Portland Zoological Society, president of the Oregon Travel Industry Council. He has held practically every office there is for the Oregon Museum of Science and Industry. And more.

Before networking was a popular buzz work, Floyd Bennett had developed contacts everywhere. He probably made and received more phone calls during his career than any living Portlander. And when the phone line was not busy, he was checking with his buddies in the local investment houses to keep abreast of how our local companies were doing.

But his first priority was, and is, his family. Elaine and Floyd Bennett have been happily married for forty-three years. Their five children and numerous grandkids never took second place to the big bank bosses.

How did this intensely committed banker and public servant get the energy for such a schedule? Every morning, for forty-three years, his breakfast included a ripe banana. Now there's a commodity that must have a special energizer as well an ingredient known as graciousness!

FRIDAY SURPRISE

Where there's an old will, there's interesting reading

*O*ne of the most fascinating volumes I have seen in a long time was sent to me recently by a former Oregonian. It is a collection of early wills copied from the public records of courts of probate. All of the documents are real, and were published in 1925 by the Title and Trust Company in the hope that their provisions might be useful as suggestions to others.

The interesting part of this booklet is that the author of each will was a well-known Oregon personality in the early part of this century. Most of them were highly successful in their own field, and all were individuals of unusual integrity and foresight. The wills have two common objectives: the proper distribution of the person's property, and the preservation and economical administration of their assets.

Possibly no family was as prominent in the early history of our city and state as the Corbetts. One of the wills published was that of a pioneer member of that family, Henry L. Corbett, whose three grandchildren (Henry Ladd Corbett, Elliott Ruggles Corbett and Hamilton Forbush Corbett) are still remembered by many citizens of this area. Some of their children and grandchildren are still active in our community's affairs.

Mr. Corbett's bequests were particularly noteworthy because they mentioned a number of philanthropic organizations that were (and some are still) doing good work in Portland: the Home, the Boys' and Girls' Aid Society, the YMCA and the Portland Academy. One provision in his will bequeathed property to the Portland Art Association for the purpose of erecting an art gallery, which thousands of citizens have since enjoyed over the years.

Amanda W. Reed, wife of pioneer philanthropist Simeon G. Reed, left a tidy sum, for those days, to Simeon Reed Winch, son of her nephew, Martin Winch, "in consideration of his having been named for my dear husband."

But by far the most significant portion of her will directed that funds from her estate be used by a group of her friends (the Reverend T.L. Eliot, C.B. Bellinger, C.A. Dolph, William E. Robertson and Martin Winch) to establish an institution in Portland for the promotion of literature, science and art. She asked that this place of learning be known as the "Reed Institute" in memory of her husband. The result, of course, was the beginning of one of our nation's most distinguished private colleges.

Mrs. Reed might be surprised at the course taken by her institution. One provision, that the Institute "forever be and remain free from sectarian influence" is certainly true these days; however, another one, "the cultivation and development of manual training," might be more difficult to document in 1994.

241

Another well-to-do pioneer, Portlander E. Henry Wemme, tent and awning manufacturer, auto buff and real estate tycoon, established an endowment fund with its main provision the purchase of "suitable real estate as a site for a maternity home for unfortunate and wayward girls." It is now a branch of our local Salvation Army program, and has served thousands of needy young women over the years.

In his will, newspaper pioneer Henry L. Pittock saw to it that his friends at the *Oregonian* were well taken care of. He wrote that C.A. Morden was to be elected manager of the paper and should be retained as such, and that Edgar B. Piper should be retained as managing editor until he became incapacitated or voluntarily resigned. Not bad employment security contracts!

The will of Dr. Bernard Daly, who was born in Ireland in 1858, and who came to Lakeview, Oregon, in 1887 to hang his shingle, has had a profound impact in the annals of education in our state.

Dr. Daly had a full career: country doctor, successful banker and rancher, state representative, state senator, his party's candidate for the U.S. Senate and House of Representatives, county judge, circuit judge, regent of the Oregon State Agricultural College, and member of the local school board for thirty years, in addition to being a businessman and capitalist. Some feel that perhaps he made more history in a wider variety of endeavors than any Oregonian of his time.

What a fascinating man he was. The late lawyer Forrest Cooper, himself an Oregonian of distinction, reminisced that Daly would walk into Eli's Cafe in Lakeview a few minutes before noon, order a bowl of soup, then gather up the cracker bowls from surrounding tables and proceed to have a ten cent meal. He lived in an untidy apartment over his bank, scrimped and saved (and never married) in order to leave as large a fortune as possible with which to combat ignorance.

Dr. Daly cut his family ties at an early age. However, he did finance the migration of a number of fellow Irishmen to his new-found home, where he created an empire of sheepmen. After he died in 1920, some of his heirs filed a suit in federal court in Portland where they unsuccessfully attacked his proposed charitable trust.

Daly's desire was that no student would have to quit school for lack of funding before his or her education was complete. Daly Educational Fund scholars are named solely on the basis of merit in a blind selection process. Using high school grade point averages and SAT scores, students are ranked in order of their probable success in college.

Beginning with $600,000 in 1922, the fund has awarded 1,413 scholarships and is presently valued at over $2 million. Scholarships are now going to the grandchildren of some of the first recipients.

The opportunities offered by this generous bequest have had monumental results in Lake County. There, the high school dropout rate is around 2 percent, and over 60 percent of Lake County graduates continue their education past high school.

The foresight and generosity of some of our state's early pioneers certainly provide a sterling example for modern-day Oregonians.

The President, "The King" and a man from Oregon

*W*hat is the connection between a former Portlander, a former occupant of 1600 Pennsylvania Avenue in the nation's capital and a deceased king? Give up? Read on!

The former Portlander is a good guy who took the rap, which many feel was grossly unfair, for some shady dealings in Washington, D.C., in which he was following orders from his commander-in-chief. His name is Egil "Bud" Krogh, Jr., a Watergate victim who served four months and seventeen days in a federal prison for his role in the Ellsberg break-in.

He first served as deputy assistant to the president for domestic affairs, primarily working on narcotics, criminal justice programs and transportation and serving as liaison between the White House and the District of Columbia. In 1972, he was appointed under secretary of the Department of Transportation.

Bud's father Egil, Sr., was my Dad's assistant at the Friday Surprise store; I always thought that Bud, like my father, was an absolute straight arrow. Unfortunately, he was in the wrong place at the wrong time, and he paid for it. For a time he was disbarred from practicing law; now he is one of Seattle's most able and prominent attorneys.

One of the saddest, and most memorable, days of my time in Senate service was visiting Bud Krogh behind bars. I just couldn't bring myself around to

believing that he deserved that penalty.

The former occupant of the White House is, of course, none other than Richard Nixon. As Krogh's boss, he was the man ultimately responsible for the entire Watergate scandal. But more than that, he was a fascinating human being who suffered from a terrible inferiority complex; a man who worshiped those who were famous, and especially those who were famous AND had money.

What is a king doing in this company? No, it wasn't a real king; it was one more famous than any of those wearing jewelled crowns. It is none other than Elvis Presley!

The story of how these three very different men came together is a rare bit of history. It is recounted in detail in a book recently published by Pejama Press (based on the names of Krogh's three children: Peter, Jamie and Mathew). Titled *The Day Elvis Met Nixon,* it is an informal look behind the scenes at the most important house in the world.

On December 21, 1970, Dwight Chapin, who was one of the stars of the Nixon administration, a man considered to be a top political strategist and a staffer who knew exactly what the fellow in the corner office wanted and didn't want, called Bud Krogh to tell him that the "King" had sent a letter to the White House asking for a meeting the President.

Presley's letter to Nixon mentioned that he was staying at the Washington Hotel, very near the White House, registered under the name of "Jon Burrows." What he really wanted were credentials certifying him as a Federal Agent so he could work with the young generation who idolized him and, at the same time, were victims of the drug culture.

What really got the juices flowing for Krogh was the mental picture of what an honest-to-goodness rock star could do to bring attention to the administration's anti-drug campaign.

Practically every session with Nixon had to be approved by the late Bob Haldeman, the crew-cut, intensely serious, and protective chief-of-staff. Much to everyone's surprise, Haldeman approved this summit meeting.

A slight glitch appeared when Elvis arrived in the West Wing lobby with his two burly bodyguards. He had a gun as a gift for Nixon; naturally, this raised all sorts of problems for Nixon's Secret Service protective detail. Bringing a gun into the Oval Office was an absolute no-no, even for Elvis.

(As a bit of historical detail, the gun was never personally given to Nixon. Like all such memorabilia, it ended up as an exhibit in the Richard Nixon Library in Yorba Linda, California.)

Can you picture this scene in the most famous office in the world? Elvis Presley, in tight-fitting dark velvet pants, a silk shirt open to below his chest, wears a dark purple velvet cape, a gold medallion, a belt with a four-inch by six-inch gold buckle and sunglasses with "EP" built into the nose frame. Nixon, on the other hand, is in a serious dark suit, the preferred uniform of his headquarters.

Bud Krogh recalls that the King was very ill at ease in the company of the Chief. It was all very formal: Mr. Presley and Mr. President.

As is usual practice, a photographer was ready to shoot pictures of the Oval Office guest. It is of some note that the picture taken by Ollie Atkins has become the most requested presidential photo of the Nixon years: 30,000 people have asked for copies!

No one was more surprised than Krogh when his boss approved Presley's request for a badge from the Narcotics Bureau as well as his offer to help the administration with the ongoing drug war. The King was so pleased that he hugged the President. Hugging Nixon? That had to be a historic gesture!

Unfortunately, it was never possible for Presley to work on the drug program. But the fact that this gentleman from Oregon had the fun of meeting a legend of the period, taking him to lunch at the White House mess, introducing him to office secretaries and presenting him with a narcotics agent badge was an unforgettable episode in an unforgettable career.

And today, when the drug scene has reached overwhelming proportions, and hundreds of thousands of young American boys and girls are victims of this curse, maybe we need another "King" who can get through to some members of this generation before it is too late.

Certainly the deceased "King" would approve of such a move. So would that very controversial president. But no one would clap harder than the Portland boy who grew up good, then was pronounced bad, and now is very good again.

Ceremony stirs memories of outstanding careers

Most any parent is happy to talk about his or her children, especially when it comes to the stage in life where they begin to make a contribution in their own community. The same is true, albeit in a little different frame of reference, for those who have been mentors and have had the pleasure of watching the growth and accomplishments of the young people they hired, trained and encouraged to broaden their career horizons.

At a very formal, yet very human, ceremony in the sedate courtroom of the Oregon Supreme Court in Salem last week, I had spinal chills as I watched Rex Armstrong of Portland invested as a judge of the Oregon Court of Appeals.

It was a rather remarkable gathering in a number of ways. First, the caliber of speakers and presenters could hardly have been more impressive: the Honorable William Richardson, Chief Judge of the Oregon Court of Appeals; Honorable Barbara Roberts, Governor of Oregon; Judy Shipler Henry, President of the Oregon State Bar; Sid Lezak, former United States Attorney for Oregon; and David Frohnmayer, President of the University of Oregon. Each of these had touched the life of Armstrong in one way or another.

Second, it was an emotional experience for the famous Roberts' political clan of our state. Present were three wives of long-time educator and legislator, the late Frank Roberts. One was completing her last day in office as governor (Barbara); one was present as a former justice of the Oregon Supreme Court (Betty); and one (Mary) was watching her son-in-law achieve a lifelong goal. Rex Armstrong is married to lawyer Leslie M. Roberts, one of two daughters of Mary and Frank. Sitting in the audience was the other daughter, Mary Wendy, winding up her own career that day as Oregon Labor Commissioner.

In the annals of twentieth century Oregon, few families have been as closely identified with public service as the Roberts crew.

In a touching recounting of his career leading to this prestigious new challenge, Rex recalled his own hundreds of days and thousands of miles on the campaign trail for Senator Mark Hatfield. Naturally, I took a bit of pride in the fact that I had hired this engaging young man and encouraged him to forge relationships around the state.

But there was another side to this somewhat political occasion, and it was a very human one. Rex's father, Ed, a political junkie like myself, served with distinction for many years in Salem in the sensitive and powerful job of chief of staff for three former Oregon governors, Douglas McKay, Paul Patterson and Elmo Smith. Rex's mother, Alice, is a long-time community activist in her own right, so their offspring comes by his public service interests naturally.

As an "adopted" father, I have watched dozens and dozens of other outstanding men and women, whose careers I helped launch, take their places in the public life of our state.

Ray Baum, a member of the LaGrande family renowned in that area for involvement in government service, started with us as an intern in the United States Senate. This outstanding gentleman is now the majority leader in the Oregon House of Representatives.

Tom Imeson has become a well known public figure. He served as chief of staff for Governor Neil Goldschmidt and is now acting temporarily in that capacity for Governor John Kitzhaber.

Over a decade ago, a bright and very focused lady, Kate Mathews, then the principal of Myers Elementary School in Salem, visited my office to inquire about doing summer volunteer work in the nation's capital. Her initial foray into politics led to further assignments in political campaigns and finally to the influential job of Director of Professional Development for the Confederation of Oregon School Administrators. Now Mrs. David Dickson, Kate is able to relate to students, firsthand, the valuable lessons she learned in the middle of the most political environment in the world.

Others of "my kids" have also had success in educational pursuits. Chris Call is a shining example; he is now the right-hand man for Willamette University President Jerry Hudson.

Two outstanding individuals who did a tour of duty in Washington have found their places in the advancement of health facilities for the Oregon Health Sciences University in Portland.

Elizabeth Geiger is the Director of Alumni and Constituent Relations, and Vic Gilliam is serving as Director for Individual Gifts for the Oregon Health Sciences Foundation.

Younger Oregonians are deeply committed to our state's natural resources. It is no wonder, then, that a number of former senate staffers have found leadership positions in major environmentally related organizations. Jack Robertson serves as Deputy CEO of the Bonneville Power Administration; Steve Hickok is head honcho of the sales and customer service division of the same outfit; and Steve Crow, who was once the Chief Clerk of the Senate Energy and Water Development Subcommittee of Appropriations, is now head of government affairs for the Northwest Power Planning Council.

When I first interviewed Tom Decker, from Albany, some in the office wondered what that "blond-haired surfer" could contribute. Well, he did, positively, in spades. He served as chief staffer for the 1980 Reagan inaugural in Washington and now is Director of Federal Government Relations for the Port of Portland. He was also responsible for suggesting another hire, his Oregon State University classmate, Jenna Dorn of Corvallis. Jenna has gone on to a particularly lustrous career in a number of capacities at the U.S. Department of Transportation and the American Red Cross, as number one assistant to Elizabeth Hanford (Mrs. Bob) Dole.

Proud? You bet. But more than that, these ladies and gentlemen of achievement disprove the too-commonly expressed concern about the new generation of leadership. As a proud "adopted" dad, I'd match them (and many others) against any challengers, anywhere.

1905 Portland Automobile Club frolics at Sandy River clubhouse

*I*n 1912, the 16.6 mile journey from downtown Portland to a picturesque spot on the Sandy River was quite a drive. It was really more of an outing! But that trip was made many times by the original members of the Portland Automobile Club, founded in 1905, to visit their striking clubhouse on magnificent property east of the city.

At the time construction started on the building, the club had 380 members. Today the Oregon AAA Club, of which I am a member along with 495,000 other Oregonians, is one of the largest and healthiest organizations in the state of Oregon. And, last week the club's board of directors celebrated ninety years of service to motorists with a dinner in the original landmark structure.

The social aspects of the clubhouse, set in the middle of twenty-eight wooded acres, received greater attention in the early days than the real purposes envisioned by the pioneer members. Some of them signed a petition opposing the building and stating that, "We believe the proper purpose of the Automobile Club is to be along different (not social) lines, such as encouraging road building, proper legislation, erection of sign boards, rather than maintaining a clubhouse which it is feared will degenerate into practically a road house."

Well, apparently there WAS quite a bit of fun and games at this hideaway in the early days. In 1915, club members reported that a number of individuals "were in the habit of entertaining women of questionable morals at the Clubhouse."

All of this didn t seem to stop the pillars of Portland from using the retreat for some memorable events. In 1912, an informal house-warming banquet was held in this sprawling complex with many prominent Portland citizens who were responsible for high-grade, hard-surface road development in Multnomah County in attendance. Among the well-known names present: Yeon, Benson, Corbett, Riggs and Wemme. E. Henry Wemme, a former president of the club (1909-1910), was considered the sparkplug of the group, and the most devoted automobile enthusiast of the time.

Wemme was also responsible, through the donation of a great deal of time and money, for work on the Mt. Hood road, the Portland-Seattle road, the Rex-Tigardville road, the Hood River road, and the Portland to Astoria and beach resorts highway.

A copy of the 1912 banquet program listed W.J. Clemens as toastmaster, with music by Fisher's Orchestra, and songs by Miss Helen Horn from the Oregon Grill.

What did they eat? First, an "auto cocktail" with no mention of what ingredients were included. On to Toke Points on shell, strained chicken okra, fillet of halibut, Roman Punch, larded fillet de boeuf (with truffles), French endive salad, nesselrode pudding, assorted cakes and camembert cheese. Wow! No wonder many of them collapsed at the clubhouse for an overnight stay!

The banquet speakers were the best of the day. Oregon's most prominent proponent of quality roads, Samuel Hill, spoke on "The Good Roads to See God's Country."

Early brochures proclaimed that in addition to the perfectly equipped clubhouse, tennis courts, bowling alleys, a swimming pool, boats and fishing would provide recreation and amusement for the club members and their guests. It was also announced that a number of bungalows would be constructed on the river bank where members could live during the summer, boarding at the club.

In looking over the membership list, I was struck by the names of so many of my relatives (grandfather, uncles, distant cousins and the like), in addition to a number of individuals who played leading roles in community activities at that time and who had been rewarded with life memberships: E.H. Beall, John T. Clemson, M.J. Delahunt, Miss H.E. Failing and Wemme among them. Old-time Portlanders would also recognize the names of prominent dentist Dr. George D. Peters, legendary ship captain Delmer Shaver, Pacific International Livestock Exposition leader Theodore B. Wilcox, merchant M. Sichel, man-about-town Philip Grossmayer, industrialist Thomas Autzen, and department store magnate (Lipman Wolfe) Adolph Wolfe.

I was particularly interested to see that my great uncle, former Oregon Governor Julius Meier, was listed as a part of the dinner committee as well as a former officer of the club. He had originally purchased the property for the Boy Scouts. Those who have visited Menucha, Meier's former estate overlooking the Columbia Gorge and now a Presbyterian retreat home, would be struck by the similarity to the original AAA structure. The main room, with its commanding stone fireplace, and the adjacent large porch are almost carbon copies of the house later built by Meier.

In later years, the clubhouse had a number of owners, fell into some disrepair, and was purchased in 1993 by local industrialist Junki Yoshida and his wife, Linda. Yoshida's main business is Yoshida Foods and the well-known Yoshida sauce. They have spent considerable time and funds restoring and modernizing the building; it stands now as a unique and charming residence.

Early minutes of the club reveal fascinating tidbits of Portland life in the early part of this century. Heavy discussion was held about the purchase of twenty-seven dining room tables, the total cost of which amounted to ninety-five dollars. Telephone service was another topic of importance. A contract was entered into with the Pacific States Telephone Company, with the firm agreeing to build a main line from Montavilla to the clubhouse and to supply unlimited service for a period of one year at twenty dollars per month.

But by far the most fascinating item related to dancing at the clubhouse. The minutes recorded that it was to be brought to the attention of members that those involved in the "habit of indulging in ragging (a form of dancing) should know that a number of members find this offensive, and therefore they should refrain from ragging while at the clubhouse." One wonders what they would think of today's dancing.

Index

A

Abraham & Straus, 54, 55
Adams, R.R. "Rube," 156, 202
Adler, Leo, 206
Afghanistan, 31–32
agricultural products, 170
AIDS, 96
Ainsworth Grammar School, 1, 43, 202
airline companies
    and Donald Trump, 67
    and Frank Lorenzo, 38, 53
    management problems at United, 53, 163
        164
    in Oregon, 91–92
Air Oregon, 91
airport security, 100
Alaska Airlines, 92
Alaskan oil spill, 37
Albania, 115
Albany Collegiate Institute, 190
Alexander, Nan, 172
Alexander's, 128
Allegis, 53
Allied Stores, 54
Alpenrose Dairy, 167
Amato, George, 114, 166
Amato, Mary, 114
Ames, Bob, 98
Amling, Jan, 21
Amos 'n' Andy, 175
Amtrak metroliners, 35
Anderson, Andy, 176
Anderson, Glenn, 87
Annenberg, Walter, 109
Antarctica, 57–58
Antique Rose Inn, 126
A.P. DeLin & Company, 190
aquarium. See Oregon Coast Aquarium
Arabian Sea, 216
Arafat, Yasser, 25
Aramony, William, 151
Arbuckle, Ruth, 44, 141, 142
archives, 157–158
Arlington Club, 63, 201
Armed Forces Extra, 10
Armishaw's, 165
Armstrong, Alice and Ed, 245–246
Armstrong, Rex, 245–246
Arnstad, Mary, 164
arts and entertainment. See also theater
    in 1894, 209–210, 217–218
    in Oregon, 87–88, 169–170
    and use of PR, 134
Ashland, Oregon, 126
Ashland Natural History Museum, 126
Astoria Hotel, 144
Astoria Museum, 126
Atiyeh, Victor, 224
Atkins, Ollie, 244

"Aunt Rosie". See White, Rose
Aureole's, 51
Austin, Joan, 149
autographs, GF's collection of, 135–136
automobiles
    racing news in 1910, 193, 194
    trends in, 51
Autzen, Thomas, 248
Avalon Grill, 128

B

Baker, Doug, 140
Baker, Howard, Jr., 8, 78
Baker, James, III, 77, 115, 116, 233
Baker City Interpretive Center, 126
Baker Hotel, 143
Baldwin Hotel, 127
Ballot Measure 5, 182
Bandon, Oregon, 81, 126
Banfield, T. Harry, 49
Bangkok, Thailand, 213–214
banks. See specific names of banks
Barbey, Graham, 187
Barnes and Noble Bookstore, 236
Barnett, Dr. Ruth, 166
Barnett, Leolyn, 9
Baruch, Bernard, 95–96, 136, 224
Barzun, Jacques, 186
Bates-Seller house, 206
Baum, Ray, 246
Bay House, 127
Beall, E.H., 248
Beaux Arts Union Station, 35
Beckett, Margaret, 220
Bed, Bath and Beyond, 178, 236
Beetle Bailey's, 126
Beirut, Lebanon, 25
Belgrano, Frank, 47, 239
Bell, Phyllis, 150, 171, 231–232
Bellini's, 147
Bement, Kenyon, 238
Bend, Oregon, 126, 193, 194
Bennett, Elaine, 239
Bennett, Floyd, 42, 239–240
Bennett, George, 81
Benny, Jack, 113, 114
Benson Hotel, 73–74, 166
Bentley, Sara, 30
Berg, Forrest, 24
Besaw's Cafe, 206
beverages, trends in, 11
Bidwell, Jerry, 98
Bijan's, 51
Bilderback, Dr. Joseph, 166
Bishop, Mabel Livingstone, 150
Blackwell, Christina, 206
Blair, Tony, 220
Blair House (Washington, D.C.), 15
Blitz-Weinhard Brewing Company, 209
Bloomingdale's, 54, 159–160, 170

Blue Heron Cheese Company, 128
Blumauer-Frank, 117
Blumenauer, Earl, 98
Bo, Mr. (Vietnamese negotiator), 18
Boeing Company, 92
Bohemian Restaurant, 165
Boivin, Harry, 93
Bolliger, Ralph, 198
Bombay, India, 216
Bonanza, Oregon, 126
Boorstin, Daniel, 4
Booth, Bob, 91
bottle bill, 205
Bounds, Doris, 50, 105, 205
Bourguiba, Habib, 161
Bowen, Gwladys, 166
Bowerman, Jay, 71
Bowers, H.C., 144
Boyle, Gertrude, 150
Bradford, Charles "Chuck," 238
Brady, Sandy, 21
Bragdon, Paul, 98
Braley, Buzz, and family, 164
Breezley, Roger L., 50, 172, 212
Brinkley, David, 75
British Royal Family, 109, 134
Brokaw, Ann Claire, 3
Brokaw, Tom, 75, 224
Brown, Maurine. See Neuberger, Maurine
Brydon, Edith Findley, 29
Brzezinski, Zbigniew, 25
Buckingham, Phyllis, 238
Buckman, Frederick, 211–212
budget. See also debt
    federal, 133, 145–146, 207–208
    state, 102
Bureau Saloon, 190
Burnett, Iverson, 144
Burns, Keith, 64
Burros, Marian, 148
Bush, Asahel, II, 189
Bush, George, 131
    and Barbara, as team, 84
    as campaigner, 195
    and Persian Gulf conflict, 95, 99
    as president, 40, 52, 104, 180
    public opinion about, 61–62
    as vice president, 8
business. See also marketing; work
    discipline in, 230
    downsizing in, 208
    entrepreneurs, 55–56, 89–90
    and executive washrooms, 151
    leaders in Oregon, 149–150, 211–212
    management at Mayo Clinic, 65–66
    news in 1910, 193, 194
    productivity trends in, 179–180, 208
    and PR spin, 133–134
    social responsibility vs. greed in, 37–38
    stock market crash, 52
    trends, 178
    and trust in management, 163–164
    tycoons, egos of, 53–54

wage and compensation disparity in, 96,
    181-182, 208

C
Cabell, Margaret Malarkey Cartwright, 202
Cadonau, Carl, Sr., 167
Calcutta, India, 215–216
Call, Chris, 246
Callahan, Frank, 13, 34
Cambridge University, 103, 219–220
Cameron, Gerry, 212
campaign reform, 96, 182
Campbell, Larry, 98
Campbell House, 126
Camp David Agreement, 136
Campeau, Robert, 54
cancer, 96
Candy Basket Factory, 128
Canyon Way, 127
Cape Arago State Park, 81
Capital Journal, 189
The Cardinal, 1
Carl Greve Jeweler, 85
Carlson, Cheryl, 21
Carradine, Keith, 113–114
Carson, Wally, 93
Carter, Ann, 206
Carter, Jimmy, 62, 72, 83, 233–234
Casebeer, Scott, 98
Castles, Jim, 198
Castro, Fidel, 115, 116
celebrities, standards for, 223–224
Chambers, Carolyn, 150
Chanterelle's, 126
Chapin, Dwight, 243–244
Chaplin, Charlie, 135
Chapman School, 209
charitable foundations, 197, 198
Charles Adams house, 206
Charles F. Berg, 24, 85, 165
Charleston, Oregon, 81, 82
Cheney, Richard, 77
children. See also education; youth
    opportunities for, 105–106, 154
    and poverty, 180
China, 177
chocolate cake, 21–22, 137–138, 148, 186
Christmas shopping, 203–204
Christopher, Warren, 233
Cipriani, Harry, 147
City of Roses train, 35
Claridge's Hotel, 219
Clark, Bud and Sigrid, 70
Clarke, Thomas, 212
Clatsop County, 143
Clemson, John T., 248
Clinton, Bill
    admired by Andy Rooney, 186
    as campaigner, 195
    and foreign policy, 233–234
    as president, 195–196
    view of economy, 180
Clinton, Hillary, 196

clothing. *See also* retail stores
  in Portland, 23–24
  trends in, 11, 51–52
Clover Club, 166
Cody, Jack, 34, 139, 201
coffee wagons. *See* Jay W. Stevens Disaster
  Wagon
Collins, Lee, 198
Collins, Maribeth, 198
Collins, Truman, 197, 198
Collins Foundation, 197, 198
Columbia River Maritime Museum, 105
community diversity, 101–102
community service awards
  for humanitarian deeds, 6
  for volunteer work, 237–238
  to women, 29–30
commuter airlines, 91–92
compensation, executive, 96, 181–182, 208
CompUSA, 236
Condomania, 159
Cone, Ed, 173
Congdon, Marsha, 150, 212
Congress. *See also* government
  changed rules for, 153
  discipline in, 229
  GF's views about Senate, 107–108
  loss of trust in, 164
  need for reform, 182
  news in 1910, 194
  public opinion about, 178
  vital issues in, 153–154
Continental Congress, 135
Cook, Vern, 174
cooking schools, 89
Cooper, Forrest, 242
Coos Bay, Oregon, 81
Copeland, Helen Jo, 149
Corbett, Alf, 64
Corbett, Henry L., 241
Corbett, Henry W., 64, 210
Cordon, Guy, 173
Cordray, John F., 217
Cordray's New Theatre, 217
Cornett, Marshall, 94
corporations. *See* business
Correll, Charles, 114
Costco, 160
Couric, Katie, 224
Crater Lake Lodge, 126
Crazy for You, 155
crime
  control issues, 12, 180
  effect on communities of, 101–102
Critchlow, Helen, 44
Cronin, Ambrose, 194
Cronin Company, 190
Cronkite, Walter, 75
Crook County, 169
Crookham, Charles, 188
Cross, Travis, 64, 93, 198, 200
Crotty, Ida, 79
Crow, Steve, 246

Cuba, 115–116
culture, American, 51–52
Curran, Jim, 239
Czechoslovakia, 59–60

D

Dagwell, Benjamin D., 201
dairies, 167–168
Daly, Dr. Bernard, 242
Daly Educational Fund, 242
Danforth, Jack, 76
Daniel, Don, 13
Darman, Richard, 133
Davidson, Jebby, 64
Davidson, Sylvia, 1, 44, 64
Davis, Edna, 79
Davis, Jefferson, 135
The Day Elvis Met Nixon, 243-244
Deaver, Mike, 78
debt, federal, 133, 151–152, 154, 163, 207–208.
  See also budget
Decker, Tom, 246
Dees, Eleanor, 79
Delahunt, M.J., 248
Democratic party
  and Bob Straub, 173–174
  regains power in Oregon, 63
Demorest, Harry, 171
Department of Agriculture, 151
department stores. *See* retail stores
Desert Storm. *See* Gulf War
Dick, Harvey, 34
Dick, Helena Biddle, 186
Dickson, Kate, 246
Dienstbier, Jiri, 60
dietary habits, trends in, 11, 51, 178
  See also foods
disaster wagons. *See* Jay W. Stevens Disaster
  Wagon
discipline, lack of, 229–230
discount stores, 160, 236
discrimination
  in marketplace, 172
  in Portland, 43–44
  against women, 149
diversity, community, 101–102
Dodd, Chris, 76
Dodson, Ruth Ann and Mark, 98
Dole, Elizabeth, 42
Donahue, Richard, 212
Dong, Pham Van, 20
Dorn, Jenna, 42, 98, 246
Dotten, Kathleen, 97
Douglas, Lewis and Peggy, 109
Dr. Wythe's Dentists, Inc., 194
Drake, Harriet, 150
Drexel Burnham Lambert, 37–38
drug issue, 12
Duberstein, Ken, 78
Duncan, Robert, 184, 199, 200
Dussin, Guss, 152
Dyke, Walter, 198

E

Eagle Rock Lodge, 128
Earth Scents, 159
Eastern Airlines
  and Donald Trump, 67
  and Frank Lorenzo, 38
Eastern & Oriental Express train, 214
Eastman, Clint, Jr., 188
Ebersole, Lee Luders, 10
economy
  health of, 179–180, 207–208
  and lifestyles, 51–52
  Paul Volker's views about, 223–224
  trends in, 96
Edgewater Inn, 81
education. *See also* teachers
  financing of, 45–46
  in free enterprise, 172
  gender bias in, 149
  of labor force, 95–96
  status of, 154, 180, 182
Edwards, Cecil, 93
Egypt, 25, 26
Eichinger, Marilyn, 150, 171
Eisner, Michael, 181
elections
  bellwether county in Oregon, 169
  and need for reform, 182
  Oregon model in, 227
Electrical Distributing Company, 190
Elephant Deli, 206
Elgin Opera House, 126
Elizabeth, Queen (England)
  PR for, 134
  as princess, 109
Ellicott, Irene, 149
Elorriaga, John A., 49–50
Emmons, Ralph, 200
Eneidi, Julius, 14
England, 178
Enterprise, Oregon, 87
entertainment. *See* arts and entertainment
entitlement programs, 207, 208
environmental issues, in Antarctica, 57
Eritrea, Ethiopia, 71
Erlichman, John, 39
Ethiopian civil war, 71
Eugene, Oregon, 126
European Economic Community, 104, 177
Evans, Jim, 75, 97
Evelyn Gibson's, 24
Evergreen International Aviation, 92
executive secretaries, 9–10
executive washrooms, 151
export trade
  bureaucracy in, 182
  in Oregon, 170
Exxon Corporation, 37

F

Fadeley, Ed, 93
Failing, H.E., 248

Faisal, King, 136, 154, 161–162
families, discipline in, 230
farmers
  bureauracy serving, 151
  priorities of, 146
Farmer's Market, 105
Farrell, Robert, Jr., 94
Federated Department Stores, 54, 55
Ferris, Richard, 53, 54
Fields, Chester, 87
Finley's Sunset Hills Mortuary and Cemetery, 209
firefighters, 5–6, 145
fire wagons. *See* Jay W. Stevens Disaster Wagon
First Interstate Bank of Oregon
  Floyd Bennett's career at, 239–240
  leaders of, 47–48
  PR expert for, 42
First National Bank of Oregon. *See* First Interstate Bank of Oregon
Flanagan House, 127
Fleming, A.P., 175
Flessas, Nick, 74
Flightcraft, 92
Flowers by Tommy Luke, 140
Food and Drug Administration (FDA), 146
food critics, 147–148
foods
  chocolate, 21
  chocolate cake, 21–22, 137–138, 148, 186
  desserts, 178
  Farmer's Market for, 105
  hamburgers, 13
  ice cream, 165, 235–236
  from Oregon, 170
  oysters, 217–218
  potatoes, 185
  trends in, 11, 51, 178
Foothill Broiler, 206
Ford, Cynthia Jackson, 149–150
Ford, Gerald, 83
Ford, Glenn, 98
Forsman, Marty, 206
Foulk, Calvin, 44
foundries, 87–88
France, 178
Frank, Aaron
  background of, 10, 175–176
  and bombing at M&F, 27
  and fire service, 5–6
  hobbies of, 135–136
  and love of horses, 111–112, 175
  photos of, 3, 122
Frank, Fannie
  family photo of, 120
  and Sigmund, 118
Frank, Ruth (Mrs. Aaron), 24
Frank, Sigmund, 190
Frank Dooly house, 206
Frank estate. *See* Garden Home Farm
Frasca, Bob, 171
Frederick & Nelson, 85

Fred Meyer
  history of, 198
  radio show for, 205
Fred Meyer Challenge, 41
Freidenrich, Bob, 24
Frenchglen Hotel, 126
Friday Surprise
  cake recipe, 21–22
  columns, 1–2
  sales at M&F, 1, 2, 118, 190
Frisbee, Don, 98
Frohnmayer, David, 225–226, 245
Frohnmayer, John, 226
Frohnmayer, Lynn, 225–226
Frohnmayer, Mira Jean, 226
Frohnmayer, Otto and MarAbel, 225–226
Frohnmayer, Philip, 226
Fullbright, William, 8

G

Gable, Clark, 118
Galleria, 85
Gandhi, Indira, 215–216
Gango, Jackie, 206
Garden Home Farm, 111–112
gardens
  in England, 220
  at Shore Acres State Park, 82
Gardiner, Marina, 9–10
Garsen, Bob, 114
Gearhart, Oregon, news in 1910, 193, 194
Gearhart Hotel, 143–144
Gearhart's Golf Hotel, 143
Geiger, Elizabeth, 246
Germany, 178
Gerry Frank Meritorious Service Award, 6
Gilbert, William B., 189
Gilbert House, 128
Gilliam, Vic, 246
Gimre's Shoes, 209
Glickman, Harry, 44
Goizuetta, Roberto, 182
Goldschmidt, Neil, 97–98, 105, 131, 228
Goldwater, Barry, 108
Goldy, Dan, 64
Golf Hotel. See Gearhart's Golf Hotel
Good Samaritan Hospital, 190
Gottesman, Peryl, 44
Goudy, Grace Collins, 172, 198
government. See also Congress; politicians;
    politics
  bureaucracies, 178
  and downsizing, 208
  female leaders in, 29–30
Graham, Billy, 68
Graham, Kay, 75
Grand Central Bakery, 128
Granite, Oregon, 126
Gray, Betty and John, 70
Grayson, Bobby, 175
Great Britain, 104
Green, Alan "Punch," 234
Green, Edith S.

and Bob Straub, 174
as congresswoman, 227
relationship with Wayne Morse, 184
relationship with Wendell Wyatt, 184
Grice, Duchesne, 220
Griebel, Emma, 44
Grimes-Moore-Seasider Hotel, 144
Grossmayer, Philip, 248
Gulf of Aden, 216
Gulf War, 95, 99–100, 133
Gunn, Henry, 43, 44

H

Haig, Alexander, 15
Haines Steak House, 127
Haiti, 233, 234
Haldeman, H.R., 77, 244
Hall, Jayne, 71
Hall, John, 94
Hall, William, 71, 234
Halvorsen, Ruth, 44
Hamburg, Joan, 169
Hampton, Connie, 21
Hancock, John, 135
Hanneman, Barbara, 63
Hansen, Clifford, 108
Happe, Rosalia, 1
Harold Kelley's, 85
Harrods, 219
Harry's, 147
Hart, Schafner and Marx clothes, 24
Hasson, Isaac, 165
Hatfield, Antoinette, 200
Hatfield, Dovie, 199
Hatfield, Mark O., 123
  career of, 199–200
  directs Reagan's inauguration ceremony,
    15
  functions enjoyed by, 195
  and Hanoi negotiations, 19–20
  as leader, 228
  and Paris peace talks, 17–19
  proposed as vice-president, 7–8, 200
  relationships with local politicians, 184,
    199–200
Havel, Vaclav, 68
Hawley, Phil, 10
Hawthorne Boulevard, Portland, 206
health care
  in England, 220
  at Mayo Clinic, 65–66
  opportunities in Oregon, 106
  problems with, 96, 146, 154, 178, 180
Heathman Hotel, 164
Heinz, John, 107
Hells Canyon, 88
Helms, Jesse, 196
Helmsley, Leona, 51, 54
Helmsley Palace Hotel, 51
Helser, Brenda, 139
Heltzel, Lillian, 1
Helvetia Tavern, 127
Hemphill, Jim, 157

Hendrickson, Ames, 44
Henningsgaard, Edith, 30
Henry, Judy Shipler, 245
Herald Center, 55
Hershey, Pennsylvania, 21
Hertz Rent-A-Car, 53
Heyburn, W.B., 194
Hickok, Steve, 246
High Desert Museum, 105, 126, 205
Highet, Lester, 14
Hill, Samuel, 248
Hillman, Don, 137
Hinson, Dave, 92
Hippo Hardware, 206
Hirsch, Harold, 2
Hirsch, Jeanette. *See* Meier, Jeanette
Hirsch, Ludwig, 2
Hirvi, Jacob, 144
Hofer, Judi, 118, 150, 176
Hoffman, L.H., 176
Holiday Farm, 126
Holman Funeral Service, 190, 209
Holocaust Memorial Museum, 191
HomeBase, 160
Home Depot, 236
homes, trends in, 12, 51
Honeyman, Nan Wood, 227
Hood River, Oregon, 127
Horizon Air Lines, 91–92
horses
    Aaron Frank's love for, 175
    at home, 111–112
hotels. *See also specific names of hotels*
    and Donald Trump, 67–68
    historic, 143–144
    trends in, 51
    as victims, 53, 54
Hot Potatoes, 185
Howison, Lt. Neil M., 158
Hoyt, E. Palmer "Ep," 166, 176, 202
Hoyt Hotel, 34
Hradilek, Thomas, 60
Huber, Frank R., 14, 190
Huber's Cafe, 14, 128, 165, 190
Hudson, Jerry, 171–172
Humason, Ivan, 210
Hussein, King, 25, 99, 133, 154, 162
Hussein, Saddam, 99–100

I

Imeson, Tom, 98, 141–142, 246
India, 215–216
Indiana University, 31
IRA, 221, 222
Iran-Contra affair, 39, 40
Ireland, Northern, 221–222
Israel, 25–26
Italy, 178
Iverson, Rich, 82

J

J. K. Gill, 160, 165
Jackson, Glenn L., 129

and Air Oregon, 91–92
influence of, 69, 226, 228
supports Bob Straub, 174
Jackson, Henry M., 108
Jackson, Phil, 10, 166
Jacksonville Inn, 127
Jacobsen, Peter, 41
Jaeger, Mary, 206
Jake's Famous Crawfish Restaurant, 13, 128, 209, 218
Jalalabad, Afghanistan, 31
Jamestown House, 222
Jansen, Dan, 211–212
Jantzen (Moore), Esther, 8
Japan
    decline of, 177
    economy in, 207–208
    education in, 45, 154
Japan Ltd., 55
Javits, Jacob, 108
Jay W. Stevens Disaster Wagon, 5–6, 122
Jennings, Peter, 224
Jensen, Hildamae, 34
Jerry's Rogue Jets, 126
jobs
    art-related. *See also* business; occupations; work
    competition for, 52
    loss of mid-management, 163–164
    trends in, 11
John Day, Oregon, 127
John Jacob Astor Hotel, 144
Johnson, Lyndon B., 77, 229
Jolly Joan's, 13, 165
Jordan, 25, 133, 154, 162
Jordan, Hamilton, 77
Joseph, George, 93
Joseph, Oregon, 87–88, 127
Joseph Art Castings, 87
Josephson's, 126
Joy, Audrey, 165

K

Kaiser, Edgar, 140
Kaiser, Henry J., 33
Kam Wah Chung Museum, 127
Kassebaum, Nancy, 234
Katz, Vera, 30, 98
Kaye, Danny, 224
Keiko, 231–232
Keisling, Phil, 98
Keller, Greg, 145
Keller, Ira, 202
Keller, Margie, 238
Kelley, Harold, 165
Kennedy, Edward M.
    as controversial figure, 107
    at party for Ribicoff, 76
    star quality of, 68
Kennedy, John F.
    and Abe Ribicoff, 76
    and chief of staff position, 77
Kerr, Donald, 105

Kihs, Daryl, 137
Kihs, Tammy and Kristina, 137
Kincaid, Robert, 148
Kiplinger Washington Letter, 179–180
Kissinger, Henry, 25, 68, 76
Kitzhaber, John, 98
Kitzmiller, John, 175
Kmart, 160
Knight, Penny and Phil, 172
Knox, William "Pete," 238
Kolar, Edward J., 49
Konditorei, 21, 128
Korea, 45
Kravits, Henry, 75
Krogh, Egil, 39
Krogh, Egil, Jr. "Bud," 39–40, 243–244
Kulongoski, Ted, 98
Kuolt, Milt, 91
Kwan, Kam Sang, 89–90
Kwan's Original Cuisine, 89–90, 128

L

labor force, training of, 95–96
Ladd & Bush Bankers, 189
Laise, Carol, 234
Lake, Anthony, 233
Lake County, 242
La Mirabelle, 148
Lane, Bill, 234
La Serre, 128
Lauder, Estee, 75–76
Lauderdale, Keeta, 29
Lawrence, Pauline, 198
Lazarus, Charles, 55–56
leaders
    business, 47–50, 149–150, 211–212
    and charisma, 161–162
    loss of trust in, 163–164
    political, 29–30, 227–228
    preparation of future, 172
    and vision, 211–212
    women, 29–30, 149–150, 227
    World War II, 229–230
Lebanon, 25
Lee, Dorothy McCullough, 33, 120, 139, 227
Lee, Janet, 21, 137
Lenard, Charles, 212
Leonard, Stew, 167–168
Lewis, Leland Stanford "Bud," 238
Lewis and Clark College, 176, 190
Lezak, Sid, 245
Lightner, W.L., 14, 190
Limbaugh, Rush, 186
Lincoln High School, 1, 43–44, 141
Linde, Hans, 64
Linder, Laree, 30
Lipman, Jessie (Mrs. I.N.), 24
Lipman Wolfe's, 24, 85, 165, 190
Lloyd, Lulu May. *See* von Hagen, Lulu May
Lloyd, Ralph, 78, 79–80
Lloyd Center, 79–80, 86
Lohr, Linda, 172
Loma Linda College, 31

Lord Bennett's, 82
Lorenzo, Frank, 38, 53
Louie, Jim, 14
Lueddemann, Hillman, Jr., 42
Lugar, Richard, 234
Luihn, Jack, 165, 238
Luke, Tommy, 140
Lusk, Judge Hall, 81
Lytle, Grace, 165–166

M

M. & H.H. Sichel's, 165
MacDermott, John, 221
MacNaughton, E.B., 10, 47, 176, 239
Macy & Co. (R.H.), 54
Mahoney, Barbara, 150
Major, John, 104, 115, 116, 178, 220
Malarkey, J.D., 210
Malheur County Wildlife Refuge, 127
Mallicoat, Maxine, 21
Mama's, 126
Mandela, Nelson, 220
manners, trends in, 12
Mansfield, Mike, 108
Manuel, Dave, 87
Marcus, Stanley, 55, 159
Margaret, Princess (England), 104
Mariam, Mengistu Haile, 71
Marion County Firefighters, 6
marketing. *See also* business
    niches, 159–160, 178, 235–236
    overseas, 182
    targeted, 204
Marsee Baking, 128, 206
Martin, Charles, 93
Marylhurst College, 172, 209
Massawa, Ethiopia, 71–72
Mathews, Kate. *See* Dickson, Kate
May Department Stores, 85, 118
Mayo, W.W., 66
Mayo Medical Center, 65–66
McCall, Dorothy Lawson, 174
McCall, Tom, 123
    as leader, 227–228
    as Oregon legend, 169, 202
    PR expert for, 41–42
    relationship with Bob Straub, 174
    relationship with Mark Hatfield, 184
McClure, James, 20
McKay, Douglas, 94, 98
McKay, Mabel, 94
McKee, Paul B., 10, 176
McMurdo Station, Antarctica, 57
McNary, Charles L., 199–200, 228
Measure 5, 182
media. *See* press
Medicare. *See* entitlement programs
Meeker, Tony, 93, 98
Meese, Ed, 78
Meier, Aaron
    background of, 117
    death of, 190
Meier, Grace, 74

Meier, Jeanette, 117–118, 120
Meier, Julius
  and Aunt Rosie, 74
  and Gearhart Hotel, 143–144
  as governor, 93, 118, 205
  and Portland Automobile Club, 248
Meier, Roger, 24
Meier & Frank (Portland)
  Aaron Frank as head of, 176
  bombing at, 27–28, 47
  chocolate fudge at, 21
  early history of, 85, 117–118, 190, 209
  early photos of, 119, 121
  Friday Surprise events at, 1, 2, 118, 190
  and Gearhart Hotel, 143–144
  memorable employees of, 165–166
  merchandising events at, 155–156
  party for elevator operators at, 203
  restaurants at, 13
Meier & Frank (Salem)
  community dinner at, 156
  ground breaking ceremony, 123
Melvin Simon and Associates, 80
Men's Grill, 13
merchandising, 155–156
Merki, Nancy, 139, 175
Merlo, Harry, 171
Metschan, Phil, 93
Meyer, Fred
  background of, 197–198
  and discipline, 230
Meyer, Harry, 198
Meyer Memorial Trust, 197, 198
Michaelson, Wes, 17
Middle East, 25–26, 99, 154, 215–216.
  See also Gulf War
Midway Airlines, 92
Milken, Michael, 37–38
Miller, Bryan, 147–148, 185–186
Miller, Edward, 218
Miller, Nash, Wiener, Hager & Carlsen, 189
Miller, Sue Harris, 29
Mills, L. Roland, 218
Millsaps-Jenkins, Florence, 10
Mitchell, George, 229
Mitchell, John, 8, 200
M.J. Murdock Charitable Trust, 197, 198
Monet's, 126
Montgomery Ward, 160
Moore, Donald, 23
Moore, Richard, 8
Morgan, Howard, 63, 64
Morrison, Edris, 166
Morse, Midge, 69–70
Morse, Wayne
  background of, 69–70
  independence of, 169
  as leader, 228
  Paris mission of, 17
  relationship with Hatfield, 200
  relationship with Richard Neuberger, 183
  relationship with Wendell Wyatt, 184
  as senator, 64, 107

Mt. Angel Library, 127
Mt. St. Joseph's residence, 206
Mount Howard tramway, 88
Moyer, Tom, 175
Mubarak, Hosni, 25, 26, 99
Mudie, Peter, 205
Muir & McDonald, 209
Multnomah Athletic Club, 34, 139, 210
Multnomah Hotel, 166
Munro, Anne Roy, 73
Murdock, Jack, 197, 198
Murphy, James H., 210
My Turn (Nancy Reagan), 62

N

Naftlin, Rose, 202
Naito, Bill, 206
Naito, Sam, 136, 206
Nancy Reagan Foundation, 62
Nangarhar University Hospital, 31–32
National Archives, 157–158
National Department Stores, 24, 85
Neiman-Marcus, 159, 170
Nemcova, Dana, 60
Nemy, Enid, 185
Nepal, 45
Neuberger, Maurine, 183, 227
Neuberger, Richard, 63, 64, 169, 173, 183, 227
New Market Theater, 210
Newport, Oregon, 127, 171
New Sammy's Bistro, 128
News-Telegram, 166
New York
  caller interest in Oregon, 169
  and Donald Trump, 67
  food critics in, 147–148
  GF's book about, 8, 147
  lifestyle trends in, 51
  theater in, 113–114
  trend for "exclusion" in, 101–102
New York Life Insurance, 209
New York Times, food critics for, 147–148
niche marketing, 159–160, 178, 235–236
Nicholas Ungar Furs, 24
Nick's, 127
Nielson's Jewelers, 209
Nike, 212
Nixon, Richard M., 130
  comeback of, 62
  and Elvis Presley, 243–244
  GF's views about, 7–8, 84
  and negotiations with Vietnam, 18, 19
  as president, 77
  PR expert for, 42
  and Watergate, 39–40, 243
Nob Hill, 206
Nordstrom, 85, 86
North, Oliver L., 39, 40
North Bend, Oregon, 81
Northern Ireland, 221–222
Northrup, Henry H., 189
Northwest Aluminum, 38
Novak's Restaurant, 126

Nunn, Warne, 198, 200

O

Oaks Park, 210
Oanh, Xuan, 18
OASIS program, 238
Oberteuffer, G.H., 139
occupations. *See also* jobs
   public opinion about, 145
   trends in, 11
Ocean House, 143
O'Connor, Basil, 176
Ohmart, Lee, 200
Ohrdruf concentration camp, 192
oil spill disaster, 37
Olds, Wortman and King, 23, 85, 190
Old Spaghetti Factory, 152
Old Stage Inn, 127
Old Town, 206
Olsen and Johnson, 175
OMSI, 105, 128, 171
Onassis, Jacqueline, 223
O'Neill, Bill, 76
Oregon. *See also specific names of cities*
   in 1894, 209–210
   Afghan shipment from, 31–32
   agricultural products, 170
   best places in, 126–128
   education in, 182
   effects of budget problems in, 102
   gender bias in, 149
   good news about, 171–172
   governors of, 93–94
   historic hotels in, 143–144
   inexpensive luxuries in, 151
   influential people in, 139–140
   map of, 124–125
   mayors in, 30, 33, 139
   museum tour for, 105
   parks in, 82, 205
   political leaders in, 227–228
   population in 1845, 158
   prominent couples in, 69–70
   relationships among politicians in,
      183–184
   tax issues in, 45–46
   transportation opportunities in, 106
   trend for "exclusion" in, 102
   uniqueness of, 169–170, 205–206
   wish list for, 105–106
Oregon American Automobile Association
   Club, 119, 247
Oregon City, Oregon, 170
Oregon City Interpretive Center, 127
Oregon coast, 81–82, 170, 205
Oregon Coast Aquarium, 105, 127, 171, 231
   232
Oregon Constitution, 158
Oregon Convention Center, 88
Oregon Electric Railway, 111
Oregon Episcopal School, 190
Oregon Garden, 128
Oregon Health Plan, 220

Oregon High Desert Museum, 105, 126, 205
Oregon Historical Society, 105, 128
Oregon Historical Society Annals, 34
Oregonian
   and Friday Surprise column, 1–2
   news in 1910, 194
   in old Portland, 166, 209
   origin of, 189
Oregon Journal, 10, 140, 166
Oregon Museum of Science and Technology
   (OMSI), 105, 128, 171
Oregon Oyster Co., 14
Oregon Products Week, 155
Oregon State Archives, 157
Oregon State Fair, 21, 137–138
Oregon Statesman, 93, 177, 189, 209
Oregon State University, 190
Oregon Trail, 170
Oregon Trail Interpretive Centers, 105
Orient Express train, 36
Original Pancake House, 14
Orpheum, 209
Osburn, John, 144
Otis Cafe, 127
Our Children's Store, 206

P

PACE, 160
Pacific Institute of Natural Sciences, 105
Pacific International Livestock Exposition
   Horse Show, 175
Pacific Northwest Magazine, 33
PacifiCorp, 211–212
Pacific University, 190
Packwood, Bob
   as campaigner, 195
   relationship with Mark Hatfield, 184, 200
Paine, Tevis, 175
Pakistan, 31
Palace Theater, 113
Palmer, Bill, 155, 156
Papa Hayden's, 206
paramedics, 145
Paris peace talks, 17–19
Parker, Dick, 91
Parks Bronze, 87
Parmenter, Ramon, 88
Parmenter Bronze, 87
Parry, Will H., 189
Patterson, Paul, 94
Paul's Wagon, 165
Paulus, Bill, 70
Paulus, Norma, 30, 70, 93, 98
Payne, Ancil, 64
Peace Corps, 31–32
Peddicord, Clarence, 28
Pelletreau, Robert H., Jr., 25
Pendleton Underground, 127
Penner, Brenda, 150
Percy, Charles, 7
Perkins, Edward, 234
Perot, Ross, 180
Persian Gulf conflict. *See* Gulf War

257

personalities. *See also specific names*
  historical legends, 81
  media stars, 67–68
  at Ribicoff's birthday party, 75–76
Peter Britt Festival, 127
Peters, Dr. George D., 248
pharmacists, priorities of, 146
Philip, Prince (England), 109
Phoenix House Center, 62
Piacentini, John, 205
Pine Valley Lodge, 127
Pioneer Place, 86
Pittock, Henry L., 242
Pittock Mansion, 128
Platt, R.T., 210
Plimpton, Martha, 114
political parties, 63–64. *See also* Democratic
  party; Republican party
politicians
  Oregon: approachability of, 224; emerging
    stars, 98; independent candidates, 169;
    relationships among, 183–184; with
    vision, 227–228
  public opinion about, 61–62, 145, 146, 196
  styles of, 115–116
politics
  in 1910, 193, 194
  in England, 219–220
  need for reform in, 96, 182
  and PR spin, 133
  trends in, 12
poll taxes, 104
Ponderosa Cattle Company, 128
Poppert, Claris, 171
Portland, Oregon
  in 1894, 209–210, 217–218
  airline schedules for, 53
  best of, 128
  discrimination in, 43–44
  downtown, 80
  livability of, 170
  names from 1880s, 189–190
  neighborhoods in, 205–206
  news in 1910, 193–194
  Northwest, 206
  old-time highlights of, 165–166
  old-time restaurants in, 13–14, 217–218
  old-time trains in, 35
  oyster tradition in, 217–218
  residents, contributions of, 33–34
  restaurant choices, 148
  stores in downtown, 23–24, 85–86
  wish list for, 105–106
Portland Automobile Club, 247–248
Portland Fire Bureau, 5–6
Portland General Electric, 42, 171
Portland Hilton Hotel, 50, 176
Portland Hotel, 14, 144, 166
Portland International Airport, 92, 106
Portland Police Sunshine Division, 238
Portland Rose Festival
  news in 1910, 194
  selection of queen for, 176

Portland Rose Garden, 128
Portland Rotary Club, 172
Potts, E.D. "Debbs," 93
Powell's Bookstore, 128, 206
POW release missions, 17–20
Prague, Czechoslovakia, 59–60
Pratt, Gerry, 198
Pray, Charles, 81
presidents (U.S.). *See also specific names*
  and foreign policy, 233–234
  GF's signed photos of, 136
  influence on subordinates of, 39–40
  at Nixon Library dedication, 83–84
  public opinion about, 61–62, 196
Presley, Elvis, and Nixon, 243–244
press. *See also specific names of newspapers*
  attention to "stars", 67
  old-time newspapers, 166, 189
  and PR experts, 41–42
  reports on economy, 179–180
Proctor, Arlitria, 237–238
Protzman, Kate, 1, 202
Providence Stage Band, 238
public relations
  media experts, 41–42
  as spin, 133–134

Q

qat, 216
Quickie's, 128

R

Raffles Hotel, 214
Ralphael's, 127
Ramaley, Judith, 150
Rankin, George, 112
Rawl, Lawrence, 37
Ray, Rob, 141
Rayburn, Sam, 229
Raynes, Marty, 67
Reagan, Nancy, 15, 16, 61–62, 224
Reagan, Ronald, 130
  and chief of staff position, 77–78
  first inaugural of, 16, 136
  as former president, 61–62
  GF's views about, 83–84
  as nation's cheerleader, 196
  and negotiations with Vietnam, 20
  as president, 40, 224
recipes
  chocolate cake, 21–22, 138
  potato, 185
Recovery of Hope Drug Rehabilitation
  Program, 238
Red Lion Inn (Coos Bay), 81
Reed, Amanda W., 241
Reed, Rose Coursoen, 210
Reed College, 241
Reedwood Friends Church, 209
refugees
  from Czechoslovakia, 59–60
  Palestinian, 25–26, 99
Regan, Donald, 78

Reiten, Dick, 98
religion
    in Czechoslovakia, 59–60
    in Oregon, 205
Republican Party
    1968 convention, 7–8, 200
    in Oregon, 63, 94
Resort at the Mountain, 128
restaurants. *See also specific names of*
        restaurants
    Chinese, 89–90
    dining cars, 35, 36
    and food critics, 147–148
    old-time, 13–14, 165–166, 217–218
    in Portland, choice of week, 148
    and PR spin, 134
    trends in, 11, 51
    in Washington, D.C., 35
retail stores. *See also specific names of stores*
    and Christmas shopping, 203–204
    dairy stores, 167–168
    in downtown Portland, 85–86
    and niche marketing, 159–160, 204,
        235–236
    prices in 1910, 194
    profitability of, 56, 204
    as victims of egos, 54
    and vision, 55–56
Rex Hill Vineyards, 127
Reynolds, Nancy, 15, 16
Rhodes (*formerly* Olds Wortman and King),
    85
Ribicoff, Abraham, 75–76
Ribicoff, Casey, 75
Rice, Orville, 6
Rich, Jesse, 13
Richard Nixon Library, 83–84
Richardson, James J., 33–34, 139
Richardson, William, 245
Rife, Richard, 206
Riley, Frank Branch, 34, 166
River Ranch House, 126
R.M. Wade Company, 190
Roberts, Barbara, 30, 97, 224, 245
Roberts, Frank, and family, 245
Roberts Brothers, 24, 85, 165, 194
Robertson, Jack, 246
Robertson, Oran B., 198
Robinson, Anne Keil, 176
Rochester, Minnesota, 65–66
Rockefeller, Nelson, 68
Rock Springs Guest Ranch, 126
Roehm, Carolyne, 75
Rogers, Kay, 30
Rogers, Roy, and horse, at M&F, 156
Rogers, Will, 113–114
Rogue Valley Memorial Hospital, 226
Rooney, Andy, 185–186
Roosevelt, Franklin, 158, 229–230
Rose Festival
    news in 1910, 194
    selection of queen for, 176
Rose Garden, 128

Rosenblatt, Millard, 24
Rosenblatt, Samuel, 24
Rosenthal, Abe, 75
Roth, Bob, 44
Roth, Orville, 137
Rumsfeld, Donald, 77

S

Sacred Heart High School, 209
St. Mary's Academy, 190. *See also* Marylhurst
        College
St. Vincent's Hospital, 190
Saks Fifth Avenue, 86
Salem
    archives building in, 157
    best of, 128
    community dinner at M&F, 156
    prominent women in, 29–30
sales tax, 45–46
Salonen, Don, 82
Sammons, Edward, 10, 49, 176
Samuel Rosenblatt and Company, 24, 85, 194
Sardam, Frank, 34, 166
Saturday Market (Eugene), 126
Saudi Arabia, 26, 154, 161–162
Schlesinger, Lee, 23
Schloth, Millie, 201
Schmidt, Ron, 41–42
Schminck Museum, 127
Schnitzer, Arlene, 150
Schnitzer, Harold, 44
Schnitzer, Sylvia. *See* Davidson, Sylvia
schools. *See* education; teachers
Schreiber, Susan, 206
Schroeder, D.R., 143
Schwab, Mildred, 98
Schwabe, Williamson and Wyatt, 209
Schwartz, Charlotte, 237
Schwartz (Meier), Laura, 24
Scott, Bill, 98
sculpture, 87–88
seafood, 13–14, 170
Sealy-Dresser, 165
Sears, Roebuck and Company, 160
Seattle, Washington, 33
secretaries, value of, 9–10
Securities and Exchange Commission, 182
security precautions
    effect on communities of, 101–102
    during Gulf War, 99–100
    in Northern Ireland, 221–222
Selassie, Haile, 71, 72, 136
Shakespeare performances (Ashland), 126
Shaver, Delmer, 248
Shelk, Linda, 149
Sheng, Sherry, 150
Sheraton, Mimi, 148
Sherry Netherlands Hotel, 147
Sherwood, Don, 237
Sherwood, James, 214
ShopKo, 160
shopping trends, 203–204, 235–236. *See also*
        retail stores

Shore Acres State Park, 82, 126
Short, Bob, 171
Shultz, George, 20, 25, 233
Sichel, M., 248
Siegel, Herb, 75
Silo, 160
Silver Falls State Park, 128
Simon-McWilliams, Ethel, 150
Simpson, Dave, 10, 176
Simpson, O.J., 223
Singapore, 214
Sleighbells Christmas Shop, 128
Smith, Cherida, 198
Smith, Del, 92
Smith, Edgar, 166
Smith, Elmo, 81, 94
Smith, John, 220
Smullin, Patsy, 150
Snake River, Oregon, 88
Snell, Earl, 94
social issues
    corporate greed, 37–38
    exclusion *vs.* inclusion, 101–102
    national problems, 180
South Africa, 220
South Pole, 58
Southworth, Mabel, 1, 44
South Yemen, 216
Soviet Union
    and Afghanistan, 31
    GF's train ride in, 35–36
    Yeltsin's visit to U.S., 115, 116
Speck Drive-In, 165
spending
    government, 46
    trends in, 51–52
Spirit Mountain Resort, 126
sports, discipline in, 230
Sportsmen Quartet, 114
Sprague, Charles A., 81, 93–94, 177
Sprouse, Robert A., 237
Standard Insurance Company, 212
State Department, 233, 234
Statesman-Journal, 30, 209
Staver, LeRoy, 49
Steamboat Inn, 128
Stein, Andrew, 68
Stennis, John, 108
Stephanie Inn, 126
Stephens, Lynda, 30
Stephenson, C.B. "Bill," 47, 239
Stepp, Billy, 166
Stevens, Jay, 5
stock market crash, 52
Storrs, Frances and John, 69–70
Storybook Lane, 167
Stout, George C., 210
Straub, Bob, 64, 93, 173–174, 202, 224
Straub, Pat, 173
Strawberry Patch, 126
Stuart, Arthur and Helen, 222
Sumpter Railroad, 128
Sunset Bay State Park, 82

Sununu, John, 77, 78, 115, 116
superstores, 160, 236
Suzi (*New York Post* columnist), 75
Swan Island, 166
Swanson, Bill, 206
Swanson, Lyn, 198
Sweden, 207–208
Sweet, Bill, 50, 91
Sweetland, Lil, 64
Sweetland, Monroe, 63–64
Swigert, C.F., 210
Swigert, Ernie, 23
Sylvia Beach Hotel, 127
Syria, 25–26

T

Taft, William Howard, 194
Target Stores, 160
taxes
    English poll, 104
    federal, 152, 180
    sales, 45–46
Taylor, Elizabeth, 68, 109–110
Taylor, John, 42
teachers. *See also* education
    and classroom discipline, 230
    in Lincoln High School, 43–44
    priorities of, 146
Tea Room, 13
technology, trends in, 12, 142
Tektronix Inc., 198
telephone service
    automation in, 142, 152
    language interpreters, 151
    and niche marketing, 235
    ring patterns, 152
Teresa, Mother, 132, 136, 215
terrorism, 221–222
Texas Air, 54
Thach, Nguyen Co, 20
Thailand, 213–214
Thatcher, Dennis, 103
Thatcher, Margaret, 103–104, 116, 130, 220, 240
theater. *See also* arts and entertainment
    analogy to merchandising, 155
    in London, 219
    in New York, 113–114
    in old-time Portland, 209–210, 217
The Dalles Interpretive Center, 128
The Lab, 236
Thiele, Henry, 14, 165
Tho, Le Duc, 20
Thorne, Jill, 150
Thornton, Dorothy and Bob, 64
Thuy, Xuan, 19
Tik Tok Drive-In, 165
Tillamook Creamery, 128
Timberline Lodge, 127
Timm, Peggy, 97
Timpe, Ron, 212
Tolly's, 127
Tomasek, Frantisek, 59–60

Tom Busch Home Furnishings, 209
Tompkins, Susan, 137
Tower, John, 107
Towey, Jim, 19
toys, 55–56
Toys 'R' Us, 55–56, 236
trains
    Eastern & Oriental Express, 214
    GF's favorite rides on, 35–36
Traub, Marvin, 54, 159–160
trends
    business, 178, 208
    dietary, 11, 51, 178
    in economy, 96
    general, 11–12, 51–52
    shopping, 235–236
    social, 101–102
    technological, 142
Trump, Donald, 67–68
Trump, Ivana, 67
Trump Plaza, 67
Tucker, Sophie, 114
Tully, Grace, 158
Tune, Tommy, 114
Tunisia, 161
Tunno, Eleanor, 218
Tu Tu Tun Lodge, 126
Twentieth Century Limited train, 35

U
Unander, Sig, 200
Under the Greenwood Tree, 127
Union Pacific Railroad Company, 36
United Airlines, 53, 163–164
United States Department of Agriculture, 151
United States Department of State, 233, 234
United States Navy, leadership in, 164
United States State Department, 233, 234
United Way, 151
U'Ren, W.S., 227
U.S. Bancorp, 212
U.S. National Bank of Oregon, 49–50
U.S. News & World Report, 179
U.S. West Oregon, 212

V
Vagabond Vintage Luggage Company, 159
Valley Bronze, 87–88
Van Ausdell, Lorraine, 29
Vance, Cy, 76
Vancouver, Washington, in 1910, 193, 194
Van Zante, Laurie, 150
Vaughan-Crownhart, Elizabeth, 69, 150
Vaughan, Tom, 34, 69, 93
vice presidents, 77
Vietnam War
    Hanoi delegation, 19–20
    Paris peace talks, 17–19
vision
    and leadership, 211–212
    in retailing, 55–56
Volker, Paul, 223–224
Vollum, Howard, 198

volunteers, awards to, 237–238
Vondra, Sasa, 60
von Hagen, Lulu May (Mrs. Richard), 79, 80
von Schmidt (Adams), Lina Louise, 202
Voss, Ralph, 47–48, 239
Vy, Mr. (Vietnamese negotiator), 18, 19

W
Wachsmuth, Louis, 217, 218
Wade, Robert M., 190
wages. See compensation
Waldheim, Kurt, 115, 116
Wallace, Robert, 48, 239
Wallowa County, 87–88
Wallowa Lake, 88
Wallowa Lake Lodge, 88
Wallowa tramway, 128
Wallowa Valley Festival of Arts, 87
Wal-Mart, 160
Walsh, Tom, 97
Walt Disney Company, 181
Walters, Barbara, 103–104
Walton, Sam, 160
Warm Spring Museum, 128
Warner Bros., 231–232
Washington, D.C.
    security precautions during Gulf War,
        99–100
    trains in, 35
Wass, O.A., 217
Wasserman, Lew, 75
Weekly Chatter, 1
Weinstein, Lee, 206
Welch, Claxton, 172
Wells, Pat, 21
Wellstone, Paul, 115, 116
Wemme, E. Henry, 210, 242, 247, 248
Wendel, Harold, 10, 24
West, Oswald, 81, 82, 205, 210, 227
Westin Hotels and Resorts, 54
whales, 231–232
Where to Find It, Buy It, Eat It in New York, 8,
        147
White, Rose (Mrs. Isam), 73–74, 120
White House
    chief of staff position at, 77–78
    GF alone in, 15–16
    and PR spin, 133
    state dinners at, 7
Whiteley, Ben, 212
White Stag Company, 117
Wilcox, Brett, 38, 98
Wilcox, Theodore B., 175, 248
Wilgenbusch, Nancy, 150, 172
Wilke, Bill, 48, 239
Will, Sandra, 114
Willamette University, 128, 171–172, 190
William Gadsby & Sons, 194
Williams, Wade "Whizzer", 44
Willison, Bruce, 211, 239
Willison, Gretchen, 48, 211
Will Rogers Follies, 113–114
wills, of early Oregonians, 241–242